FUNDAMENTALS

OF VEDIC ASTROLOGY

Vedic Astrologer's Handbook I

Lotus Press
Vedic Astrology Titles
by Bepin Behari

FUNDAMENTALS OF VEDIC ASTROLOGY
Vedic Astrologer's Handbook
Volume I

PLANETS IN THE SIGNS & HOUSES
Vedic Astrologer's Handbook
Volume II

MYTHS & SYMBOLS OF VEDIC ASTROLOGY

Fundamentals
of
Vedic Astrology

VEDIC ASTROLOGER'S HANDBOOK I

Bepin Behari

Edited by Kenneth Johnson

LOTUS
PRESS
Twin Lakes, WI

All requests should be directed to:
Lotus Press, P.O. Box 325, Twin Lakes, Wisconsin 53181
Web: www.lotuspress.com   Email: lotuspress@lotuspress.com
(800) 824-6396

2nd U.S. edition 2003

ISBN: 0-940985-52-7

Library of Congress Control Number: 2002108742

Printed in the United States of America

CONTENTS

EDITOR'S
FOREWORD

When Westerners approach the study of Hindu astrology, they are usually looking for something quite definite. They are looking for a *spiritual* astrology — a discipline which will throw light (*jyotish*) on their karma, their spiritual path, their ultimate purpose. The psychological emphasis of astrology in the West has proven somehow insufficient for their needs; they feel compelled to go beyond psychoanalysis to the techniques of enlightenment.

But to the seeker, no matter how earnest, Hindu astrology seems, at first, somewhat daunting. Various writers on the subject have stressed the predictive element in Hindu astrology — giving one the impression that here is a science concerned primarily with externals, an astrology which is far more focused on worldly matters than our own.

Surely, we say, there must be more. An ancient spiritual culture such as India *must* have an astrology which embodies the philosophical principles of Yoga and Vedanta. But how do we get beyond the surface level and contact the spiritual core of the science? The Hindu astrological scriptures, even when they are available to us (and they are often difficult to obtain), contain hundreds of rules and mathematical formulae to be memorized, and are written in the language of medieval India, a culture and world view entirely foreign to most of us.

Bepin Behari seeks out the yogic principles which underlie the ancient writings. He elucidates the spiritual core upon which the rules and formulae have been based. In so doing, he restores to us the vision of the early Vedic astrologers. As David Frawley has remarked in his introduction to Behari's *Myths and Symbols of Vedic Astrology*, he preserves a "deeper and older wisdom tradition."

But if there is much that is old in Behari's work, there is also much that is new. Bepin Behari is a species of "Renaissance man." An economist by profession, he is also one of modern India's most widely published astrologers. He maintains a lively interest in Western psychology (especially Jung) and in quantum physics. He has been deeply influenced both by Theosophy and by traditional Hindu philosophy. All of these influences find a place in his work.

Behari is uniquely qualified to give Westerners a sense of the spiritual astrology they seek. He focuses on the inner principles upon which Vedic astrology is based, then defines those principles in the light of contemporary psychology and scientific speculation. He joins the ranks of those who seek to re-formulate Vedic wisdom for the modern world so that it may regain its rightful place as a truly integrated path which encompasses science, religion, psychology, and life in general. During the middle years of the twentieth century, Dane Rudhyar — another Renaissance man who was deeply influenced by Theosophy — gave Western astrology a thorough re-structuring which made of it a deeply meaningful form of psychology. Behari, in giving Hindu astrology an equally thorough restructuring, makes it a true spiritual science.

Fundamentals of Vedic Astrology, Vedic Astrologer's Handbook I is the second of Behari's works to be published by Passage Press (*Myths and Symbols of Vedic Astrology* was the first). Many more are planned. The *Handbook* is intended primarily as a teaching manual, though it is a teaching manual enriched with philosophical speculation and spiritual exegesis. The first volume covers the basic principles of the art, while the second is devoted to an extremely detailed treatment of planets in the various signs and houses. The third volume will deal with predictive techniques and with synthesizing all the information into a practical but spiritual method of interpreting the horoscope, while the fourth will be comprised of essays on various astrological topics.

Hindu astrologers have never pretended that their art is simple. Behari will demand your full attention. You *will* study! But those who take the time to master the techniques offered in the *Fundamentals of Vedic Astrology* will find the spiritual astrology they have been seeking. They will also find unexpected gems of wisdom in the more philosophical portions of the book.

To all those about to enter Bepin Behari's rich inner world: Happy wandering.

Kenneth Johnson
March 1991
Santa Fe, New Mexico

PREFACE

Vedic astrology has its roots in ancient Vedic occultism. The Vedic seers considered the Jyotish Shastra, which dealt with the knowledge of the future, as an important limb of the Vedas. The antiquity of the Vedas themselves is lost in archaic times and any effort to fix their origin is beyond human capability. The authorship of the various scriptures is attributed to several different seers, but none of them claimed originality. They merely recorded the wisdom they had heard or remembered. Time has not tarnished their work. During the course of human civilization the intellectual horizon of mankind has expanded and new lights have begun to shine from the ancient wisdom. With every new revelation, the ancient wisdom becomes yet more profound. But as yet, we have not succeeded in identifying the original foundation upon which the superstructure was raised, or the eternal spring from which these drops of nectar are drawn.

Vedic astrology is not inductive. Its principles are not founded solely upon celestial mechanics by way of which generalizations can be made for application to posterity. Vedic astrology reflects the understanding and perception of ancient spiritual teachers regarding the facts of life. If the receiving instrument was not perfect and the reflecting medium free from every distortion, the understanding of this mysterious life-process could not be everlasting. Even when perception was free from any bias, the imparting of the knowledge had to be very carefully accomplished. Especially when the wisdom had to be transmitted over a long period of time, the language had to be such that the impact of time was minimal. Only a language which arose from the very nature of the objects and relationships it was designed to express could be useful in this regard. The most important handicap arose from the psycho-spiritual equipment possessed by the student, who had to comprehend the messages conveyed by the seers. Generally, a student interprets or bends the wisdom to suit and fit his own experience, understanding, and psychological propensities.

The ancient seers did not inquire merely out of intellectual curiosity. They wanted to understand the laws of nature so that they could adapt themselves to these laws and enlighten the paths of other seekers. Astrology was "enlightenment" in the sense that its manifestation resulted from the process of enlightening the Eternal Darkness or Nothingness. Jyotish Shastra is related to the nature of light and the radiation of various objects (especially the celestial entities), but this process had a purpose and a direction as well as a carefully defined nature and specific laws. Several occult scriptures concern themselves with different aspects of this process of manifestation and one cannot hope to comprehend the sublime nature of Vedic astrology unless it is approached from a wider perspective.

The *Yoga Sutras* indicate the goal of one's intelligence and the process by which distortions in the same may be eliminated. Once an individual is able to attain clarity in perception, there are immense possibilities for him. Patanjali, author of the *Yoga Sutras* which are of such great value in these present times, tells us that the clarity attained by yogic practices can enable the practitioner to concentrate on the Sun and know the secret it holds with regard to the working of the solar system and the inhabitants dwelling therein. The basic principles of Vedic astrology resulted from this kind of attainment. By going to the very source, it is possible even today for students to understand the deeper meanings of celestial relationships. Unless one is able to attain perfection in yogic discipline, it is useless to ponder over the basic astrological tenets or seek to comprehend and intuit their deeper implications. Engaging in the necessary yogic practices, the related metaphysical knowledge coming from the archaic past should also be intensively studied.

The present study is a modest attempt to present merely a portion of the ancient astrological knowledge of the Vedic Aryans. The author has been merely an infant, trying to understand the spiritual nature of astrology and other occult literature of the East. He is not a professional astrologer and does not claim infallibility in his predictions. But his acquaintance with the subject for the last fifty years has shown him that a proper and unbiased approach may be very rewarding for the student, and reveal to him the purpose of his life and how to grapple with his everyday problems effectively so that, over the course of several incarnations, he succeeds in establishing a harmonious balance with Nature. The author has also learnt that the use of this approach in predicting the future of others proves effective in counseling. A large number of individuals with whom he has come into contact have felt that Vedic astrology has a distinct role to play in providing peace, stability and confidence in everyday human relationships. In the present work the author hopes to carry this message to a wider audience, especially to those with whom he cannot come into personal relationship and contact.

A prerequisite for astrological prediction is the realization of the existence of cosmic unity. In almost every occult tradition and wisdom religion of the East, the basic identity of microcosm and macrocosm has been emphasized. But an application of this principle in predictive astrology is often overlooked. Planetary combinations affect the universe in a very mysterious manner. An understanding of the mechanism by which planetary impulses impinge upon the manifested universe, are received by the earth and deflected to the individual, as well as the manner in which different individuals receive them in order to evolve toward their archetypal destiny, is essential in order to gain an insight into astrological forces. A synthesis between esoteric religious philosophy (and in fact all such religions come from the same source, so there should be no basic difference between them) and various astrological concepts helps in understanding the code of relationships and hence the various suggestions made during astrological counseling. Generally this is a neglected aspect of astrological studies. The reader is strongly urged to see *A Study in Astrological Occultism* by the author (available from Passage Press). The sections dealing with the Cosmic Man and his basic impulses, and the constitution of man in light of the Seven Rays and Principles, should prove especially helpful in throwing new light on the subject.

In astrological prediction, it is important to examine the nature of planetary combinations, the nature and strength of the planets and their influence on the bio-psychological field of the individual. The complete human individual consists of various subtle sheaths, has certain inherent impulses received at the time of birth, and is related to different levels of manifestation. These characteristics are reflected in the pattern of planetary combinations. During the course of worldly evolution and the emergence of individualized human souls, different kinds of concretization take place, both in the individual as well as in the manifested universe. But the basic link is never severed. The different houses in the natal chart and the planetary connections with the houses reflect these eternal relationships, and are the basis upon which the nature of the individual, his course of unfoldment, and the direction towards which his life is moving can be known. For a proper understanding of oneself, this knowledge is very helpful. The trials and tribulations of life, the selection of a career, the pleasant and sorrowful experiences in human relationships and one's basic temperament are all deciphered from the natal chart. The first volume of the *Vedic Astrologer's Handbook — Fundamentals of Vedic Astrology* — deals with these subjects.

The nature of planetary influence depends upon the basic characteristics of the planets themselves. The Vedic astrologer does not consider the planets as inert orbs of different chemical composition: they are living, spiritual force-centers with their presiding deities, their specific functions and their history. These living occult forces are not restricted to the astrological realm. Life is much more expansive than mere astrological predictions can suggest. The Vedic seers have described the nature of the planets in many kinds of esoteric language. A Hindu occultist, T. Subba Rao, has emphasized that the key to the secret meaning of these zodiacal signs, planets, asterisms, etc., should be turned several times in order to decipher their meanings at various different levels. He has offered the following rules which, at the first level of such an exploration, may help the enquirer in ferreting out the deeper significance of the ancient Sanskrit nomenclature used in the old Aryan myths and allegories.

1. Find out the synonyms and other meanings of the terms which are used.

2. Find out the numerical value of the letters comprising the word according to the methods given in ancient Tantric works.

3. Examine the ancient myths or allegories, if any, which have any special connection with the word or concept in question.

4. Permutate the different syllables comprising the word and examine the new combinations formed, and their meanings, etc., etc.

In fact, such are the rules for deciphering the hidden meanings of all the esoteric or wisdom religions of the world, including Christianity and the Kabbalah. In order to examine some of the deeper meanings of Vedic astrological signs, planets and lunar mansions, the author has written *Myths and Symbols of Vedic Astrology*, published by Passage Press. The nature of planetary influences can be better appreciated if the chart of an individual is examined against the background of information given in this study, especially the section on the asterisms or lunar mansions which reveals special qualities of the planets in different horoscopes.

The planetary periods or dashas are the crux of astrological predictions. An individual may be very capable, but his latent faculties may not be useful to him unless he is able to use them. Money in the bank does not enable an individual to enjoy the comforts of living unless he draws that money for the purpose. The timing for the fructification of any result or the occurrence of any event is a special aspect of Vedic astrology. Elaborate guidelines have been given to work out the time period in which any planet will come into full play and thereby precipitate its influence. This aspect of the subject will be presented in *Predictive Techniques of Vedic Astrology*, Volume III of the *Vedic Astrologer's Handbook*. On the basis of various methods indicated there, it is hoped that the reader will be able to draw some realistic inferences about everyday human struggles.

In the preparation of this study, I have been helped by many friends and colleagues. M. M. Mistri, an architect by profession but an expert on horary astrology, and Biman Behari, an atomic physicist and practitioner in bio-rhythmic predictions, did much to help me in the preparation of the book. But the interaction with the team of friends and experts around Robben Hixson deserves special mention. Robben is a very discerning intellectual who is ever eager to harmonize different lines of thinking without imposing his own thinking or personality. He strives to achieve perfection in every bit of one's action, for which he is prepared to incur many personal inconveniences. Erna Wilson and Ken Johnson typed, edited and went through the manuscript in great depth, highlighting things which needed special consideration and attention. As a result of the interaction with Robben, Erna and Ken, the book has assumed a radically different appearance from what it was in the beginning; in its present incarnation it evolved substantially. It is now difficult for anyone to identify which ideas arose from whom, but the final form has an identity of its own and I trust is much more useful than the original presentation. I alone am responsible for any shortcomings which may come to light.

The author would like to make a special request to his readers: as this study is likely to fall into the hands of individuals living in different social and geographical backgrounds than the author's, they may experience reactions to planetary influences in a different manner than what has been described herein. They are welcome to share their insights and questions with the author.

Bepin Behari
C-505 Yojana Vihar,
New Dehli-110 092
INDIA

INTRODUCTION

Order, harmony and bliss are the foundations of our existence and, provided they are directly experienced and understood, can be profoundly effective in guiding mankind and reducing its sorrow. Today this is not so — disorder, conflict, and brutality abound in the world. Modern civilization has lost its goal and light and stands at a crossroads.

For millennia, sages, philosophers and thinkers sought knowledge of the conditions and events surrounding them. Many divergent views emerged from this search. With increasing awareness of the laws operating in the universe, mankind adapted itself to existing conditions and survived. As knowledge grew, mankind replaced its ancient gods with science and technology. Logic replaced magic. Scientists became the priests of the day but human bewilderment persisted. Perplexity and pessimism increased.

As human learning advanced, assumptions were made and hypotheses tested to explain the relationship between man and the cosmos. Each individual approached his life according to his understanding of the universal laws. When he found an approach that satisfied him, he shared it with others to help them. The acceptance of these approaches by others depended upon their own level of understanding and the conditions of their own lives. In this way, a vast amount of basic knowledge became available.

The relationship between man and the world around him has been variously interpreted. Many highly evolved intellectuals who have had uncommon experiences and are sensitive to the different forces impinging upon their lives have postulated that physical existence is paralleled by a nonphysical counterpart. Exploring further, they have proposed an invisible subjective progenitor of mankind. Many of them have described it as the Divine Father; and some call it God.

Hindu philosophers and sages went into great intricacies along this line of thinking. They developed a system of relationships in which events in the everyday life of an individual and his society could be worked out in great detail. This system was presented to assist each individual in comprehending his own unique pattern of existence, and to show how the course of individual development was in harmony with social and universal development. The system was designed for practicality.

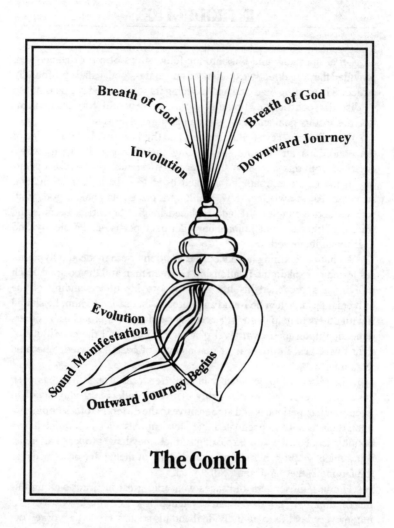

The Conch

Three features of this system are very significant. First, it recognizes the existence of a "subjective reality" behind the veil of "objective manifestation." Wherever there is an "objective" existence, there is a "subjective" counterpart to it. That there is an "objective present" means that there is also a "subjective past." The "objective present" and life's direction flow from this "subjective past." Second, the Hindu system recognizes that there is rhythm, circularity, expansion and direction in life at the different levels of its manifestation. Social and physical scientists have explored the forms of human existence and have shown us various facets of this rhythm, while poets, musicians, painters, and mystics have expressed the same truths in different ways. Third, the system recognizes that dissolution is inherent in all phenomena. Nothing remains permanently in the same form. Everything ultimately dissolves into subjectivity and finally into nothingness. Different names have been suggested to describe this ultimate state of immutability.

These conditions have been symbolically represented by such images as an ever-expanding circle, the ascending heights of mountain peaks that ultimately vanish into nothingness, a serpent eating its own tail, and by a conch.

Hindu philosophers attached considerable importance to the conch. It essentially epitomized their esoteric teachings. It reminded them of the process of cosmic manifestation. To them, the sounding of the conch expressed the human determination to cooperate with cosmic forces.

The conch was sounded at the beginning of every auspicious activity. It invoked the divine subjective energy present at every moment in every being. It announced the individual's dedication to the inner guiding force and his willingness to accept the final consequences of his present activity in the interest of harmonious natural order. Every god was symbolized as holding a conch in one of his hands. This showed his adherence to the natural evolutionary principle.

The significance of the conch in the evolutionary process can be explained in many different ways, and the astrological forces operating on man can be characterized by the sounding of this conch. The invisible spirit manifested itself from "subjectivity" to "objectivity" and became polarized as "involutionary" and "evolutionary" impulses. These were sustained and energized by the three basic attributes: harmony (sattwa), activity (rajas) and inertia (tamas). This highly surcharged field of activity was further motivated to change under four urges: goal oriented behavior (artha), righteous motives (dharma), desire oriented activities (kama), and the urge toward disentanglement and retirement (moksha or liberation). These urges made human society come together and proceed according

EVOLUTIONARY IMPULSES

Numericals stand for
NAKSHATRAS (ASTERISM)

ATTRIBUTES (GUNAS)	BASIC MOTIVATIONS
RAJAS	DHARMA
TAMAS	ARTHA
SATTWA	KAMA
	MOKSHA

to the basic impulse vivified by the subjective universal spirit. In this stupendous task, many forces variously represented as gods, deities, fairies and divine spirits cooperate and help the evolutionary forces to proceed according to their preordained destiny.

Over the last thirty years, astrophysical research and space voyages have probed outer space, and the mystery of the origin of life has become even more baffling. Scientists like Sir Fred Hoyle have speculated on the possibility that life originated elsewhere and was transmitted to this earth through extraterrestrial bodies. Ancient sages and occult seers indicated that life on earth began long ago when powerful evolved beings arrived from the planet Venus to direct the course of human growth and evolution. Earlier sages spoke of this phenomenon in more mystical terms.

Astrological philosophy does not enter into the controversy of this ultimate question. It does not speculate about the causes of the conditions that exist in the world. Astrology merely describes relationships between the occurrences of objective phenomena and planetary dispositions and leaves the explanation of causation to be worked out by philosophers and scientists. It has, however, provided information on various links between the different natural spirits and deities, planets and human beings. Every event taking place on this earth is related to invisible divine forces.

Astrological predictions are concerned primarily with four areas. In genethlialogy (the science of casting nativities), planetary influences are delineated according to their locations at the moment of one's birth or conception. General or mundane astrology deals with influences affecting social groups, nations, or humanity as a whole. It includes predictions relating to meteorology, seismology, husbandry, etc. State or civic astrology deals with the destinies of nations, kings, or the rulers of nations. It describes the nature, auspicious or otherwise, of a moment chosen to initiate a course of action. The fourth branch, interrogatory or horary astrology, provides answers to a client's questions based on the planetary situation at the moment the question is asked. Besides these, astrology is also applied to medicine and military strategy. These are simply special variants of the above primary forms.

The origin of astrology is lost in antiquity. In Vedic civilization, astrology was the very basis of daily life. In order to harmonize their daily lives with the laws of nature, the ancient seers revealed the nature of extraterrestrial influences on everyday life. In ancient China, the belief in an intelligent cosmic order found expression in correlation charts that juxtaposed natural phenomena with the activities and fate of man. For a long time, it was a universal practice there to have a horoscope cast for each newborn by a professional astrologer. These horoscopes were consulted and interpreted at all decisive junctions of life, particularly on the eve of a marriage.

Since the decipherment of hieroglyphics, ancient Egyptian knowledge concerning planetary influences on the spirit in man has come to light. Religious rituals (even those concerning births and deaths), architectural designs (including the great pyramids), and the lives of Pharaohs, were all correlated with planetary influences.

In Mesopotamia, astrologers regarded the planets as potent deities whose decisions could be changed through supplications, liturgy, or theurgy (the science of persuading the gods or other supernatural powers). The library of King Ashurbanipal, which contained about a million tablets, revealed the Assyrian's great reverence for Sin (Moon), Shamash (Sun), Adad (the weather god) and Ishtar (Venus). Hebrew astrologers made extensive use of the relationships between planets, numbers, and sounds. They deciphered the esoteric teachings of their scriptures and the implications of contemporary events on this basis.

Such beliefs were current in Greece, Babylon, and other ancient civilizations. Royal patronage was bestowed at many places for such astrological studies. Ardashir I, when he founded the Sasanian Empire in Iran, had a substantial number of Greek and Indian astrological works translated. Under the wisest emperors of Rome, a school of astrology existed wherein the occult influences of the Sun, Moon, and Saturn were secretly taught. During the late fifth and sixth centuries of the Christian era, Byzantium had such astrologers as Hephaestion, Julian of Laodicea, Proculus, Rhetorius, and John Lydus. In the late Middle Ages, universities in Paris, Padua, Bologna and Florence had chairs of astrology. The revival of ancient studies of the Humanities encouraged this interest, which persisted through the Renaissance and into the Reformation.

The study of sidereal influences has ever remained confined to a select group of students. Medieval alchemists revealed many of the esoteric relationships between the planets and the natural process of nuclear fission (the process which alters the atomic composition of elements, thereby changing base metal into pure gold), and between the planets and the transmutation of the spiritual and moral nature of man. They veiled their findings in garbled language, however. Students could comprehend their meanings only if they were given the keys to the various esoteric blinds. Annie Besant, under the influence of the famous British astrologer Alan Leo, studied Hindu astrology, but found it too casuistic and mystifying. Her mentor, H.P. Blavatsky, in *The Secret Doctrine* and *Isis Unveiled*, showed that the course of cosmic, terrestrial and human evolution was controlled and guided by planetary forces.

Astrology degenerated with the advent of materialism. When the votaries of astrology lost the metaphysical keys and began to practice it in order to earn money, or prognosticated to satisfy the whims and fancies of their clients, the deeper meaning of astrological prediction was lost. Its votaries were cultivating a mere husk. The astrologers in Rome and elsewhere came into disrepute because of their penchant for making money. Ignorant of the esoteric basis of astrology, they evolved a system entirely based on mathematics; instead of transcendental metaphysics, they began to consider the physical celestial bodies as the material basis of causation rather than merely the means for transmitting spiritual power. In order to understand the extraterrestrial powers energizing life on earth, it is necessary to step beyond the physical world of matter and enter into the domain of transcendent spirit.

$$* * *$$

Scientific research has opened new dimensions of life. J. B. Rhine of Duke University has pointed to the possibility of a sixth psychic sense. Clairvoyance, clairaudience, and precognition are being recorded with increasing frequency. Edgar Cayce's clairvoyant teachings stressed the relationships between physical disease and planetary influence. C. W. Leadbeater, Geoffrey Hodson, and Phoebe Bendit have documented their findings on the existence of non-human entities on this earth. Despite skepticism about UFO reports, eminent scientists, including Fred Hoyle, have begun to consider the possibility of life on Mars. Photographs and astronomical data sent by various space probes have compelled astrophysicists to speculate seriously on the possibility of life on Jupiter as well as on stars in other galactic systems. The uniqueness of our terrestrial existence is not only seriously challenged, but the outer and inner dimensions of the human body are being explored as well. In addition to the experiments of the Kirlon brothers in the Soviet Union, Dr. P. Naendran of Madras has designed a machine to photograph the human aura. It exposed impending diseases.

As a result of such findings, the scientific approach to "life" has changed radically. Scientists at the International Symposium held at Moscow in 1956 to discuss the origin of life on earth realized that they could neither define, nor unequivocally recognize "life," but they were nevertheless certain that there was such an entity to be recognized.

In 1975, 116 American scientists, including eighteen Nobel Laureates, took the unprecedented action of issuing a statement that condemned astrology. Carl Sagan, widely known for his television series *Cosmos*, called the action "authoritarian." Founders of modern science such as Tycho Brahe, Johannes Kepler, Isaac Newton and Albert Einstein would certainly have lamented this self-imposed blindness to expanding the horizons of human knowledge. When the skeptical scientists were questioned as to the basis of their statement, they replied that they had signed it out of a "religiously felt conviction." Even Jayant Narlikar of India, an astrophysicist, called astrology a mere pseudo-science. Eminent astrologers have consistently made spectacular personal and world predictions in spite of such a strong lobby against astrology's growing popularity. The outstanding evidence of the mystic nature of astrology, whose laws are still undiscovered by modern scientists, should be explored in depth if the scientists wish to maintain their credibility.

Through the ages, eminent men have advocated and practiced astrology. Historians record that Caesar, Pliny and Cicero believed in astrology. Marcus Antonius never travelled without the astrologer recommended to him by Cleopatra. Augustus, when ascending the throne, had his horoscope cast by Theaganes. Before his invasion of India, Alexander of Macedon consulted astrologers. Cicero's best friends, Nigidius, Fiulus, and Lucius Tarritius, were great astrologers. Vitellius dared not exile the Chaldeans because the astrologers had announced that the day of their banishment would be the day of his death. The Emperor Hadrian was a learned astrologer and predicted important events of his day. Such eminent intellectuals and scientists as Sir Isaac Newton, Bishops Jeremy and Hall, Archbishop Ussher, Dryden, Flamstead, Ashmole, John Milton, and Steele believed in astrology. Cardan and Kepler were among its ardent supporters. Newton traced the origin of the signs of the zodiac prior to the voyage of the Argonauts. Kepler was an astrologer by profession and became an astronomer in consequence. We find Regiomontanus, Tycho Brahe and others among the votaries of astrology. This suggests that the refusal of modern scientists to consider its impact on human affairs is a symptom of deeply rooted schizophrenia.

It would be more intelligent of modern man to gradually try the efficacy of astrological prognostications, and remember that they depend upon the erudition, experience and psychic faculties of the astrologer. If the predictions are fruitful, it would then be advisable to base daily decisions on planetary directions. This sagacity made Elizabeth I, Napoleon, Lloyd George, Edward VII, Roosevelt, Churchill and others consult astrologers. General Pinochent in Chile is reported to follow the stars. Sri Lanka, before choosing the exact minute in which it became a republic, took astrological advice.

The Sunday Times reported that there was documentary evidence that Mossad, the Israeli intelligence service, regularly used astrologers, most notably in the raid on Entebbe. Sheikh Yamani had one in London and organized OPEC meetings according to astrological advice. Indira Gandhi, Lal Bahadur Shastri, and Rajendra Prasad had great confidence in astrologers. American President Ronald Reagan consulted an astrologer. According to a report by Jon D. Miller of Northern Illinois University's public opinion laboratory, nearly two-thirds of American adults read astrological material, while twenty-six million of them read it regularly. About 5,000 professional astrologers practice in the United States and there are 50,000 part-time practitioners. In the United Kingdom, astrology is assigned a respectable status. The faculty of astrological studies at Hayward Heath compiled a list of astrological consultants who have completed a five-year training course and abide by a code of ethics that prevents them from writing an astrological column for the press. In fact, in modern times there is a great desire for scientific inquiry into the rationale of stellar relationships.

Carl C. Jung, the eminent psychologist, explained astrology in very simple words. He said, "We are born at a given moment, in a given place, and, like a vintage year of wine, we have the qualities of the year and of the season in which we are born. Astrology does not lay claim to anything more." This principle is a source of great enlightenment and may even open new lines of intellectual inquiry which could clear many of the cobwebs from the mind of modern man.

To survive, modern science must discover new methods of research. The fundamental principles of nature will not always yield to laboratory tests. The current experimental method will be inadequate to discover the truths of the nonphysical world. Dreams are realities which no sane individual would deny, yet it is impossible to repeat dream experiences. Inquiry into dreams and their impact on human consciousness has not been abandoned simply because dreams are unrepeatable. The Indian seers laid down rigorous requirements for those who wanted to delve into occult subjects but they did not deny any sane person the right to inquire. Perfection in astrological prediction depends upon intensive practice of meditation and perfection with regard to key mantras which open one's subconscious mind to the cosmic impulses that enable the practitioner to prognosticate the future.

Patanjali, in the *Vibhuti Pada* of his *Yoga Sutras*, indicated the type of meditation practice which could enable any student to gain knowledge of the past and future, knowledge of the meaning of sounds uttered by living beings, knowledge of previous births and of the time of death. Krishnamurti explained the process of apprehending the future when he stated that when the mind has become somewhat sensitive it naturally observes more, whether of tomorrow or today. It is like looking down from an airplane and seeing two boats approaching from opposite directions on the same river; one sees that they are going to meet at a certain point, and that is the future. The survival of modern physical science rests on its ability to leave terra firma and take an eagle's view from the sky. Only this can reveal to them the rationale of astrology and other occult sciences.

The ancient Eastern occultists not only indicated the various principles of prediction, they also enunciated the basic principles which enable stellar repercussions to take place. The basic principle of this relationship between the distant planets and worldly affairs is the existence of a magnetic force which is called by such names as the anima mundi, sidereal light, the astral light, akasha, noosphere, etc. Whatever the name, the essential feature of this field of "energy-consciousness expansion" is its complete coverage of the solar system. The entire universe is psychically and magnetically linked with an invisible thread of affinity.

The significance of time is unique in the cosmic ideation. In fact, time is an illusion. It is only perceived at the lower levels of existence. As the consciousness swings up, the illusion is gradually eliminated. With yogic practices, the disciple is capable of functioning on the plane of Eternity or the Eternal Now and can see the universal forces operating in their cosmic expanse. There neither the origin nor the end exist; everything is the present. In the Eternal Now, everything just exists. Once that level of existence is contacted, the future becomes an open book.

The astrological seer functions at the level of the Eternal Now. But even a common astrological student who is earnest and purifies his consciousness to understand the laws of nature can understand the impact of the various planetary impulses. He must, however, give attention to different astrological aids in order to understand how these interrelated impulses of cosmic ideation affect man and the society in which he lives and moves.

✳ ✳ ✳

The natal chart, known as the horoscope, is the most important basis on which astrological prognostications are made. It may be defined as a map of the sky and the planets at a certain moment, typically the moment of a person's birth. The planets move along the path of the ecliptic (the apparent path of the sun against the stars). To specify their positions at the time of birth, or at any moment of time, a reference point is needed to identify the position of the planets in relation to the earth. This reference point is the point of intersection between the path of the ecliptic and the equatorial horizon. But due to the retrograde motion of the equinoctial points along the ecliptic, these points intersect earlier in each successive sidereal year. Thus, over a number of years, the precise position of these coordinates becomes difficult to ascertain. The rate of precession is now identifiable; however, this aspect of the problem is very complex and has given rise to different schools of astrology. For the present, it is sufficient to note that the horoscope cast for one's birth is a charting of the planetary positions in the sky at that exact moment.

When examining any horoscope, it is important to realize that planetary positions are gauged in relation to both the zodical signs and the asterisms — i.e. further extensions of the ecliptic. When the planets are charted in relation to the equinoctial points, they are naturally related to these twelve signs of the zodiac and twenty-seven asterisms. The zodiacal point with which to begin the vernal equinox has been disputed by different astronomers, but there is agreement upon the beginning points for the signs of the zodiac and the asterisms. Signs and asterisms both begin their cycles at the 0 degree point of the zodiac.

For predictive purposes, it is essential to realize that these signs, asterisms, and planets are radiating centers which discharge their various influences into the vast "energy-consciousness" field of operation. The asterisms are very powerful influences which continuously send their impulses throughout the universe. To maintain balance in the cosmic whole, there must be order in the discharging of these impulses. As they radiate towards earth, they meet another type of specialized radiation. These second radiations come from the signs of the zodiac. When they reach the earth, these influences merge with one another to affect different entities on earth. None of these impulses affect us in their pure form.

On their way to earth, these impulses encounter more astrological phenomena. These are the planets. Planets are positive forces which impel the arousal of certain activities. They are causative impulses. The planets impart specialized energy substances, but their causative forces are influenced by the radiations coming from the signs and asterisms. We may think of the asterisms as climatic conditions in which the planetary

**ASTROLOGICAL IMPULSES
AS PART OF THE COSMIC
MANIFESTATION PROCESS**

radiations are like actors playing a role. While the planets are releasing certain influences, the general atmosphere produced by the signs and asterisms changes the planetary radiations. In order to understand astrological influences, the relationship between planets, signs and asterisms must be fully grasped.

The entire interplay of these forces takes place in what is known as Kala Purusha. This concept is basic in Hindu astrology. Kala means time and Purusha is man, but the term may be better translated as the Cosmic Man. The cosmos constitutes all that exists. The planets, signs of the zodiac, asterisms, the earth, its vegetation, animals, and man together form Kala Purusha. The Cosmic Man includes all these but he is much more. He is constantly imparting evolutionary impulses, as expressed by the signs of the zodiac, the asterisms, and the planets. Individuals at different rungs of the evolutionary ladder experience these influences differently.

The impulses reaching a person must pass through that person's immediate environment. Many kinds of occult forces surround the earth and the individual. The Sun enjoys a special importance in arousing such forces. In the morning when the Sun rises, it radiates its most powerful influence. When it reaches the midheaven, it draws all that is best from the individual — it extracts his faculties from him and pours them upon the external world. At the time of sunset, the sun gathers together the individual's active energy and blows it towards the invisible counterpart of one's life, seeming to drain the life-force from the physical vehicle, making the individual dormant and inert. At midnight, when the Sun traverses the nadir, it links the individual's ego to the eternal plane of his existence from which everything has arisen. This activates the core of the individual's being, his very heart. Other specialized influences percolate around these cardinal points. The circle, beginning and ending at the eastern horizon, describes the complete celestial cycle. It is divided into twelve parts, each concerned with a different aspect of life. Each of these twelve subdivisions has seven layers of influence which, in order to successfully examine the planetary influences operating on them, must be carefully understood by the student of astrology. These subdivisions, when related to the signs of the zodiac and the asterisms, constitute the horoscope.

There are many methods of charting the twelve houses. Some are circular, some rectangular, some box-like formations, and others in geometrical form, but they all represent the 360° of the celestial horizon. The astronomical positions of planets are indicated in these house divisions according to conveniences provided by the format of the chart. On the basis of such a chart, the astrologer must transcend the physical-astronomical diagram and enter into the realm of spiritual forces in order to predict the effect of the various forces impinging upon the individual. Ancient seers have given various correspondences between the different planetary and zodiacal forces and spiritual powers in great detail. Even the division of the horoscope into houses has been analyzed in depth. Each house has been divided into sections and each section is associated with various deities of a specific purpose. The large number of these super-physical powers, influencing the minutest part of a horoscopic house division, must be carefully studied before a final decision is made. A comprehensive study of astrology will reveal a new relationship between man and the non-physical influences around him.

PART I

BASIC INFORMATION

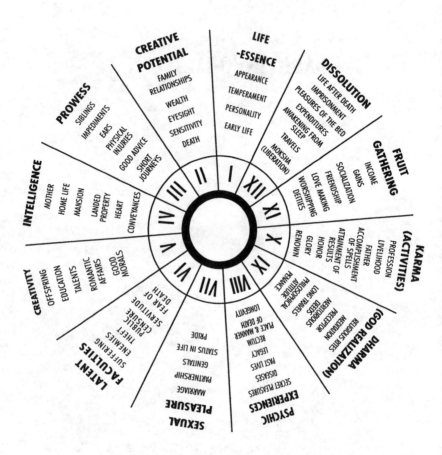

SIGNIFICANCE OF THE HOUSES

1
BHAVAS
THE HOUSES

The horoscope or natal chart consists of twelve houses or bhavas. Each house is basically comprised of thirty degrees, though the exact size may differ depending on the latitude of the birthplace and the time of year.

FIRST HOUSE

The First house or the eastern horizon is the most significant house in the horoscope. It represents the very being of the person, his *elan vital* and birth potential. It is a reflection of the spark fragmented from the whole. It is the soul incarnated, the creative urge of the individual. It expresses the inner fire and signifies the rajasic propensities.

All the qualities of the incarnating soul are contained in this house. Unless the seed of a specific quality or event is contained in this initial spark, other planetary indicators in the horoscope will not find suitable opportunities for manifestation. It not only reflects the individual's personality and potential, but the possibility of his achieving any desired result.

The First house represents the physical body, head and brain, general appearance, attractiveness of the face, and the impact of the personality. The height, the hair and its texture are also connected with it. The person's nature, his capacity to enjoy the pleasures and struggles of life, the pleasures and pain destined for him are indicated by this house. Wisdom acquired from earlier lives is shown here as well. The First house represents the beginning of an event, a journey, or any activity undertaken by the person.

The First house in a natal chart is called Adi, meaning the "beginning." It represents the beginning of all sentient beings, of all thought and idea; it stands for initial imagination, inspiration and aspiration. This house is also called Udyam, outgoing energy, or the power of taking the initiative and energetically participating in any activity. It is also called Deham, signifying the physical vehicle, and thus indicates the general state of health; it is also known as Rupam, for it symbolizes the form, identity, or mode of expression contained within.

The First house is Kshetrjan, "the knower of the field," suggesting that all experiences are garnered and stored here to be transmuted into wisdom. The Seventh house represents the kshetra, the field or area of experience that the soul must confront in the given incarnation.

SEVENTH HOUSE

The Seventh house is known as Kalatra Sthanam, the place of wife, groin, and the royal citadel. It represents the polarity of the First house. The First is the beginning while the Seventh is the ending: it leads to dissipation of the seminal fluid — marital relationship and sexual enjoyment being the primary means of such dissipation. The First house provides vitality and initiative, while the Seventh leads to depression; the First encourages onward progress, while the Seventh stands for a break in the journey. This house represents how the soul will employ the energy and vitality entrusted to it. Business partnerships, social relationships, and the expression of bodily urges are some of the characteristics of this house.

The Seventh house is the field of one's experience. Such activities are confined not only to sexual relationships, but are also linked with the enjoyment of food, the acquisition of beautiful clothes, perfumes and flowers, victory over enemies and even the "control of lustful men and women." From this house one can delineate business partners as well as the decorations and acquisitions of royal favor.

The Seventh house in its deeper implications represents the gross materiality out of which the soul must rise. Thus the nature of one's attachments, whether to wife, business and trade, royal favor or professional advancement should be reckoned from this house. The house has been assigned kama (desire and passion), dyuta (gambling), mada (pride), loka (world) and marg (way, the path). These Sanskrit words all describe the opposite polarity to the self (First house). Yet one's life partner, according to the spiritual view of human relationship, is actually a channel for fulfilling the Divine purpose. Vehicles, the path, and the loins — these Seventh house experiences exist together with their polarity factor, the self, in cooperation with God's plan.

The Seventh house is the field of experience, but the actualization of that experience is signified by the Tenth house. The latter therefore is known as the house of profession.

TENTH HOUSE

The Tenth house represents the midheaven where the Sun is at its highest glory. It is known as the house of the father, glory, royal patronage, profession and the karma of this present incarnation. Esoterically, the

Tenth house is the externalization of the Fourth, which is the container of that primeval seed that blossoms forth during the course of various incarnations. The Fourth and Tenth houses are intimately connected with the Moon and the Sun respectively — the Moon being the reflection of the Sun, which for each individual is the reflection of the Divine on earth. The Tenth house, connected with the Sun, draws the individual toward his future whereas the Moon reveals the past.

Success in life is determined on the basis of the Tenth house. The avenues through which past forces may lead the individual toward the future are also represented here. This externalization process occurs when the individual involves himself in mundane activities that bring him into contact with the world at large. For most people, this comes about through their profession. The classical texts therefore speak of trade, honor from one's sovereign, governmental activities, administrative jobs, and fame. Some of these texts also mention "riding a horse" while others speak of the Tenth house as tending toward the sky or of the nature of the sky. These epithets symbolize the soul being drawn toward its final goal.

In exoteric astrology, the Tenth house represents profession, honor, the quality of leadership, karma of the soul, father, government service, and achievement in the material world.

FOURTH HOUSE

There is a close link between the Fourth and the Tenth houses. While the Tenth signifies aspirations, ambitions, public standing and all matters outside the home, such as career, profession, and social status, the Fourth is the source from which all these spring. The Tenth house, as we indicated earlier, draws the individual to the future, while the Fourth reveals the past — the environment into which one is born, the family support one gets, the landed property, vehicles, clothes and ornaments one receives as well as the emotional nature one has inherited. All these things reveal the type of karma the individual has already generated. This karmic past is called sanchita karma. The primeval seed from which the evolutionary pattern flowers is contained in the Fourth house. In this sense this house is linked with the Hiranyagarbha,[1] the Mother Principle in Nature. It also stands for one's biological mother, as well as the heart, emotion, and intelligence.

---

1   In the *Upanishads,* Hiranyagarbha (literally "golden egg") is one of the names given for the creator of the universe. Behari uses the word to describe an inner creative principle or "seed" which forms the basis of one's psycho-spiritual developement.

All these are the basic wherewithal with which the soul embarks upon its worldly journey and fulfills its destiny as signified by the Tenth house. Symbolically, the Fourth house is represented by a tent or pavilion; it is also said to be a "medicine of supernatural efficacy," a metaphor which reveals the occult qualities of this house.

In exoteric astrology, the Fourth house stands for home, private life, transport facilities, landed property, mother, diseases of the chest and peace of mind.

The First, Fourth, Seventh and Tenth are very important houses. Planets are very energized there and their effect on the unfoldment of the person's life is very significant. These are the cardinal houses: all the important events in one's life hinge around them. They are known as angular or kendra houses, implying that they are the center or core of the chart. Taken together, they represent the celestial cross on which the Divine Child is crucified so that he may finally return to his father in heaven and ascend to his rightful throne.

FIFTH HOUSE

The Fifth house represents creativity. Creation is an essential quality of the Divine spark. The process of manifestation for which God assumed objective form was procreation, and, as such, creativity is an essential component of Divinity itself. Procreation implies giving rise to a new life, and that urge stimulates the creative impulse when this house is favorably disposed. This creativity can take place on different levels of manifestation. On the physical level it takes the form of children, but when it operates on an emotional plane it may manifest as the pleasures of life or in the realm of mental creation — authorship, or the expression of new ideas in the arts and crafts. Thus some of the significations of this house are education, progeny, intellect, management ability, courtship, speculation, artistic talents and "festival occasions when different musical instruments are played."

Considered from a deeper perspective, all creative arts are reactions to accumulated karma. The Fifth house expresses an individual's reaction to his past. In this sense, the Fifth house is important in modifying past karma so that new opportunities, more helpful to the attainment of the final goal, are realized. Ancient seers related this house to wisdom, religion, traditional laws, intelligence, occult knowledge, intuitive perception of the future, socially accepted forms of courtship, and progeny. All these are externalizations of inner creativity.

As the fruits of this house have far-reaching effects for the individual's course of life, it is considered a very auspicious house. Any connection between this house and the cardinal houses is conducive to great benefits.

NINTH HOUSE

The Ninth house is one of the bases of the Spiritual Triangle formed by the Ascendant (First house), Fifth house and Ninth house. These houses are important for spiritual growth. Creative activity produces the favorable conditions whereby spiritual progress is expedited. The Ninth house is said to represent religion, philosophy, austerity, worship and poorvapunya or the accumulation of auspicious karma from past lives. Unexpected help and encouragement to one's efforts result from this condition. Exoterically, the house is a significator of religion and philosophy, but esoterically it symbolizes discipleship and contact with great enlightened masters. This house also signifies one's approach to life, or understanding of the diverse forces at work around us.

The Ninth house represents God's grace and has a special affinity with Jupiter. Under its influence, the individual leads a spiritual life. Many aspects of life which move toward the goal of spirituality are indicated by this house. Classical texts therefore considered this house to rule destiny, pilgrimages, paternal wealth, Vedic sacrifice, nourishment, exertion for the acquisition of learning, splendor, purity of mind, generosity, and charitable or other virtuous deeds.

The First, Fifth and Ninth houses form the triangle which represents the spiritual nature of the person concerned. The First house shows the potency and possibilities of the soul. The acme of personal development and the direction to which the life force should flow are indicated by this house. The Fifth house signifies the limitations which the individual's creative activities and past karmas impose upon his involvement in earthly life and professional activities, as well as on his enjoyment of both mundane and post-earthly life. The Ninth, representing God's grace, reveals the possibility of special benediction, or past karmas which yield the fruits of success. For the auspicious fulfillment of one's life mission, it is essential that the nature and disposition of the Spiritual Triangle be considered carefully.

ELEVENTH HOUSE

The Eleventh house represents the creative activities of matter. There are cults in India which believe in intensifying the sexual urge, acquiring much money and indulging excessively in alcohol and narcotics to attain the goal of happiness. Their tradition is based on the assumption that greater intensification of material bondage is an end in itself — the members of this cult do not believe in a life beyond. By indulgence, one receives a greater impetus toward material gains. The Eleventh house represents all the tendencies and cravings that arise from this kind of activity. These proclivities are expressed as material affluence, extra-marital relationships, receipt of material wealth, love of ornaments and pearls, realization of one's wishes and any other situations which concern personal pleasures, friends, acquaintances, clubs and social gatherings, or monetary income.

The Eleventh house in its deeper implications also indicates that dissipation of man's material substance which destroys the physical chains so that a new birth may take place. But this can occur only when the individual has already acquired great spiritual merit. Generally speaking, this house represents friendship, high-class conveyances, prosperity, a good social life, satisfaction of personal needs, gains, hopes, the elder brother, arrival, and other worldly means of enjoyment flowing to the individual. It is said to be the house of income and receipts.

THIRD HOUSE

The Third house is an important base of the Triangle of Maya represented by the Seventh, Eleventh and Third houses. When the cosmic ideation penetrates the material sheaths and intensifies them, enormous strength, courage, valor, enthusiasm and energy are needed. All these are different expressions of the Mahat or Mind Principle. To experience the process of manifestation, the soul meets many different experiences as it proceeds through the world; man encounters different emotions and relationships. These are symbolized by the Third house. Prowess is its most important characteristic; collaterals, colleagues, companions and the immediate environment are among the experiences met by the soul in its journey, while classical texts state that courage, death, siblings, travels and the death of parents are also to be predicted from this house. But mention of spiritual teachings as one of the significations of this house reveals the deeper implications of the experiences garnered in this stage: the soul learns its lessons from the experiences encountered here. Difficulties and obstructions are the teachers of these basic lessons.

Exoterically, the Third house signifies the mind, siblings, short journeys, asthma, cough, consumption, chest, and the practice of pranayama, the breathing exercises which precede yogic meditation.

The Triangle of Spirituality represented by the First, Fifth and Ninth houses and the Triangle of Materiality or Maya represented by the Seventh, Eleventh and Third houses together form the mystic hexagon. It symbolizes creation resulting from the interaction of spirit and matter, generation as the outcome of the interplay of fire and water. As a Tantric insignia, it is a powerful talisman for mastery of the power of nature. In any horoscopic prediction, the nature and struggles of man, his possibilities for spiritual upliftment and the difficulties encountered in living out his destined course are described by the disposition of these houses.

Manifestation has emerged from the bounded eternity which has been described by occultists and metaphysicians in many abstruse terms. Astrologically, the interlaced triangles represented by the forces of spirituality and materiality have emerged from the great chaos — which is very tranquil but always in a state of creativity, containing all that ever was or will be. This creative chaos is symbolized by the Second, Sixth, Eighth and Twelfth houses.

SECOND HOUSE

The Second house is related to speech, family relations, faith in sacred tradition, eyes, gems and other forms of wealth, jewels, metals, and death. But it is also related to the sacred word Om, the Pranava. The sacred word is triple in its constitution, which reveals the different aspects of manifestation linking it with the primordial essence in its creative aspect and finally leading back to the Original Cause. The sacred word has tremendous mantric power — it links the evolving entity with his eternal counterpart and opens the channel for the downpour of tremendous spiritual force.

Speech, eyes, wealth and family relations are indeed an efflorescence of the everlasting life force expressed by the Gnostic term *Bythos*,[2] which means "depth," the Great Deep from which everything has emerged. Speech is a link between creative energy and creative action. Eyes link the beholder with the object perceived, the understanding of which depends upon the state of the inner perceiver. Wealth of the type signified by this house arises not so much as a result of one's activities but a result of past karma; it comes from inheritance, property, interest accruals and sources over which the individual has no decisive control. Even the family relations signified by this house refer to those relationships into which the person is born and are distinctly different from relationships with siblings, the mother, father, wife and others which are directly assigned to different

---

2   *Bythos* (Greek). In Gnostic symbolic language, the *Bythos* is variously termed the Great Deep or Abyss of Profundity (see G. R. S. Mead, *Fragments of a Faith Forgotten,* University Books 1966). As Behari remarks, the liberal meaning is "depth."

houses. The human relations signified by this house refer to those contacts which form the close blood-ties (binding cultures and ethnicities). They are also formed from the karmic past. Thus one finds that the Second house refers to creative potential as distinct from creative action, and that it links the individual's life with one aspect of his eternal component. It is significant to note that the Second house refers as much to creative potential such as speech, etc., as it does to death.

EIGHTH HOUSE

The Eighth house represents another aspect of the eternal component, different from the Second house in many ways. Generally, the Eighth house is related to longevity, death, the rectum and its diseases, but there is much more to this house than the standard interpretation implies. It will be better understood if the relation between the Eighth house and the Second, Sixth, and Twelfth is examined.

The Second house, related to Om, is intimately linked with the creative impulse while the Sixth, represented by Shakti or Mahamaya, contains the six primary forces of Nature in germinal form. The Eighth house symbolizes the chakras or hidden organs of man through which the Kundalini Shakti or Serpent Power flows. Esoterically, this house refers to the Vishnu aspect of creation, Vishnu implying expansion. The Eighth house is thus the storehouse of expansive energy latent in the microcosm. The Twelfth house represents life after death and is related to the Pancha Mahabhutam or five basic elements. In a way, the Twelfth house is a symbol for water functioning as the universal solvent of the alchemists. In fact, that is what death does: it reduces everything to its ultimate constituents.

Seen against the background of the four mystic houses, one can realize that the Eighth house represents the hidden aspects of one's life. The rectum is the most concealed portion of the body, but it is also the seat of the Serpent Power from which all siddhis arise, whether they lead to death, knowledge or discipleship.

In essence, the Eighth house signifies all things hidden; the rectum, serious diseases, concealed wealth, lotteries, knowledge of the hidden laws of Nature, gains or losses from market fluctuations, psychological afflictions or mental sufferings which would be unseen to others and even death — which is in fact the hidden existence of the individual after the close of life. Thus the Eighth house symbolizes the powers in Nature embodied as the Kundalini Shakti. All these spring from the Great Deep, the *Bythos* which exists forever. According to the karma of the individual, a portion of it is brought before him to bear.

SIXTH HOUSE

The Sixth house represents the struggle-experience of the soul during its sojourn. As it proceeds on its material path, the soul meets with resistance. The nature of this opposing force is also an aspect of the eternal component of existence. Thus the Sixth house shows struggle, difficulties, opposition of various kinds, litigation and servitude. Through these experiences, however, the individual develops his latent spiritual powers. When diseases and difficulties depress the individual, he gains strength by overcoming his depression. Exoterically, therefore, the Sixth house represents fear, difficulties, enemies, ill health, debt, servitude and the fear of death. Essentially it is the house of difficulties.

TWELFTH HOUSE

In the Twelfth house all individual forms of existence merge with the eternal stream of the life-force. Exoterically it is characterized by death, the cessation of all activities, expenditures, the end of the journey, voyages overseas, imprisonment, the pleasures of the bed (signifying the close of all mundane activities) and all kinds of misfortune. From the Twelfth house, astrologers also prognosticate mental agitation, discharge of debt, "termination of one's appointment," "renouncing one's couch," and loss of one's wife as well as entry into heaven. Dream experiences and psychic phenomena are indicated by this house. In the background flows the eternal life-force which is at last deciphered from this sign. Finally everything returns to the shoreless ocean of immutability; this house shows the process of this return at different levels of existence.[3]

---

3   Readers desiring to study the deeper significance of the houses should read Chapter 4: 'The Man on the Cross' in the author's *A Study in Astrological Occultism,* Bangalore, India: IBH Prakashana, 1983. See also Chapter 2: 'The Heavenly Man'. These chapters discuss the rationale of relating various attributes to the different houses.

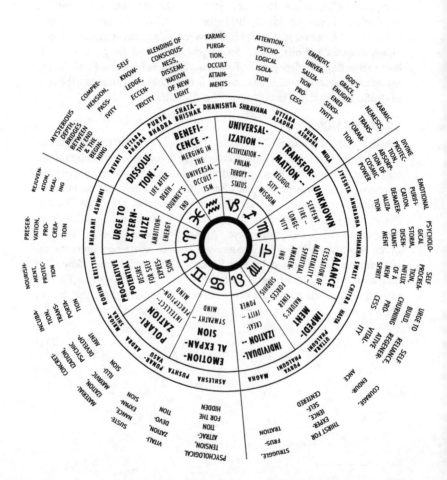

SIGNIFICANCE OF THE SIGNS

2
RASHIS
THE SIGNS OF THE ZODIAC

The zodiac is a twelve-fold division of the Sun's apparent path along the ecliptic. Twelve segments of sky have been given names and certain constellations associated with each. The constellations do not precisely match up with the zodiacal signs, which are best understood as symbolic representations of the divisions of the ecliptic. The constellations form imaginary figures which are associated with special influences flowing through their area. The influences work differently at different levels of manifestation. An understanding of these influences is derived from the characteristics suggested by these signs of the zodiac. When a natal house comes under the magnetic radiation of a zodiacal sign, the nature of that house is affected by that energy. Similarly, when a planet comes into this zone of radiation, the zodiacal influence vitally colors the effect of the planet upon the individual concerned. Students of astrology study the zodiac in order to work out the sum total of astrological influences and arrive at valid conclusions. The characteristics of the signs are merely suggestive, and the student — using his own understanding of the life process — has to reach an intuitive comprehension of the zodiacal influences.

There are twelve signs of the zodiac, represented by animals, insects, and some articles in common use. The ram, bull and lion are the animals representing the first, second and fifth signs of the zodiac; the crab, scorpion and fish represent the fourth, eighth and twelfth. The scale or balance and a pitcher are connected with the seventh and eleventh signs. The centaur, a creature from Greek mythology which sports the head, trunk, and arms of a man and the body and legs of a horse, represents the ninth sign. The unicorn, another mythical creature, represents the tenth sign — which is also represented by a goat. A couple, male and female, represents the third sign, while a virgin or maiden represents the sixth. Some of these signs of the zodiac have been linked with other symbols as well. Besides the symbols, there are other characteristics attributed to them. One must study the symbols intensively to understand the special features of each sign. We shall describe them only briefly, leaving much to the imagination and understanding of the reader.

MESHA
Aries ♈

Mesha is the name given to the first sign of the zodiac. The Sanskrit word Mesha means a ram or sheep, but other synonyms given to it are more connotative. Aja means the unborn, Vishwa refers to the whole or the universe, Kriya stands for motion and activity, and Tambura is a musical instrument, while Adya implies the first primeval cause of the manifest universe. Though Aja means the unborn, it refers to the "unborn-but-existing-in-eternity." Mesha symbolizes the unborn or unmanifest potential chafing to externalize itself: it stands for subjective-objective unity. Aries represents the future possibilities of creative energy, the world-to-be rather than the world-as-it-is. Thus, some of its attributes are ambition, aspiration, dream-like consciousness, the desire to multiply and expand. There is always newness in whatever Aries influences, but there is also a certain amount of contradiction. Aries is full of vitality, always eager to explore new lands and propound new theories. It represents the stage when the bud is ready to burst into flower but is not yet a flower; it shows the qualities of an adult though it is not yet an adult. There is a fire burning within, sex eager to express, and the desire to dominate — but in all these efforts there will be some form of restriction, some limitation or impediment of the bubbling potential. A person under this influence may become a dictator, an autocrat capable of passing the most cruel orders, but his heart may remain very clean, ready to forgive and pardon the guilty.

Esoterically, Aries maintains a strong link with the central invisible Sun God which makes the sign fiery, penetrative, restless, and eager to attain the highest in every field. This impulse impels the individual to dwell in subjective realms, unexplored universal ideas, ideals not yet achieved. His preoccupation is to make those inner, subjective, unexplored ideals objective and real. The impossibility of the task often makes the individual desperate, despondent and miserable.

The ancient seers considered Aries as masculine, fiery, a cardinal or movable sign[1] of the zodiac. Mars is intimately related to it: this planet is said to be the lord of the sign. The Sun is exalted here, implying that it is in possession of its best nature. Saturn is the weakest planet in this sign. The root or basis of Aries lies in Spirit, but both its conflict and its purity

---

1   Behari often uses the older terms "movable," "fixed" and "common" rather than "cardinal," "fixed" and "mutable," the more familiar terms in the West.

arise from the paradox inherent in making spirit manifest in a world of matter.

VRISHABHA
Taurus ♉

Vrishabha, the bull, is the second sign of the zodiac. The bull has been assigned a respected place in most world religions as a symbol of all the auspicious things in life. Social position, security, ease and comforts, wealth, progeny, vitality and a passionate nature are some of the characteristics of this sign. This is so because at this stage the unborn potential (Aries) becomes a creative urge which makes objective manifestation possible. At this stage there is a simultaneous attraction and repulsion which produces tremendous sexuality, materiality, and enjoyment of the pleasures of life. And yet the activity, motion, and adventurous spirit of Aries is lacking here, which makes the person comfort-loving, passive, content, and desirous of staying close to the birthplace rather than moving around in search of new experiences.

A bull is physically powerful. It has a tremendous capacity to breed. The very word Vrishabha means any male animal, anything best or eminent in its class. The maleness of Vrishabha symbolizes its role as a storehouse of procreative energy. When engaged in an activity, the Taurus person can work unceasingly at it, even if it is repetitive, till the desired result is achieved. There is a symbiotic relationship between the Taurean individual and his environment. Just as an oak tree becomes a permanent part of its landscape, a Taurean will want to "belong" to a permanent scene. Even so there is no satiety and stasis; there is always an urge to be creative and continue the evolutionary movement.

Taurus is feminine, earthy, and a fixed sign. These characteristics, however, must be carefully understood. Taurus is considered feminine, earthy and fixed because these qualities reveal the special creative nature of the sign. Procreation is the most sublime function of the female. The feminine nature is passive, yet full of desire and emotion centering on the female role in creation. Sexual activity is the supreme goal of the female. The earthiness of Taurus describes it as "downward," that is, "earth-ward" movement. Taurus represents the nature of the individual rather than his activity, as indicated by the fact that it is "fixed" rather than moving in any special direction. No planet is debilitated in this sign because the creative cannot let any force remain negative: the Moon is exalted here and Venus owns the sign. These suggest a zone of influence where consciousness and sensitivity are in a highly alert condition.

MITHUNA
Gemini ♊

Mithuna, which means a pair, twins, sexual union or a junction, is the third sign of the zodiac and stands for divine creative activity, which is made to operate by the polarization of Spirit and Matter. Though the sign is named the twins, it is in fact a trinity. It represents the Father, Mother, and Holy Ghost; it also represents the three gunas, namely sattwa (harmony), rajas (activity), and tamas (inertia). Emblematically, the sign represents a male (Father) and a female (Mother) seated in a boat. This suggests a journey or an involvement in the creative process of manifestation. Gemini stands for Mind or the Mahat Principle. This principle creates duality, polarization, and the birth of intellectual perception. Esoterically, it stands for the interaction between objectivity and subjectivity.

In predictive astrology, Gemini shows the qualities of quicksilver, a mysterious metal which is highly elusive and susceptible to a wide range of fluctuations. Heat and cold both affect the sign very easily. There is a sparkling quality to it, often brilliant and intuitive. Though it has a great deal of mystic potential, Gemini's approaches and expressions are basically materialistic. Conflict and instability are important characteristics of the sign. Contentment, satisfaction, stability, and tranquility are not to be found in Gemini. Depression, suicidal tendencies, excitement, experience, and a great thirst for indulgence may arise. These could very well be related to the discovery of the meaning and purpose of life. Gemini is very active on the subjective plane.

Gemini is a masculine sign, airy in nature and containing the mixture of movable and fixed qualities which define a common sign. Gemini is most effective at higher subjective realms, always eager to act and achieve but not terribly effective in yielding concrete results. No planet is exalted or debilitated here and Mercury rules the sign.

KARKATA
Cancer ♋

Cancer, the fourth sign of the zodiac, provides pliability, emotion, and the quality of sympathetic appreciation. Its action is decisive, and its hold invincible. From its grip, no one can extricate himself without shedding some blood. Inwardly it is a little shaky about itself and uncertain of its power and potential, which often makes it an easy target for birds of prey. Sages consider the sign to represent the four aspects of Parabrahman: sthula (physical), sukshma (subtle), bija (causal), and sakshi (the Silent Watcher). It also represents the four states of consciousness: jagrata (wakeful), sushupti (the dream state), turiya (deep sleep) and nirvana or samadhi (deep meditation). These attributes are suggestive of the fact that Cancer has a wide range of operation and operates in the subjective as well as the objective realm of manifestation. Esoterically, Cancer stands for the interaction of time and space on the involutionary path of the soul. It is related to the Hiranyagarbha of the Hindus and the *Bythos* of the Greeks.

Cancer is feminine, watery and movable. Water is adaptable and can assume any shape depending upon the vessel in which it is kept. Water is formless, colorless, and odorless, but it is also the sustaining energy of all life. Cancer provides sustenance: the differentiation of cosmic ideation in space and time is an expression of this life-sustaining force. Being feminine in nature, Cancer is very productive provided it is met by the right kind of unity force. Cancer never feels at ease with inaction; it desires to be engaged in some kind of movement — even mere displacement, or movement without much significance.

The Moon owns this sign, showing its great expansive capacity. Jupiter is exalted here, which reveals the protective quality of the sign. Mars is debilitated, signifying inaction as the most trying experience for Cancer.

SIMHA
Leo ♌

Leo, the fifth sign of the zodiac, is symbolized by a lion and is characterized as masculine, fiery and fixed. The significance of the lion symbol is understandable when we realize that the primary quality of this radiation is the Divine urge towards procreation. This is the stage wherein the Cosmic Man darts forth his creative thread of Primordial Light into the labyrinth of chaotic matter, establishing different force centers which lead ultimately to the individualization of man. At this stage the spiritual principles transform themselves into material forms. Leo represents creativity, the articulation of the Divine Nature in man; it is Divine Nature objectified.

Fire is the Divine symbol of penance, creativity, and purification, but it is also an element of Nature which cannot adapt itself to anything else. Fire cannot exist in active form in anything else. Leo is self-centered, aspiring, ambitious, and arrogant; it is fierce in action, calculating in sexual encounters, choosy in social relationships. Etymologically, simha means "the protector of its followers," and those who align themselves with this sign will have much natural force at their command. One supreme quality of Leo is its suddenness, aggression and frontal attack.

The Sun owns this sign but no planet is exalted or debilitated here. There is a grace and glow radiating from the Sun. No force which furthers the evolutionary impulse by procreating, or by protecting and leading its followers, can ever experience restrictions on its capacity. This is why no planet is debilitated here. Simha is one of the most mysterious signs of the zodiac.

KANYA
Virgo ♍

Let no one suppose that Kanya, the sixth sign of the zodiac, is weak because it is feminine, earthy and a common sign. Virgo has a very special significance in the manifestative process. It represents consciousness-in-bondage, but with an understanding that the shackles can be cast away. It represents that Divine discontent which impels the aspirant onto the path of discipleship where mass is converted into energy and matter is subjugated to Spirit. Virgo contains within itself those finer forces of Nature which express ideals and strive for perfection; it is that energy which suffers for the growth and fruition of a child's desire. Virgo arouses conscience and suffering for a noble cause.

Virgo is owned by Mercury which is also in its exaltation here. Venus is debilitated in this sign. Virgo produces intense activity in the realm of the intellect and psychic consciousness, where there is no place for personal pleasure and enjoyment. There is little of merriment produced by this sign, but for the attainment of siddhis there is no other sign which can be so helpful. Virgo is indeed very difficult to comprehend. It is the only sign in the zodiac symbolized by a single human figure and its mystic nature is enhanced by the fact that it is a maiden, not a married female adult. Hindu scriptures link it with Prithivi, the Earth, or Aditi, Celestial Space. The way Virgo influences the individual is difficult to describe. It symbolizes the Female Power (shakti). Yavanacharya described Virgo as holding fire in one hand — the significance of this statement becomes clear only when one pursues the symbolism of fire. There is not a thing or a particle in the universe which does not contain some kind of latent fire. Virgo holds within itself the power which enables everything to grow. Just as a mother tenderly guides the growth of her child, even suffering for her child, so Virgo cares for the manifest universe.

On the superficial level of existence, Virgo produces suffering, disquiet, and movement of an undesirable nature. But for inner quietude and tranquility, the grace of the World Mother whom this sign represents is essential. The maiden is shown seated in a boat, holding a chaff of grain in one hand and fire in the other. The maiden is Virgo's primary symbol;

the boat, the fire, and the handful of freshly cut grain are secondary. Moving in the current of manifestative flow, the creative potential moves to provide food and sustenance for its children. This is a sign of great sensitivity. It represents energy concealed in matter.

TULA
Libra ♎

Tula, the seventh sign of the zodiac, represents that stage of cosmic ideation in which Spirit is completely immersed in matter. At this stage, the soul is ready for a change. Wherever Libra appears, materialization is intensified and the indicated aspect of life has become ready for spiritualization.

Libra is enigmatic. There is a seeming quietude at the surface, but inwardly there is dissatisfaction. The existing state of affairs does not meet the psychological requirements. This sign represents a critical balance between Matter and Spirit; the fullness of materiality is not enjoyed because there is an inner quest for the life Divine. Both forces being of almost equal intensity, the aspect of life affected by Libra has fullness — but that fullness is not satisfying. This situation arises due to the dawning of spiritual awareness. Libra bestows material riches but does not allow the person to enjoy them. The sign is rightly represented by a scales of balance, symbolizing that this is where immersion in materiality ceases and spiritual awakening begins.

Libra is masculine, movable and airy. These qualities show the method of its operation. Libra does not depend upon other influences to be effective. Wherever and however it operates, it will create an impact. That is its positive or masculine quality. It can never remain stationary: it will always impart a thirst for greater and greater achievement. Whatever one's level of prosperity, Libra will always induce the ego to thirst for more. Outwardly, however, it does not create much of a show, for a great deal of its operation is psychological, for which reason it is said to be airy. Venus owns the sign, signifying that the sign is operating primarily in the realm of materiality. The Sun's debilitation and Saturn's exaltation in this sign have connections with this trait.

The seventh sign of the zodiac is full of deeper implications, and an understanding of its mysteries might unveil many clues to the finer forces in Nature as well as those hidden dimensions of human beings which can be employed either for useful or nefarious objectives. Many of the meanings of this sign are suggested indirectly by such attributes as Tauli (weigher), Vanika (merchant), Yuka (the link), and Tula (balance).

VRISHCHIKA
Scorpio ♏

Yavanacharya called Scorpio a deep opening in the earth whose correspondence in the human individual extends over the middle portion of the body represented by the genitals and the anus. The sign represents a cavity, a hiding place, a hole in which Vasuki, the Serpent Naga, surrounds and protects the precious gem. Naturally, this is a mysterious sign. The appellation Vrishchika (scorpion) is significant. This insect practices a very primitive form of animal association yet for the most part leads a strictly individualistic life. It avoids others except to fight to the death; the victor usually devours the victim. A scorpion is sensitive to heat and dies easily when exposed to the rays of the Sun in a closed container. These characteristics point directly to the occult nature of this sign.

Scorpio signifies energies which, if properly managed, could lead to a tremendous unfoldment of psychic power. But unless this process of unfoldment is perfectly understood, any activation of it is likely to lead to untold misery. It is related to hidden aspects of life, especially connected with the kundalini. Though the activities of an individual will be guided by this energy at various levels of his existence, the ways in which this energy manifests are not well known; Scorpio's impact is often considered difficult to comprehend. In ordinary individuals this energy works on the sex life, and sexuality is secret. Secrecy rules supreme in other aspects of life as well. But if the kundalini is controlled and well regulated, there is the possibility of harnessing psychic and other occult powers. Scorpio is the pit, the hidden recess of the earth where the Serpent Power is hidden, awaiting arousal. Unless one is careful, many dangerous and destructive possibilities can emerge from this sign.

Scorpio brings much conflict, destruction and chaos. The Serpent Naga which symbolizes this sign was used in the churning of the Great Milk Ocean when the gods and demons retrieved the immortalizing nectar. That churning power resides in Scorpio: the eighth sign creates chaos wherever it strikes. Turmoil, upsets, and unexpected developments arise. All these difficulties sooner or later produce the nectar of immortality. The special feature of Scorpio is its directness in achieving the result.

Scorpio is feminine, watery, and fixed. The Moon is debilitated here and no planet is exalted. Mars owns this sign. These characteristics emphasize the creative nature of Scorpio. Only when some favorable force or active agent operates on it can the sign be effective in producing its results. Generally its influence is not commendable. It may be sensitive but it can also be disruptive. Vindictiveness, impetuosity, selfishness, determination and tenacity are important traits of this sign. Scorpio's watery nature emphasizes its imponderable depth.

DHANUS
Sagittarius ♐

Sagittarius is the centaur — a horse-like beast with a human upper part holding a bow and shooting an arrow toward the sky. The Sanskrit name for the sign refers merely to the bow, the arrow, and the shooting. The geometrical symbol is comprised of a cross, and one arm of which becomes an arrow pointing upward.

All these symbols reveal the transforming effect of this sign. Sagittarius symbolizes the transformation of beast into human being, of the base nature into more noble qualities. But this transformation creates turmoil, challenge, confrontation and spiritual wanderings. One's existence becomes a spiritual quest, but it is not a peaceful process. It produces a radical change. Sagittarius is masculine and fiery. The spiritualizing process will require that materiality be burnt away. For this reason, the radiation has to be powerful, purposeful, effective and well directed. These are the qualities emphasized by masculine fire. Sagittarius is a common sign, containing both fixed and movable properties. This means that the ninth sign can unsettle the life-style as well as consolidate it, depending on the astrological circumstances. Whatever the effect of this sign, life's unfoldment under its impact reveals the future destiny of the struggling soul. This makes the sign auspicious.

The eighth sign leads to an awakening of consciousness. If this impulse operates on a spiritualizing level in the ninth sign, the various aspects of human nature are harmonized with the universal principle. A greater affinity is created between the separate consciousness of the individual and the universal consciousness of the Divine. Individual characteristics become universal ones. If this sounds vague, it is because the change may occur on any number of levels, in all of which the individual approach is destroyed and the natural process of change is cultivated. In this way Sagittarius is deeply religious. This also explains why Jupiter has ownership of this sign. No other planet has any special impact on this sign unless it operates under Jupiter's authority and jurisdiction.

Sagittarius, the ninth sign, is the dharma of the cosmic deity. It leads to the unfoldment of the Divine Essence. The outflow from this sign is God's grace, but such an influence cannot be expected to produce a life of ease and comfort. God's grace does not imply a reinforcement of one's traditional beliefs, habits and superstitions. As a matter of fact, life under this impulse is subject to radical transmutation: everyday experiences can be transformed into ideas and ideas into ideals. Sagittarius enables the Divine Spirit to illuminate the inner man.

MAKARA
Capricorn ♑

The nature of Makara is shrouded in mysterious references and allusions which cannot be easily described by the exoteric laws of nature. All these allusions refer to the central meaning of the sign — which has little to do with the word makara, meaning crocodile. Rather, the sign is associated with the Tropic of Capricorn which, in Theosophical literature, is the seat of the guardians of this globe. The tenth sign is related to the spiritual impulse which guides the world towards its destiny. Capricorn refers to the involvement of the individual in the process of the universalization of human energy. During the interaction of such forces there may be hardship and suffering. Under this impulse, consciousness begins to link up with thought currents and vibrations from higher realms of existence and the governing powers of the universe. On the material level, there may be difficulties and dissatisfaction, but inwardly the result of Capricorn is extremely satisfying.

When Capricorn begins to operate, past karmas are activated. Consequently, many unusual events begin to take place. The past accumulated forces are worked out so that the burden is lessened and sensitivity is heightened for absorbing fresh inspiration. The inner light concealed under the deceptive mask is released. Disillusionment, destruction of traditional values, and a new alignment of forces all occur under this influence.

Capricorn is considered feminine because the changes which take place under this sign completely re-create the individual, making him ready for the onward spiritual journey. The situations one confronts under Capricorn are not necessarily the result of one's immediate doings, but follow from past actions; there is much working out of destiny and fate. The sign is earthy. The realm of operation of this sign is mundane existence. Whatever happens under this sign makes us capable of sustaining further pressures on the soul's journey. Capricorn is movable, implying that there will be considerable change under its impact.

The basic forces flowing through this sign can also be understood by its relationship with Saturn, which owns it, Jupiter, which is debilitated here, and Mars, which is exalted. The deep acting effect of this sign often brings excruciating pain and tormenting psychological experiences. Any kind of religious advice, exoteric philosophy, or ritualistic practices will seem offensive to it. The sign is well disposed towards hard work, trying to harmonize the Self with universal thought currents and the individual's spiritual destiny. One has to be careful in deciphering the impact of this sign because it is extremely active, highly potent, and deep acting.

KUMBHA
Aquarius ♒

Aquarius is both the water-bearer and the water flowing from the pitcher. Water stands for the cosmic life force, the universal solvent which quenches the thirst of all and transmutes base metal into gold; it absolves the individual from all sins and purifies his heart. Under this sign, the evolving soul hopes to be a conscious cooperator with the universal creative power. This generally involves the sacrifice of personal comfort, pleasure, and convenience, thus causing considerable suffering. In Indian metaphysical thought kumbha, the pitcher, is associated with human existence. The physical body is compared to a pitcher. The shape of a pitcher is at first conceived in the mind of the potter. In the same manner, the final destiny of a man is carved out for him by God. Water conserved in a pitcher sustains life by quenching human thirst or irrigating plants. A human individual is also intended to help and guide others towards their fulfillment. This is the essential characteristic of Aquarius.

Esoterically, the sign represents the release of the universal life force contained in an individual. Water flowing from a pitcher appropriately suggests this process. In order to become a conscious cooperator with the universal creative power, the individual's restrictive barriers must be broken, which is by no means a happy experience. Wherever Aquarius appears, there is reaction and opposition. Difficulties arise. Material propensities become more intense in opposition to the impulse and the consequent frustration is greatly heightened. Exoterically, therefore, this sign is considered inauspicious and unfortunate, bestowing frustrating results.

Aquarius is masculine, airy and fixed. It is owned by Saturn, but the sign does not provide suitable conditions either for exaltation or debilitation of any planet. The effect of this sign is purposive, effective and deep acting. It does not simply provide conditions under which others can act, but has its own direction. Under this sign the turmoil in one's life is immensely increased as the individual begins to work in accordance with the divine plan and annihilate his personal ego. In this task, Saturn is ruthless in achieving its goal. It completely destroys traditional moorings. The influence of Aquarius is primarily on the psychological plane. The effect is also consolidated so that it becomes permanent. The name of the sign also has a relationship with kumbhaka, meaning holding the breath in yogic practices whereby the individual hopes to link himself with the Supreme. This sign orients the individual towards attaining this goal.

MINA
Pisces ♓

The ancient seers gave to this sign not only the name Mina, which means fish, but also Antyaya, which means the end, and Yasha, which means glory. All these are veiled references to the stage of achievement where the struggle is over and one has reached the end. During the Piscean process there is constant progress. At the end, the acme of achievement is realized. This is the stage beyond which there is nothing further to achieve. It is the end, the cessation of all efforts. The weary traveler goes to bed to enjoy a peaceful sleep.

The symbol for Pisces is two fish, placed in such a way as to represent the positive and negative discharges of electric vibration leading to complete assimilation of one into another. At this stage, there is no movement, no further excitement; tranquility reigns supreme within the individual. Pisces is the cessation of all worldly efforts, the final merging of the individual into the universal. It bestows much peace and comfort, making the fish a symbol of auspicious benediction and fertility suggesting that all ambitions have been satisfied.

Esoterically, Pisces represents the impulse under which duality ceases and only life in its fullness remains. There is no conflict, no contradiction, no more trishna or lust for life. The cycle of necessity which causes rebirth has ended, and all karmas have been annihilated. The individual has attained Nirvana, his ultimate equilibrium.

It would be deceptive to consider this a sign of death, the end of all. Instead Pisces represents the preservation of the essential seed which can blossom when the next cycle of evolution begins. In Pisces, there is a great deal of meditation and reflection, contemplating past experiences so that life's journey can begin again in full possession of those seeds of experience. Wherever the Piscean impact falls, such reflection will be vitally important.

Pisces is feminine, watery and common. From these characteristics, it is evident that this sign is related to the preservation principle. The primary function of the female is to procreate, to nourish the seed till the appropriate time for a new birth arrives; the feminine is receptive and protective. That is also the quality of water, which sustains and preserves life. As a common sign, Pisces can become movable or fixed. Jupiter owns the sign, which again emphasizes the same characteristics. Venus is exalted here and Mercury is debilitated. Sensitivity and intuitive openness are developed here. Intellectualization, analysis, reason and logic will not be very successful at this stage. Venusian surrender and Jupiterian spirituality are helpful, but Mercury's connection with the material world must necessarily bring some kind of disappointment: spirituality brings only frustration when the ego is attached to material impediments.

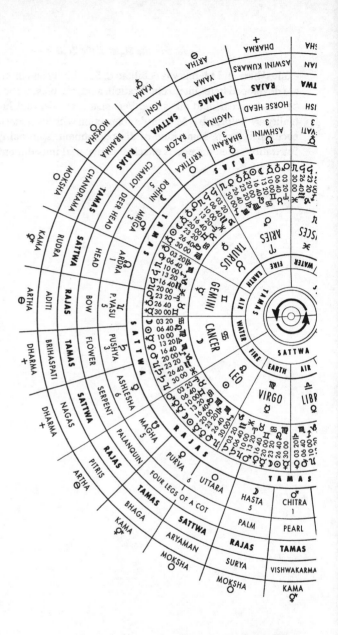

LUNAR MANSIONS
COSMIC

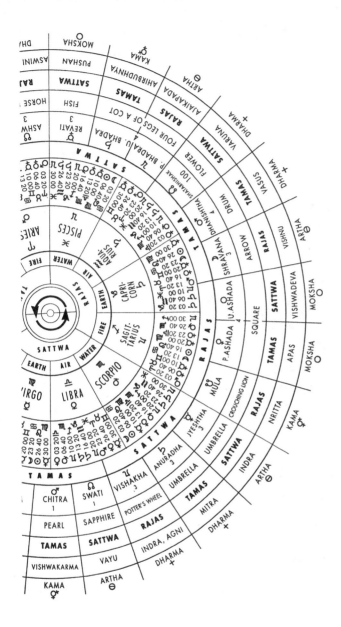

AND SIGNS IN
PERSPECTIVE

3
NAKSHATRAS
THE ASTERISMS OR LUNAR MANSIONS

The nakshatras are the central axes around which Hindu astrology revolves. Their origin is unknown. Even the Vedas give exhaustive references to them. Planetary influences are significantly altered under the impact of the asterisms. These lunar mansions, as they are called, should be studied carefully.

The Moon has a special relationship with the nakshatras. The association of the Moon with different asterisms fundamentally alters the character of a horoscope. The very nature of the Moon becomes different in certain nakshatras. When a planet is placed under the direct radiation of a lunar mansion, it is not necessarily the planet's basic nature which flows to the recipient; instead, a nakshatra influence reaches the individual. The planetary periods in the life cycle of an individual, which are a peculiar contribution of Hindu astrology, flow from the position of the nakshatras. These characteristics of the nakshatras make them very special, requiring careful examination of their nature and mode of operation.

At one time there were twenty-eight nakshatras forming the circle of 360°; but at some historical epoch of which we know but little, one of them was omitted. Presently, Hindu astrology recognizes twenty-seven nakshatras. Beginning with the initial point of the zodiac, 0° of Aries, each nakshatra consists of 13° 20′ on the path of the ecliptic. Each nakshatra is further divided into four parts known as padas, which means "feet." Each nakshatra as well as each pada is associated with a different planet. All these factors must be carefully appraised in order to predict the future of the individual.

The three gunas — sattwa, rajas, and tamas — also affect each nakshatra differently. Within the primary flow of a guna, there will be a secondary and tertiary flow from the other two. These attributes reveal the inner propensities of the asterisms in their various shades and nuances.

The nakshatras are also categorized according to the four basic motivations of a human being, artha (meaningful action), kama (passional action), dharma (righteous action), and moksha (liberation, karma-less action). When a nakshatra is so categorized, it reveals the general impulse of that nakshatra.

Each nakshatra has a dual role. When an individual passes through involutionary stages of development, the effect of the asterism will be of one kind, while its impact on those who are on evolutionary paths will be different, though related to the same basic impulse.

1. ASHWINI

The first lunar mansion extends from 0° to 13° 20' along the ecliptic, (i.e., 0° to 13° 20' Aries) and represents the mystic process of activating primeval energy in its latency. Symbolized by the head of a horse, it stands for power and beauty. Its pulsation is rhythmical. Its deities are the Ashwini Kumars who had the capability of bestowing youth to the decrepit sage Chyavan and providing life force to the tree burnt by the poison of the great serpent Takshat.[1] The first nakshatra imparts a great healing touch, regenerative potential, physical power and stamina. It also gives a capacity for leadership and a thirst for sensation.

Ashwini is motivated by rajas or the activity principle, and has dharma or righteousness as its basic direction. Mysterious Ketu, the descending node of the Moon, is its ruling planet, but its four parts are governed by Mars, Venus, Mercury and the Moon consecutively. Thus, though its basic planetary affinity lies in abstract conceptualization, the different phases of its growth and unfoldment can respond favorably to all other evolutionary impulses connected with mental and physical sensitivity and sociability.

2. BHARANI

The second nakshatra extends from 13° 20' to 26° 40' (Aries) and is symbolized by the female generative organ. It has less reference to sex than to other concepts. The symbol suggests that this nakshatra is concerned with the preservative principle in nature; it also serves as a link between the Primeval Source and the manifested event. Bharani represents the bridge between father and offspring. The creative seed passes through it, nourishing it, yielding the final fruit of human birth. The presiding deity of the asterism is Yama, the god of death, who rules over souls in the state between incarnations. This nakshatra's role is the preservation and release of the Golden Egg (Hiranyagarbha). Working primarily under the rajas or activity principle, it guides the soul in materialistic as well as spiritual growth, but its impulse being artha or

---

1   See Behari, Bepin. *Myths and Symbols of Vedic Astrology,* Salt Lake City, Passage Press, 1990, p. 172.

meaningful action, the soul wants to achieve results in both worlds. This nakshatra can arouse a deep urge to investigate occult knowledge, while on the materialistic side it may impart an excessive desire for sexual indulgence.

Venus is the planetary lord, providing affinity with both extremes, but the four quarters of the asterism are governed by the Sun, Mercury, Venus and Mars respectively. The overall influence of Bharani is sensitivity and sociability along with an acute sense of beauty and comfort, but in its various phases there may be egotism, activity, mentation, dedication and social leadership. Bharani is the productive zone of Aries where originality and impulsiveness are much in evidence.

3. KRITTIKA

Krittika extends from 26° 40' to 40° 00' (26° 40' Aries to 10° 00' Taurus). Only its first quarter lies in Aries while the rest of it falls within Taurus. Two major qualities of this asterism are to be expected. It is symbolized by a razor which is used both for curative as well as murderous intentions. Its presiding deity is Agni. The god of fire has the power to provide enormous vitality, courage and tremendous strength, but if this power is not properly utilized, the repercussions can be devastating. Possessing the possibility to achieve results of both kinds, Krittika holds the universe in its hands.

When creativity is accentuated, the asterism heightens the urge to reproduce, to sow the seeds of new generation, or to achieve the kind of artistic perfection which interprets celestial beauty and harmony. On the destructive side, it impedes all the forces which encourage evolution. Krittika can be a highly antisocial force.

Though rajas is the important motivation, there is an undercurrent of sattwa or harmony in Krittika. Whatever the action, desire is very much accentuated under this asterism: the nakshatra is predominantly guided by kama or the passional nature.

For evolving souls, Krittika arouses deeply dedicated Divine service, while for those who are materially inclined, the impact of this asterism is experienced as a quarrelsome disposition and efforts directed by selfish considerations.

4. ROHINI

Extending over 40° 00' to 53° 20' of the zodiac (10° 00' to 23° 20' Taurus), Rohini is praised as one of the most auspicious of asterisms. Various synonyms for the asterism are Vidih, meaning a sacred command, Viranchi, referring to Brahma, the god of creation, and Sakat, which means a chariot or carriage. The chariot serves as a symbol for this asterism. Rohini is an incubator of creative potential. It has the quality of the Great Deep (*Bythos*), where every seed, every idea is preserved and nourished until the right time for its birth and fruition. Rohini leads to worldly pleasures, attachments and infatuation, to the world of sensual illusion. Everything experienced under this impulse has a quality of newness, a sense of childlike delight and the desire to experience more and more of the same.

The Moon has a special relationship with this asterism. In a state of mystical ecstasy, Rohini can guide the individual to an overpowering experience of the Divine or a sense of dedication to some spiritual mission. It leads the individual into some kind of symbiotic relationship with those in whose company one may receive some sort of transcendental experience.

Rohini can also produce deep involvement in sexual relationships which transcend traditional and social boundaries, but these would generally be induced by strong impulses of attachment and a state of intoxication. The lordship of the asterism is assigned to the Moon and its four quarters to Mars, Venus, Mercury and the Moon, but these all operate within Taurus, which is governed by Venus. All these characteristics of the nakshatra bestow upon it a quality of earthiness. This also explains the asterism being attributed to the caste of Sudras, the base of the four divisions on which social existence depends.

In spiritual terms, Rohini imparts the ability to "engineer" divine power, while on the materialistic side its chief preoccupation is with social progress, wealth, and sensual pleasure.

5. MRIGASHIRA

The name Mrigashira means literally the head of a deer, but there are other synonyms for this nakshatra which more directly indicate its characteristics. These are Soumya, which means auspicious, agreeable, and having the qualities of Soma;[2] Chandra, relating to the Moon; Agrahayani, referring to the full-moon day of the month of Agrahayana; and Udupa, meaning the Moon. These names suggest that the asterism is intimately linked with the auspicious qualities of the Moon. In occult literature, the Moon is the guardian of the Earth as well as a reflection of the godhood

---

2   Soma was a deity who personified the nectar of immortality, called amrita; the word is sometimes used as a synonym for the Moon.

in the psyche of the individual; thus this nakshatra symbolizes the reflection of the eternal in each individual mind.

Mrigashira extends from 53° 20' to 66° 40' (23° 20' Taurus to 6° 40' Gemini). It is symbolized by the deer's head and ruled by the Moon. But the tertiary quality of Mrigashira is tamas, while that of Rohini is rajas. These are small differences, but they have important repercussions regarding predictions. At this stage, the concretization of the abstract Divine impulse takes place. The creative impulse of nature begins to assume material form. This asterism is linked with the basic constituents of the universe which are called tanmatras.[3] Its operation in the multiple realms of the abstract, spiritual, mental, perceptual and physical is suggested by the planetary lordship of its four quarters assigned to Sun, Mercury, Venus, and Mars, while the Moon has overall control of the asterism. These planets impart energy, agility and inquisitive intellectual endeavor. One of the special characteristics of Mrigashira is the quality of tamas, leading to materialization, but there is an equally powerful urge towards moksha or liberation. On the spiritual level, Mrigashira imparts intelligence while on the materialistic side it expresses itself in pure egotism. There is an element of contradiction in the effect of this asterism.

6. ARDRA

Ardra extends from 66° 40' to 80° 00' (6° 40'to 20° 00' Gemini). The asterism is affected by all three gunas; rajas is the primary attribute, tamas the secondary, and sattwa the tertiary. Its motivational impulse is kama, the passional nature of man. Within the overall influence of Mercury, ruler of Gemini, Rahu or the North Node of the Moon governs the asterism itself. Its four quarters are guided by Jupiter and Saturn. The presiding deity of the nakshatra is Rudra, the god of destruction.

It is interesting to note that the asterism's name, Ardra, means green, fresh, soft and moist, but its rulership is assigned to the god of destruction and its planetary lordship is bestowed on Rahu, a karmic planet which generally precipitates much misfortune; even the lords of the four quarters, Jupiter and Saturn, are mysteriously linked with occult training and renunciation. Thus this asterism destroys material reality and the soul's involvement in illusion — which, however, becomes difficult to renounce. It is symbolized by a precious stone or a human head, both of which suggest the mind, which on the one hand imposes upon experiences

---

3   tanmatras: the faculties of smell, taste, touch, sight and hearing.

its own version of "reality" while at the same time the mind may be the principle destroyer of illusion and ignorance.

The nature of mind may best be expressed through the study of esoteric law, but on the materialistic side it expresses itself as conflict.

7. PUNARVASU

Punarvasu extends from 80° 00' to 93° 20' (20° 20' Gemini to 3° 20' Cancer). It is an asterism radically different from Ardra. At this stage, the nature of cosmic ideation undergoes a radical change. Symbolized by a bow as well as by a house or resting place, this asterism represents a new beginning with a mission to carry forward. It is assigned to the Vaisya caste, whose primary function is to provide the necessary wherewithals for the sustenance and preservation of society. As the Sun sustains the universe, so Punarvasu sustains the aspect of life that it affects.

The presiding deity of the nakshatra is Aditi, the mother of the Adityas or Suns. A paradoxical term, "Visible Infinity," is said to represent the asterism. In order to comprehend this limitless expanse, one must understand the function of naada, the primeval sound, and bindu, the center of consciousness. The union of the two produces material or objective forms of manifestation. The primary impulse of this asterism is the union between sound and Divine consciousness. It crystallizes abstract ideas. The creative agents are given a fresh impetus for the performance of their work at the mental or intellectual level. The asterism provides a resting place for the downward flow of Divine energy, enabling it to function with greater zeal and increased vigor when the need arises.

Punarvasu may encourage discipleship — the orientation of one's life so as to come across the mighty powers of the spiritual world. It may also lead to a further intensification of worldly duties. In such situations, the asterism accentuates kama manas, the passional nature in man.

8. PUSHYA

Pushya is a unique asterism with several special features. It extends from 93° 20' to 106° 40' (3° 20' to 16° 40' Cancer), completely within Cancer, the sign ruled by the Moon. The Vedic deity Brihaspati, represented by Jupiter, the adviser of gods and men, presides over it, but Saturn, which is specially associated with tamasic or inertial proclivities, has planetary ownership of the asterism. Jupiter promotes expansion, protects and nourishes, while Saturn concretizes, condenses and crystallizes nebulous matter. The combined effect of these two planets stabilizes energy and enables it to grow in an entirely new form. At this stage, the subjective aspect of cosmic ideation becomes objective as an archetype.

The asterism is symbolized by a flower, a circle, or an arrow. Though these symbols emphasize different aspects of this nakshatra, they all highlight certain aspects of its mysterious qualities. They refer to vibrant tranquility, absence of undue agitation, faith in oneself, and fullness of life. Such a psychological structure can exist only when the individual has attained a stage of growth where there is full faith in the Divine plan and an unflinching confidence in oneself. At this stage, the ego can combine within itself the cosmic heights and the deepest levels of the inner self. Purification of the psyche and an intuitive perception of the Divine plan are unique characteristics of Pushya.

It is important to note that Pushya, though functioning under the rajasic impulse, gets a secondary attribute of sattwa and a tertiary one of tamas. The primary motivational urge is guided by dharma or righteousness. It is the penultimate asterism in which the rajasic guna is primary. Immersion in materiality is almost complete under Pushya, and consciousness reviving the memory of its primeval nature is unfolding. Those on the spiritual path will experience tranquility of mind but, rajasic as well as tamasic tendencies still being present, there may also be considerable mental agitation. The caste assigned to the asterism is that of Kshatriya, the warrior, which implies that there will be much purposeful activity under this asterism.

9. ASHLESHA

At the Ashlesha level, cosmic ideation has reached its lowest depth of materialization, after which must begin the task of consolidation. Not only does the asterism mark the culmination of the rajasic attribute at the primary level, it also prepares us for producing a spiritual impact due to sattwa guna at the secondary and tertiary levels. The asterism is ruled by Mercury but the deity presiding over it, the Naga or serpent, is replete with esoteric significance.

The asterism extends from 106° 40' to 120° 00' (16° 40' Cancer to 0° 00' Leo) and marks the termination of an important phase of cosmic ideation. Much of the significance of Ashlesha lies in understanding the serpent symbol. Ashlesha is an intense energy capable of great spiritual attainment as well as material immersion. Duality is one of its important characteristics. The serpent symbol reveals a complex and often misunderstood psychological factor. Persons born under the influence of this asterism are often contradictory characters. They are deeply philosophical, thoughtful, austere, self-reliant and reclusive, but they can, on occasion, display crude selfishness and treacherous, immoral and venomous proclivities. They cannot bear humiliation. Under favorable conditions they can have much spiritual insight and possess hidden knowledge of the finer forces of Nature. The Mercurial intellect, benefic as well as malefic, is in affinity with Ashlesha.

Ashlesha imparts intellectual and mental development and enables its beneficiaries to undergo radical transformations in life — transformations which occur in the most unexpected manner. Afterwards, an entirely different condition of existence prevails.

10. MAGHA

Magha extends from 120° 00′ to 133° 20′ (0° 00′ to 13° 20′ Leo). the asterism is presided over by the Pitris, Vedic immortals considered to be the progenitors of the human race; its planetary rulership is assigned to Ketu, the mysterious descending node of the Moon.

The primary guna, tamas, imparts inertia, while the secondary and tertiary attributes, rajas, suggest that one experiences great contradictions and an urge to make life purposeful. One aspect of Magha produces tremendously swift action, while other parts of it put the brakes to this tendency, directing the energy towards stasis. Such an interaction leads to psychological tension and a sense of frustration.

The symbols associated with this asterism — a palanquin, a house, or a chariot — all suggest the importance of the human body as a vehicle of the Divine. Regeneration, creativity, involvement in worldly responsibilities are all exemplified by the Vedic Pitris, who are celestial powers obedient to the Supreme Lord in carrying out his mission of manifestation. Janak, another synonym for this asterism, refers to the same function. Magha is concerned with sustaining and assisting the evolutionary impulse; in discharging this responsibility, its primary task is to overcome the various obstacles to the fulfillment of that particular dharma.

The primary impulse of Magha is metempsychosis; it leads to transmigration of the soul and involves the ego in the evolutionary process. Under its impact, those who are evolved and on the spiritual path enjoy great power and glamour; they attain prestigious status. Those who still have a great attraction to earthly pleasures will undergo servitude. Generally speaking, Magha shows idealism amidst material surroundings — an easily misunderstood situation. Persons under the influence of this asterism are often suspected as to their integrity and honesty of purpose. Misunderstood by their friends and relations, such people are a little sad in spite of their missionary idealism and zeal. But that is what all missionaries suffer.

11. PURVA PHALGUNI

This is an auspicious asterism, bestowing fortune and immense opportunity for creative involvement. Purva Phalguni extends from 133° 20' to 146° 40' (13° 20' to 26° 40' Leo). It occupies the central part of Leo and is motivated by the primary urge kama, or passion. The asterism is presided over by the Vedic deity Aryaman, who bestows riches, affluence and material prosperity. The Vedas speak of Aryaman as a deity who protects his devotees and makes them victorious over their adversaries. The passional nature or deep attachment represented by kama is altered by Purva Phalguni. In spite of great attachment, there is a unique quality of grace, self-reliance, and enormous creative action. The association of Aryaman as well as Bhaga with this asterism and its placement in the middle of Leo very appropriately describe its basic nature. Under this asterism the king arrives, the war is waged, and the religious observances begin, but the next phase of development has not yet been disclosed.

Thirst for experience is a rare quality with vast potentiality. When the god of fortune smiles on a person, when ample opportunity for creativity is provided and the thirst for new experience glows and becomes acute deep within him, the person's life-force assumes new dimensions. One cannot often predict the areas in which this asterism will grow and fructify. Purva Phalguni stands for the expression of dynamic energy. It enables the soul to work in the external realm in order to discharge the Divine responsibilities entrusted to it. The basic feature of this asterism is its readiness to plunge into activities.

The asterism may bestow victory and domination, but if the soul is still under materialistic influence Purva Phalguni will lead the individual to debauchery, gambling, and black magic.

12. UTTARA PHALGUNI

Uttara Phalguni extends from 146° 40' to 160° 00' (26° 40' Leo to 10° 00' Virgo). Uttara and Purva Phalguni, though considered as two separate asterisms, in fact represent one unified whole. This is signified by the connection of Aryaman and Bhaga with these asterisms; in their general disposition, these Vedic deities are much alike. But despite an essential unity, they also have certain distinctive characteristics.

Uttara Phalguni provides the basic energy, the inner urge or eagerness to act, and tremendous confidence in one's own capability. Under favorable conditions, Uttara can help in achieving concrete results, producing a tangible output from nebulous ideas. No amount of difficulty can withhold its progress. Uttara Phalguni represents that courage and endurance which descend on seasoned fighters who are confident of their inner strength, the righteousness of their mission, and the final victorious outcome of their efforts. Uttara Phalguni enables the ego to develop all the skills which result from its battles in the realm of materialism. It is an asterism of ambition, difficulties, and righteous struggle.

On the spiritual side, Uttara Phalguni may bestow ambition and the urge for righteous struggle, but on the materialistic side its impact is felt as a great attraction to black magic.

13. HASTA

Hasta, which means the palm of a hand, is the thirteenth asterism, covering 160° 00′ to 173° 20′ (10° 00′ to 6° 40′ Virgo). The asterism lies completely within Virgo, the reservoir of Nature's finer forces. The basic features of this nakshatra are described by the various appellations for it: it is known, besides Hasta, as Bhanu, Aruna and Ark. Bhanu means the Sun as well as a ray of light; Ark likewise means a ray of light or the Sun, and also the essence of an herbal plant; Aruna refers to the color of the morning dawn, or the dawn personified as the charioteer of the Sun. These names point to great vitality, the advent of a new beginning, and the tremendous regenerating energy which sustains and nourishes others but is completely self-reliant. At first sight it appears that the asterism should more appropriately have been in the zone of Leo, ruled by the Sun. But when we understand Virgo as an embodiment of Nature's finer forces which need to be uncovered, developed and put to use furthering the mission of life by one's own efforts, the positioning of Hasta within Virgo seems apt. The primary radiation of the asterism provides a tremendous impulse towards self-reliance and control over that outgoing energy which is always ready to proceed further. The primeval impulse of Hasta is duration, wherein lies Time. This nakshatra provides the basic foundation which makes further expression of manifestation possible. It should not be thought that Hasta provides congenial conditions for the existence of the individual and his growth. One must struggle to express his inner vitality and potential for growth here.

Hasta is owned by the Moon. It is pervaded by tamas, inertia, at the primary and secondary levels, but rajas or activity operates at its tertiary level. Its motivational urge is moksha or liberation. The presiding deity of the asterism is the Sun in its regenerative aspect. Hasta has the quality of impelling the individual to change, to take new shapes and grow in a new direction. It provides immense opportunities for growth and expansion. This process of growth results from the inner urge to march ahead, while external conditions exert resistance. Thus conflict and different levels of crises result. Resistances manifest as impediments, difficulties and obstructions.

Souls who are guided on the path of renunciation, the nvritti marg, receive opportunities for public service and become leaders of a renaissance, while those on the materialistic side of growth find themselves in conditions of penury, somehow eking out subsistence for themselves. Having been assigned to the caste of Vaisyas whose primary function is to work for the sustenance of society and to engage in commerce and trade without the objective of personal (abnormal) profit, Hasta is concerned with making the individual a sustaining power in the community.

14. CHITRA

Chitra extends from 173° 20' to 186° 40' (23° 20' Virgo to 6° 40' Libra). Since half of the asterism lies within Virgo and half within Libra, it comes under the influence of both Mercury and Venus. The asterism itself is governed by Mars. The four quarters of it are influenced by the Sun, Mercury, Venus and Mars. Thus we find that Mars, Mercury and Venus, which are concerned with the bridge that links physical existence with the spiritual level, play an important part in Chitra's meaning. In fact, Chitra represents a great surge toward building and reaching into new levels of achievement. For this reason, one finds wonder-workers, leaders, highly erudite persons, and extremely honest philanthropists born under this star. The ownership of the star is assigned to Tvashtar, the celestial architect, and it is symbolized by a pearl.

The pearl is a precious gem extracted from a stinking oyster. The celestial architect is concerned with chipping off unwanted attachments. The process is painful, but it has to be borne in order to attain perfection and achieve one's pristine purity. The hidden perfection can only be externalized with great insight and a tremendous courage to fight and bear severe ordeals. Mars, which owns the asterism, does not accept defeat. Any confrontation provides it with added incentive to fight and attain its goal. When the soul reaches the stage of Chitra, it has already crystallized the goal of its mission, which requires achievement at every cost. The attempt made at this level is primarily on intellectual and inspirational planes. That is why one finds the asterism extending from Virgo, owned by Mercury, to Libra, owned by Venus. Venusian inspiration lightens the burden of the struggling ego. The first two quarters of the asterism, governed by Sun and Mercury, fall in Virgo which is owned by Mercury and represents the struggle taking place on the intellectual plane. The confusion at this stage may arise due to lack of clarity and confidence with regard to one's ideals. But the last two quarters of the asterism fall within

Libra, the sign owned by Venus. Under this impulse, the realm of social relationship becomes important.

Chitra's field of operation is basically the world of matter as is signified by tamas operating at all three levels of impact. The primary motivation for Chitra comes from kama, the passional nature. It is space, the stage on which the celestial drama is played, which becomes the chief attraction for this asterism. Those who are fired by aspiration toward a spiritual goal and have experienced the delights of spiritual endeavor will involve themselves in building a new society, but those who are still attracted to materiality may very well live the life of a pig in the mud. Those who are not able to imbibe the full power of this asterism may become smug, self-contented, and conceited. They may turn out to be good-for-nothing, self-indulgent individuals.

15. SWATI

Swati lies in the middle of Libra, extending from 186° 40′ to 200° 00′ (6° 40′ to 20° 00′ Libra). Though the sign in which this asterism is placed is ruled by Venus, thus heightening earthy sensitivities and material attachments, the asterism itself is governed by Rahu, a karmic planet which activates the superphysical forces. To regulate them, the four quarters of Swati are assigned to Jupiter and Saturn, which have a significant role in developing spirituality. Jupiter encourages righteous behavior while Saturn stifles the materialistic proclivities by producing frustration. Swati functions under the primary and secondary attributes of tamas, while on the tertiary or external level sattwa prevails. The presiding deity of the asterism is Vayu, the god of air. Swati primarily operates as a chalice through which the Divine spirit flows to the physical level of manifestation, establishing a direct link between the inner impelling force and external activities and relationships.

Coral is a symbol of this asterism. Coral produces its offspring from within its own being. This feature of coral symbolizes the stage of evolution during which the Spirit is still encased in outer physical sheaths while its further evolution depends upon the unfoldment of its inherent potential. At this stage of manifestation two primary impulses, the centrifugal and centripetal forces, express themselves as attraction and repulsion and come prominently into operation. The subjective spirit has the natural inclination to expand, while the material sheaths restrict the process. The equilibrium attained by these opposing tendencies enables the individual to maintain stability. A unique synthesis between the inner spiritual urge and outer materialistic attraction characterizes this asterism.

The primary motivational impulse of Swati comes from artha, or meaningful activity, which, when aroused under the Venusian impact, gives intense involvement in surrounding conditions. To persons on the evolutionary path, this passion may turn out to be an intense devotion to work, religion, family or anything which expresses higher values of life. Impinging upon those who are yet struggling with the materialistic side of life, Swati is intensely pleasure-seeking. But whatever happens and in whatever form it is expressed, it leads to some psychological change in outlook. There will always be a kind of airiness, expressed as vague dissatisfaction with the world around oneself.

16. VISHAKHA

Vishakha extends from 200° 00' to 213° 20' (20° 00' Libra to 3° 20' Scorpio). The three quarters of the asterism assigned to Mars, Venus, and Mercury lie within the zodiacal zone of Libra, but the last quarter, under the Moon, is in Scorpio, giving a dualistic character to the asterism. The potter's wheel as a symbol of the nakshatra represents the great turmoil and whirlwind produced by this influence. The symbolism emphatically points to transformation.

Tamas, sattwa, and rajas operate at the primary, secondary and tertiary levels, indicating the wide range of expression of this nakshatra. There is no quality in the universe which is beyond its reach. The dual rulership assigned to Indra and Agni is also suggestive. The three quarters of Vishakha within Libra provide affluence, comfort, and the pleasant experiences of life, which all come under the domain of Indra, the king of the gods and ruler of heaven. The last quarter of the asterism, falling in Scorpio, is full of the trials and tribulations which are essential for every kind of transformation; these experiences are guided by Agni, the god of fire.

Unique features of the asterism are non-attraction, a special type of dissatisfaction with the existing conditions of life, restlessness, and a great psychological turmoil raging within. Such an impulse often leads to infidelity in married life, non-fulfillment of promises in personal relationships, and minimizing the contribution of others. Non-attraction to the existing conditions of life is not necessarily repulsion. Infidelity does not arise due to any fault of the partner, and letting down one's friends does not arise due to their lack of warmth. Instead, these reactions are produced by a feeling of emptiness at the core of one's being, expressed outwardly as restlessness.

The primary impulse of Vishakha can be described as psychism. For the spiritual person trying to lead himself to the higher goals of life, this asterism can impart the quality of tapas, the purificatory austerities, but for those engrossed in the material aspects of life, it leads to the experience of various restrictions. Whatever its outer expression, Vishakha imparts a sense of righteousness.

17. ANURADHA

Anuradha extends from 213° 20' to 226° 40' (3° 20' to 16° 40' Scorpio). The asterism itself is governed by Saturn, but the sign in which it lies is ruled by Mars. Saturn and Mars do not have affinity with each other; they vibrate on different realms of existence. Naturally, there will be stress and strain produced by this asterism. The presiding deity is Mitra, a Vedic god expressing certain aspects of the Sun. A synonym for the nakshatra is Maitram, implying friendliness. The symbol representing it is a lotus flower. The secondary attribute of the asterism is that of sattwa, harmony, but the primary and tertiary attributes are both tamas, inertia. Thus the basic impulse of Anuradha is guided by a sense of righteousness producing harmony and good social relationship, but its outer expression will be grossly materialistic. Anuradha aims at friendliness, but its outward expression fails to reveal this inner motive of action.

Mitra is worshipped in the Vedas as a special power which brings men together. He is the god of friendship and cooperation among humankind. Under the benevolent influence of Mitra, earlier efforts succeed and hidden powers begin to open up. Mitra as the light of day heralds the dawn, and the beginning of new possibilities. The motivational urge of Anuradha over which Mitra dominates is that of dharma, which indicates that the new beginning should always be towards righteous efforts and spiritualizing one's life.

The astrological symbol for Anuradha is a lotus flower. There are several layers of meaning to the word padma or lotus, but all of them point to the regenerative quality latent in the individual. The lotus symbolizes the soul's thirst for union with the Source, even though it may fall once again into incarnation. There may be a spiritual urge but not complete redemption from material bondage. Under Anuradha, latent yogic powers begin to manifest and there is emotional purification. The aspirant craves union with the Master, though he may not unite with him quite yet.

Anuradha lies in the Martian zone of influence, being within the parameters of Scorpio, ruled by Mars. The impulses flowing from this planet provide adequate and appropriate courage as well as the competence to uncover the latent powers or siddhis leading to attainment of the light of dawn, the real understanding of one's own nature. Courageous endurance in the service of Divine love may be considered the keynote of the asterism.

18. JYESHTA

Jyeshta extends from 226° 40' to 240° 00' (16° 40' Scorpio to 0° 00' Sagittarius), marking the termination of the primary impulse of tamas or inertia. At this stage, though the tamasic proclivities remain primary, sattwic attributes have begun to flow freely at the secondary and tertiary levels. The ruling planet is Mercury, whereas the zodiacal sign belongs to Mars; the four quarters of the nakshatra are ruled by Jupiter and Saturn. The Vedic deity is Indra, the king of the gods. The asterism is symbolized by an umbrella or an earring, both of which are status symbols indicating worldly and spiritual attainments. What seers call the Serpent Power (kundalini) is the primeval energy flowing through this asterism. It greatly energizes and strengthens any aspect of life affected by its influence. This force is capable of bestowing immense power on those who can rightly develop it, but it is dangerous if such control cannot be maintained.

Jyeshta means eldest sister and middle finger, as well as eminent, distinguished, and honorable. Its synonyms, such as Kulisatara, (Indra's star), Satamakha (Indra's sacrifice), and Suraswami (Indra, the god of gods), all refer to the most important of the gods. The asterism activates the best, highest, and most coveted qualities. Describing the asterism as "sister," which implies respect, also ascribes a generative power to the asterism. Jyeshta produces conditions which sustain society.

Jyeshta bestows honorable status. The earring and umbrella are both status symbols. The development of Kundalini Shakti or the Serpent Power opens up the possibility of subjugating Nature's finer forces and directing them to effective and supernormal uses. It also unveils hidden spiritual knowledge and wisdom. At this stage, the individual qualifies himself to embark upon a new direction. There is significant psychological change. For those who are on the spiritual path, this asterism opens the flood-gate of Divine benediction, but for individuals who are still attracted to worldly values the power and status bestowed upon them makes them arrogant, conceited, and dangerously proud. With artha as the motivational impulse, any action undertaken is purposeful.

19. MULA

Mula is the starting point for a radically different kind of influence. The sattwic attribute begins to dominate with this asterism. Mula extends from 240° 00' to 253° 20' (0° 00' to 13° 20' Sagittarius); the asterism and Sagittarius begin together. The zodiacal sign is governed by Jupiter, but the asterism is assigned to Ketu, the South Node of the Moon. Whenever a new guna begins at the primary level, the planet assigned to the asterism is Ketu because some abstraction has to be concretized and an idea is to be made manifest at the physical level. It implies a new opportunity but also onerous responsibilities, because much hardship must be borne in carrying out a new mission or disseminating any new ideas in a tradition-bound environment. Mula represents this stage of manifestation and is one of the most misunderstood asterisms. It is considered inauspicious; its synonyms are Asura, meaning an evil spirit, and Akratubhuj, which has a similar meaning. The presiding deity is named Nritta, who is also a demon. The asterism is symbolized by a lion's tail or an elephant's goad, both of which suggest dangerous possibilities if the asterism's influence is not properly absorbed. The ancient seers categorized Mula as belonging to "the butcher's caste." These indications emphasize the invincible quality of the asterism and the ruthlessness of its impact. The motivational impulse coming from kama makes the asterism intense.

Mula means the root, the foundation or lowest part of anything, especially the trunk of a tree from which the branches and foliage grow. After Mula, the process of manifestation is strengthened to branch out in various directions, to blossom and bear fruit. The trunk can be said to mark the end of one phase and the beginning of another. Mula marks the end of materialism and the beginning of the spiritual process.

But the process is not very pleasant. In Mula, the past proclivities have to be completely annihilated. This requires the ruthless action of a demon-like god. The occult literature speaks of a stage when the feet of the disciple have to be washed in the blood of his heart. Such action takes place under this asterism. It eradicates past karma. It is only when life becomes pure and tamasic tendencies are transformed that inner purity and the enduring goals of life can blossom. The elephant's goad inflicts pain in order to direct the animal in the right direction. Mula directs individuals toward their destined goals.

Mula is motivated by kama, the passion for carnal indulgence. When this craving is resisted, an intense opposition from the passional nature arises. Any impediment to one's carnal passion is violently resisted, and consequently the struggle ensues. Mula makes the individual violent and cruel in this sense. His mental balance is disturbed. Transformation takes place when the mental disturbance is controlled.

Mula is male by sex, a butcher by caste, a dog by species, a demon by temperament, and human as far as the animal type is concerned. The masculinity expresses the positive quality of nature; the soul wants to act, achieve, and attain a goal rather than be a passive recipient of the fruit.

The cruelty of the butcher is typical of Mula: its action is decisive and will brook no obstruction. In perpetrating its effect, it will be ruthless. By showing Mula as human, its purpose in transforming human animality into spirituality is suggested. The transmutation of animality, materiality, and self-centeredness into sympathy, spirituality and altruism is the most important characteristic of Mula.

The primary impulse of Mula is to arouse mumukshattwa, the urge for liberation. But in the process, the necessary transformation involves much discomfort, which makes the asterism troublesome. The unfortunate, demonic impulses are expressions of a karmic nemesis which the spiritual aspirant accepts joyfully. On the path of materialism Mula becomes cruel and possessive.

20. PURVASHADHA

Purvashadha extends from 253° 20' to 266° 40' (13° 20' to 26° 40' Sagittarius). It is completely within Sagittarius which is ruled by Jupiter. The asterism itself is assigned to Venus. The Vedic deity presiding over the asterism is the water-god Apas. The primary sattwic impulse permeating the asterism is affected by rajas at the secondary level and tamas at the tertiary level. The symbol assigned to the asterism is the elephant's tusk. The motivational urge of the asterism is moksha or liberation.

These characteristics indicate that the asterism is a spiritual influence. Venus will sensitize the recipient to intuition and other higher forces of nature. This heightened sensitivity and greater alertness, though outwardly they may appear as listlessness, are the most important qualifications for transformation and the dawn of spirituality. New experiences are gained in such a milieu. Possessing the pliability of water, the asterism functions as a life-sustaining influence.

One exceptional result of Purvashadha is the discovery of new possibilities, the externalization of latent faculties, and the uncovering of one's most valuable qualities. These are all symbolized by the tusk of an elephant. The tusk is the most valuable part of an elephant's body, a sort of externalization of the inner possibilities of the animal. Under Purvashadha, many unknown and unexpected possibilities come to light. Divine wisdom may flash, hidden knowledge may be revealed, and intuitive faculties may be sharpened. The experience and illumination received under this asterism is intended to purify and spiritualize the life conditions.

Under the influence of this nakshatra, the mind is activated and the individual begins to reflect on Divine law. But this reflection is not a purely mental process; it is a perception of diverse natural forces operating at their innermost depth which illumines and transmutes his animal nature into divinity. This asterism may be regarded as God's grace which, to an unripe mind, produces pride and conceit.

21. UTTARASHADHA

Uttarashadha extends from 266° 40' to 280° 00' (26° 40' Sagittarius to 10° 00' Capricorn); its first quarter lies in Sagittarius and its latter three quarters in Capricorn. The asterism, which is itself assigned to the Sun, comes under the influence of both Jupiter and Saturn. It is also presided over by Vishwa Devata, meaning "the universe as God," which makes the asterism intensely concerned with humanity at large as well as being very powerful. Its primary attribute is sattwa, harmony, while at the secondary level rajas operates and at the tertiary level sattwa again prevails. Moksha is the primary motivational impulse radiating from this asterism. A small cot or the bed-rod is its symbol.

The rods of a bed or the bed itself as a symbol for the asterism denotes a place of rest or relaxation. The rods are important accessories which finally produce the bed. Even the bed is not "rest," though it provides the necessary conditions whereby one may enjoy rest and recuperation. By providing the necessary conditions for the externalization of universal principles in human individuals, the asterism produces the psychological orientation for discharging our ultimate responsibilities and karmic debts. At this level, the individual acquires the faculties symbolized by the bed or the bed rods which later enable him to attain his final rest, Nirvana — liberation. This seems far-fetched, but in actual observation, one finds that Uttarashadha leads to a kind of universal or cosmic unity under which the individual loses his personal considerations and begins to think in terms of oneness. The asterism does not lead to rest in the physical sense; rather, it leads to activity and change. Uttarashadha enables the individual to be earthly in action, but the stimulus for each action comes from some kind of spiritual goal. Each earthly involvement will be explained in terms of the higher objectives in life.

The planetary relationships of this nakshatra indicate that it can lead the individual toward mantras, tantras and other rituals which propitiate the various celestial powers. Some individuals under the influence of this asterism may even be found engaged in penance and austerities to obtain supernatural powers. This is because the personal defenses of the individual have broken down and his personality is shaken; his old values and supports are crumbling down. Sacrificing one's personal life on the cross of universal consciousness is always painful, and that process is intensified at this stage. The influence of Vishwa Devata can be felt through intellectual development and the urge towards socialization. The foundation of harmony is empathy, and the rod of the bed represents the essential human relationships which depend on empathy for their endurance.

The entire life of the individual may seem barren and without any core. This experience flows directly from the universalization of individual consciousness. This subjective recognition makes the person very humble, and sometimes introspective or self-centered.

ABHIJIT

Abhijit is the nakshatra which, as indicated earlier, was included among the lunar mansions during the Vedic period but presently, for most purposes, is not taken into account. However, the importance of this asterism can be gauged by the fact that Lord Krishna named Abhijit as his own particular nakshatra, and by the fact that the presiding deity is Brahma, the creator of the manifest universe. The asterism is categorized as Vaisya, thereby accentuating its influence in sustaining the established social order. Generally, Abhijit provides a creative impulse and its association with destructive activities is not conducive to success. For coronation, waging war, or long journeys this asterism is still considered in order to decide the most likely circumstances to occur. Forming a part of Capricorn it can support benevolent, universalizing undertakings which are intended for the general good. Otherwise, the effect of this asterism is not likely to give favorable results.

22. SHRAVANA

Shravana extends from 280° 00' to 293° 20' (10° 00' to 23° 20' Capricorn). Capricorn, in which this nakshatra lies, is ruled by Saturn, but the asterism itself is assigned to the Moon. The influence of Shravana must therefore operate in a very uncongenial milieu. The presiding deity is Vishnu or Hari, the preserver of the universe. In spite of the difficulties arising from the Moon-Saturn combination, Shravana provides the impulse which helps sustain the established order against any opposing force. The primary attribute of the asterism is sattwa, the secondary is tamas, and the tertiary is rajas, implying that Shravana will support any activity which leads to harmony, though it may have to confront difficulties during the process due to tamasic proclivities creating certain impediments. The primary motivational impulse energizing this asterism is artha, which represents purposeful action. Shravana is male by sex, outcaste by caste, a monkey among the species, a man by temperament, and a quadruped among the animals.

The essential feature of Shravana is the Great Silence, upon which subsists the entire scheme of manifestation. The asterism leads one to meditation. If someone is still on a materialistic path and in need of considerable experience to equip himself for a spiritual orientation, he will develop those qualities under Shravana.

Shravana means "listening," the necessary quality which leads to alertness. Only after subjugating personal emotions and thoughts can one listen to that cosmic music which reveals the beauty and harmony of the universe and purifies the inner nature of man. Shravana can enable one to attune himself to Naada, the cosmic ideational sound which leads to one-pointedness. This requires the persistence of a mongoose and the eager intellect of a monkey. A person engaged in preparing himself for this kind of life is often isolated from his friends, almost like an outcaste.

23. DHANISHTA

Dhanishta is a mystical nakshatra under which many adepts and seers are born, while for ordinary men of the world it brings untold miseries and deprivations. The primeval energy emanating from this asterism is the tremendous life-force which, when properly absorbed, leads to spiritual attainments. Those who are yet unprepared for its impact may actually be "burned up." They are deprived of their material conveniences and suffer from great penury.

Dhanishta extends from 293° 20′ to 306° 40′ (23° 20′ Capricorn to 6° 40′ Aquarius). Aquarius is ruled by Saturn, which restricts the growth and expansion of material riches. The asterism itself is assigned to Mars, which externalizes that which lies concealed within. Such a conflict is similar to that of Shravana, though under Shravana the turmoil rises at the mental level and guides the ego in earthly confrontation. Dhanishta's primeval motivational urge, dharma or righteousness, goads the individual to proceed undaunted in spite of the unfriendly external situation. That is why this asterism is generally considered inauspicious.

The symbol assigned to the nakshatra is the mridangam, a drum-like musical instrument. The very word dhanishta means a drum, as well as bamboo-cane. Both of these musical instruments are hollow on the inside, but they resound and reverberate the tune played by the musician. Depending upon the skill of the musician, the nature and contribution of the instrument may be assessed. The force of Dhanishta may be similarly reflected on the plane to which it is directed. The flute attracts devotees to dance to the tune of Lord Krishna; Shiva sounds his small dumaru (a drum-like musical instrument) under the spell of which the entire universe dances. Under Dhanishta, the basic impulse is to purge the soul of all that it considers its own so that God's plan for it can be unfolded smoothly; this is the stage when the individual may function like a reed through which Divine music is played uninterruptedly and without any distortion.

An important point to remember is that the first half of the asterism lies in Capricorn and the latter half in Aquarius. The influence of Capricorn stands for trial. The person under this influence has to purify and universalize himself. Under Aquarius he becomes a martyr in the name of God, working for Nature and the universal spirit. He investigates and reveals the unifying principles in life, attuning his own existence so as to flow like a river, energizing the sattwic harmony in all life.

24. SHATABHISHAK

Shatabhishak, which extends from 306° 40' to 320° 00' (6° 40' to 20° 00' Aquarius), has the quality of producing ultimate harmony in spite of trials and tribulations. Its central purpose is to achieve and protect natural harmony.

Saturn is the ruler of Aquarius, within which the nakshatra lies, whereas Rahu is the ruler of the asterism itself. The combined influence of Saturn and Rahu makes Shatabhishak very acute. The one hundred stars constituting the constellation symbolize a thousand-petaled flower, furthering its intensity. Sattwa pervades the asterism at its primary and tertiary levels while the secondary attribute is tamas. Pracheta, a synonym for the asterism, signifies Manu, Daksha, and Valmiki, which are the names of mighty progenitors of the human race, at different levels and in different realms of its evolution. From all these significators, it is evident that Shatabhishak is concerned with very important aspects of human development.

Varuna, who presides over the asterism, is one of the earliest Vedic deities, vested with illimitable cosmic knowledge. This knowledge, however, is aimed at producing practical results. Varuna directs the mysterious power of wisdom and activities to the world so that individuals under Shatabhishak are radically transformed and a new ray of light shines through their lives. These persons will be guided in their actions by a new approach to life. They will be able to throw a radically different light on various worldly problems.

Rahu, as the planetary lord of the asterism, and Saturn, the planet under whose sign the asterism falls, produce trials and purification of the ego. Under the combined influence of these planets, the individual consciousness linked to materialism becomes lonely and depressed under the stress of purification. Shatabhishak people are rarely happy with themselves. Life to them is a duty, not an experience of personal gratification.

The asterism leads to a blending of the individual consciousness with the universal: it leads to the experiencing of Infinity, the Illimitable. A mystic feeling of the sea enters the picture. Such an experience entails immense psychological expansion, sacrifice and pain. The asterism is categorized as a butcher, suggesting that only with the ruthlessness of a butcher and the strength of a demon can the expanding consciousness of Shatabhishak be borne. Shatabhishak makes one's life idealistic and almost dreamy because only under such conditions may the universal cosmic bloom take place.

25. PURVA BHADRA

Purva Bhadra is associated with cosmic stability and imparts a tremendous amount of fearlessness. It extends from 320° 00' to 333° 20' (20° 00' Aquarius to 3° 20' Pisces). Jupiter is its planetary lord. Three quarters of it, ruled by Mars, Venus and Mercury lie within Aquarius, ruled by Saturn. The last quarter, under the Moon, lies in Pisces, a Jupiterian sign. Sattwa is the attribute of the asterism at both its primary and secondary levels, while at its tertiary level rajas predominates. The presiding deity of the asterism is Aja Ekapada, a Vedic god with much esoteric significance. The sword is its astrological symbol. Of the four primeval motivations artha, implying meaningfulness, is related to this asterism. It is categorized as male by sex, Brahmin by caste, a lion by species, and a man by temperament. The animal of the first three quarters is the human, while the last quarter is symbolized by an aquatic animal.

The Vedic deity Aja Ekapada represents the unborn, transcendent cosmic energy symbolized by the one-footed goat. The goat is a simple, harmless, milk-producing animal which requires almost nothing for its sustenance. In the Vedas, Aja Ekapada is an infinity, an entity without motion or speech. He is the unpolished creative energy which produces the different levels of existence — heaven and earth. Under his rulership, Purva Bhadra enables the individual to stand completely alone, without aid or support from any external source. Often this tendency is expressed as eccentricity, originality, and rebellion; one is unmindful of the opinion of others. For those on the path of spirituality, it is expressed as an irresistible urge to work for certain universal principles without any consideration for one's own personal welfare and advancement. Those on the materialistic path will become self-centered, maniacal, rebellious, antisocial and conceited.

Self-reliance as a feature of Purva Bhadra is expressed by the sword symbol. The sword is an instrument of attack as well as of self-defense. Courage, vision, and self-involvement irrespective of consequences, are needed in the work towards universal unity. The asterism urges the individual to fight with a missionary zeal in behalf of that goal.

Purva Bhadra makes the discharge of energy one-pointed and directs it to an objective ideal. A fearless approach combined with anguish and sorrow are characteristic of this asterism.

26. UTTARA BHADRA

The nature of the forces flowing through Uttara Bhadra is difficult to describe. It lies completely within the Jovian sign of Pisces; it extends from 333° 20' to 346° 40' (3° 20' to 16° 40' Pisces). The deeply esoteric nature of the asterism is, however, expressed by assigning its rulership to Saturn and naming Ahir Budhnya, the Serpent of the Deep, as its presiding deity. It is assigned a symbol suggesting the four stars which constitute the asterism and form a square with two stars in the east; the same set of stars divided between the two Bhadras are said to represent twins. Sattwa (harmony) operating at the primary and secondary levels with tamas (inertia) operating at the tertiary level suggest that though the asterism may be linked with materiality, resistance, difficulties and opposition at the beginning, it will create a harmonious impact in the long run. Not the detachment of an enlightened mind, but passionate involvement of an emotional nature characterizes this asterism.

Ahir Budhnya, the presiding deity, is also Ahi-Vritra, the dragon of the deep sea which lies concealed in primeval darkness. The dual principles of light and darkness, heat and cold, are emphasized by Aja Ekapada and Ahir Budhnya. They are in eternal conflict and represent the two fundamental principles of creation. These principles govern fire and water, heat and cold, and are personified by Agni, representing fire, and Soma or the Moon, representing water. They are the two primary elements, and with reference to Uttara and Purva Bhadra, they represent a unity symbolized by the four legs of a cot: the four legs represent two sets of twins, each within itself containing the dual or opposing qualities. Purva Bhadra, ruled by Aja Ekapada and governed by Jupiter, lies three-quarters within a sign of Saturn. Uttara Bhadra, ruled by Saturn and presided over by Ahir Budhnya, lies completely under Jupiter. The opposing qualities contained in the totality of Bhadrapada are differentiated between Purva and Uttara Bhadra. These two well-polarized forces which constitute the manifested universe are again moving toward unity. Uttara Bhadra, is of the nature of Soma, the Moon, which is associated with water and has the quality of passivity. The passivity of darkness is the mysterious source from which all other forms of creation have arisen. It is the outstanding characteristic of Uttara Bhadra.

Uttara Bhadra becomes very powerful whenever it is associated with any planet. Though it has complete passivity and non-action, it is also highly dynamic whenever an active force impinges upon it and the latent energy within it is vigorously activated.

Uttara Bhadra enables an individual to comprehend the wisdom concealed in different forms of manifestation. The wisdom of the serpent must manifest here. Whatever happens to the individual, there is growth and expansion of consciousness. Under the impact of this asterism, there is an opportunity to preserve, protect and cooperate with the Divine plan despite any hardships that may arise in the discharge of that responsibility. The urge toward transformation often makes the individual thirst for something better and thus produces considerable dissatisfaction. But ultimately there arises complete indifference to every worldly relationship.

27. REVATI

Revati extends from 346° 40′ to 360° 00′ (16° 40′ to 30° 00′ Pisces), in a sign which is ruled by Jupiter and symbolized by a pair of fish. The asterism itself is governed by Mercury, the son of Jupiter, and is also symbolized by a fish. It is presided over by Pushan, a deity with the primary function of nourishing the universe — hence he is known as "the nourisher." The name of the deity also means "the measurer of the sky." All three levels of this nakshatra's operation are pervaded by sattwa, suggesting complete integration between its basic urges and outward expression.

Revati stands for the great womb in which the Sun lies dormant until the next Manvantaric impulse begins again and a fresh cycle of manifestation sweeps through infinity.[4] It links the end with the beginning. The symbol of the fish is auspicious because it aids procreation and rapid growth. It helps one to become many, easily and rapidly. While so doing, it also makes an individual outward-turned and considerate of the feelings and comforts of others. Under Revati, creativity produces extroverted tendencies. A new life begins for individuals under its influence.

Arising from the desire for spiritual unity caused by Jupiter and the penance and suffering caused by Saturn, under which material craving is completely annihilated, the individual is reborn in wisdom — again sig-

---

4   A Manvantaric impulse may be loosely defined as a cosmic cycle
    encompassing aeons of time.

nified by Jupiter, ruler of the last quarter of this asterism as well as planetary lord of Pisces.

Under the impact of Mercury, the planetary lord of the asterism as a whole, the individual attains pure awareness born out of intense spiritual dissatisfaction with external forms of religion. The exaltation of Venus in the last quarter of Revati, the quarter owned by Jupiter, produces an overpowering sense of quietude, especially if it reposes there with the Moon, lord of Rohini, representing the foster mother of Krishna's brother and protector Balarama. Venus, being related to sex, encourages procreative activities which enhances the impact of Revati.

Whether we consider the impact of Revati on the individual or in relation to the cosmos, it leads to an infinite expansion of awareness to boundless duration, the dwelling of the seed of future growth in the infinite sea of quietude. Revati refers to the involvement of the soul in self-preserving activities which extend from eternity to eternity.

The basic impulse of Revati is that of dissolution, in which there is a desire to merge with the infinite, with death, the Great Deep. In everyday life, it expresses itself in quietude and equanimity, but nothing in it can be expected to be maintained in its concrete form. In Revati, there is always a turn toward the core, toward the center of everything. Everyday experiences are turned into spiritual attitudes.

4
GRAHAS
THE PLANETS

Nine celestial bodies are considered as planets in Hindu astrology. These are the Sun, Moon, Mercury, Venus, Mars, Jupiter, Saturn, Rahu and Ketu. Technically speaking, the Sun is not a planet but a star, and the Moon is a satellite. The Nodes of the Moon, the points where the Moon crosses the path of the ecliptic, are also included as planets and are named Rahu (North Node) and Ketu (South Node). The ancient seers may also have known of the trans-Saturnian planets. They give a location for Mahapata in Shravana asterism at the time of the *Mahabharata*; this may refer to the modern Uranus. Another planet called Sweta, placed in Purva Bhadra, may have been Neptune; and yet another celestial body in Krittika could have been Pluto. It is difficult to correlate the modern planets with those mentioned in ancient texts. However, the reason for basing predictions on the nine celestial force-centers mentioned above lies in the correspondence between the chakras in the human body and the planets. Yogis activate these chakras to expedite their spiritual development. For most people, that awakening takes place over many lifetimes. The activization process was linked with the seven planets, while Rahu and Ketu represented the karmic impediments we all must confront.

Hindu astrology, while describing the various planets and their effects, does not necessarily refer to the physical or astronomical planets: though these are linked with certain unseen powers, it is the higher powers themselves which govern planetary influence. This is a subject with which many people are unfamiliar and which has led to much confusion and scientific debate. Presently, the physical experimental sciences have begun to accept the reality of nonphysical forces and their impact on human life. Visual perception is no longer the criterion of truth or falsehood of any phenomenon. Hindu astrology assumes the presence of forces which are beyond the perception of man's physical senses but which guide the destiny of human individuals as well as earthly events. These forces operate according to laws which are studied under yoga and metaphysics. Astrology was a part of a well-coordinated system of spiritual sciences.

As indicated above, the nine planets represent the celestial force-centers. Differentiated influences flow through them. Planetary influences pass through signs, asterisms, and houses before reaching the individual. Predictions cannot be generalized. Correct interpretation depends on an understanding of all the relevant factors as well as an understanding of the spiritual laws operating on the universe and man. Unless one has an intuitive comprehension of this interrelationship, predictions cannot be accurate. In interpreting planetary influences, it is necessary to know the basic impulses of the planets as well as how those impulses are modified under different conditions. Presently, we shall indicate the essential characteristics of the planets:

Sun	Positive Spark of the Divine Spark. The fragment of primeval fire which ensouls every speck manifested on Earth. The withdrawal of this fire leads to the cessation of life itself.
Moon	Receptacle of the Life Spark. The Moon is the queen of the solar system. Receiving the life-force from the Sun, the Moon directs it to Earth, taking motherly care of the manifestation of different forms of life.
Mercury	Polarization of the Life Spark. The triad of Atma-Buddhi-Manas (soul, consciousness and mind) is linked with Mercury, which controls the movement of the polarized energy. Mercury stands at a crucial stage in the development of intelligence, which is essentially bipolar in character.
Venus	Electrical Spark resulting from the polarized Life Spark. Electricity and magnetism are the attractive power of Venus, which also enables the individual to radiate that scintillating spark which bestows grace, beauty and sociability.
Mars	Generation of Electrical Fluid. Mars is the blood circulating in every human being, but it is much more than that. The warmth and latent fire in every living entity is represented by Mars. As the commander-in-chief of the planetary hierarchy, it is engaged in manifesting the Life Spark radiated by the Sun in every form of creation. The Sun puts the Spark at the inner core of the entity while Mars brings it to the surface.

Jupiter	Distribution of the Electromagnetic Fluid of Divine Energy for human development and expansion. Jupiter tends the manifesting entity like a gardener, protecting the planet from rough weather and providing the necessary nourishment.
Saturn	Boundary of the Electromagnetic Field of Divine Energy for the present stage of human growth and development. Many more psychic faculties and powers will be bestowed on human beings when they have mastered the powers assigned to them under the present dispensation. The impact of the trans-Saturnian planets will be felt when additional chakras are assigned to man. Saturn is the "ring-pass-not" of human consciousness.
Rahu	The Nodes represent the Law of Divine Manifestation. At our level of existence, they represent the Law of Karma. The two Nodes have differentiated functions. Rahu is linked with past karma. When the individual is ready, Rahu brings back those karmic forces for release. Rahu produces situations which cannot be easily comprehended and which give rise to atonement.
Ketu	Rahu and Ketu together represent a demon who stole nectar from the gods during the churning of the cosmic sea. They are linked with the Dragon of the Deep Sea, symbolizing karmic nemesis, and also bestowing wisdom.

THE SUN ☉
The Soul of the Universe

Described as the Soul of the Universe, the Sun represents the life-force which vivifies, animates and enlivens the solar system. The Sun provides the gravitational pull that holds the planets together. It provides the energy which sustains them. The rays of light irradiated by the Sun animate life on earth. When the final dissolution takes place, the solar system will merge in the Sun. Hindu philosophy postulates several Suns operating at different levels of existence, but each of these is linked together, expressing themselves as the soul of the Kala Purusha. (Kala Purusha will be discussed later.)

The fragment of Divinity which constitutes each entity is represented by the solar ray. As long as solar energy reaches the individual and is absorbed by him, he lives; when the flow stops, his life ends.

The solar ray is linked with the innermost essence of the human individual. The atman or soul is represented by the Sun. It is Purusha as distinct from Prakriti. Together Purusha and Prakriti constitute the creative force, but Purusha is the male, who acts, who represents the positive or yang polarity of the life-force. The Sun is always concerned with the life-force, but never interferes with its evolution. As such, he is the "Silent Watcher" of every human being, vitally concerned with the well-being of the soul, never interfering in its activities but always ready to assist when we are willing to receive his guidance.

As the Silent Watcher, the Sun is associated with Sahasrara, the Crown Chakra, which when aroused leads the individual to Nirvana, or the liberation after which there is no more rebirth. The Sun gives human evolution its vital impetus toward perfection. This is an extremely difficult task; the Sun's impact cannot always be expected to give comfort. Often it is very strenuous. The work of the Sun resembles the pelican which tears open its breast to feed its "seven little ones." The vitality, grace, regal demeanor, and the impact of one's personality result from the radiance of the Sun. The highest level at which the Sun operates is indeed the reflection of the One Reality, the universe as Brahman. The Sun is thus the central generative impulse of cosmic manifestation. The other principles in Nature are merely differentiated aspects of the One Reality, the true Sun. Man is a multidimensional manifestation of the solar radiance. The different aspects of human personality are expressions of that radiance at various levels.

The Sun operates from the inner depths, illuminating the mind and soul, arousing spirituality and making the personality glow with radiance. Under the influence of the Sun, materialism, egotism, and wrong-doing are eliminated. Man identifies himself with others while at the same time maintaining his individual and regal status.

The solar ray seeks, strives, finds and conquers. It does not yield under any circumstances, and finally, even after delays and impediments, victory is achieved. No truly solar individual will relish any interference in his plans. He will aim at capturing the seat of power. He will enjoy shaping the lives of others; but in his private life he may be inflexible, unyielding, cruel and dictatorial. The intuitive understanding of truth and the underlying causes of world events are easily perceived by him. He may even display tremendous control over his physical reactions. His thinking will not necessarily follow logical steps, but he will arrive at his conclusions in a flash. In his method of teaching he will be direct, correcting mistakes ruthlessly and using short-cut methods to reach the end result. Outwardly determined, matter-of-fact and rigid, inwardly he will be kind and royal — like a stern father watching his son fight his battles, protecting him from a distance, coming to his rescue only when absolutely necessary. The Sun operates majestically, invisibly, protective, but without disturbing other levels of existence. The Sun acts discreetly, pointedly, effectively, and always keeping the final end in view.

Being such an overpowering planet, the effect of the Sun is very significant. The strength and uniqueness of a natal chart depends upon the disposition of the Sun. The various attributes assigned to the Sun describe the basic nature of the solar impulse. The Sun is assigned sattwa guna, which indicates its basic goodness, harmony and purity of intelligence. It is associated with gold and copper, the former as a symbol of purity and precious nature, the latter for its electrical vitality. The Sun rules the East, suggesting auspicious beginnings. The Sun only moves forward; it is never in retrograde motion.

The Sun is most powerful in the Tenth house, signifying the relationship of the individual with his external environment. There the Sun takes one to the center of power. Being such a domineering influence, the Sun in the house of marriage (the Seventh house) is not conducive to happiness. Individuals with this placement will find cooperation with others very trying, and there will be misunderstanding and friction with one's spouse. In the house of creativity, the Fifth, the physical production of offspring will be restricted, though there may be one or two children — but there will be a great deal of mental creativity. Such individuals may be able to propound philosophical ideas with freshness and mass appeal. With the Sun in the Fourth house, the individual will be able to dive deeply into the depths of the cosmic psyche — as a result of which, in spite of his great empathy, he will be misunderstood. In the Ascendant, there will be baldness and sharpness of personality. The individual will be full of ideas and eager to implement them, but he will meet with impediments when he tries to actualize his plans.

In the Third, there will be trouble with siblings, but few barriers to the realization of one's dreams. In the Sixth house, there will be easy victory over competitors and all difficulties will be quickly surmounted.

The Sun is related to the heart, and to blindness if afflicted. The Sun is the light and life of the universe, and any impediment to its flow seriously affects the light coming from one's eyes. Being the soul or heart of the universe, it is also related to one's heart (though in this regard the Moon is also important). On the basis of the Sun's placement in a horoscope, the astrologer may predict one's relationship with the government, father or husband; the Sun also reflects the enthusiasm, refinement and idealism of the person. A haughty nature, tyrannical disposition and argumentative temperament are also related to the Sun's disposition in a horoscope.

Whatever the impact of the Sun, it provides the life-force, works from the center of one's being, and always guides the individual toward his peak of achievement.

THE MOON ☽
The Cosmic Mother

References to the Moon in ancient religious literature are replete with contradictions. Sometimes considered male, sometimes female, at times bestowing wealth, honor and intelligence, while on other occasions inflicting death-like maladies, nourishing poisonous plants, and encouraging sorcerers, the Moon remains enigmatic. The Vedas say that the Moon carries the golden rays of the Sun. In Blavatsky's *Secret Doctrine*, the Moon is described as the Insane Mother. In the planetary hierarchy, the Sun is king and the Moon is queen. None of this reveals the true nature of the planet or its importance.

The Sun is the Soul of the Universe, and the flow of the Sun's rays is channeled through the Moon. The Moon does not shine with its own light but reflects the life-giving energy flowing from the Sun. This energy sustains life and acts as an agent of destruction as well; the Moon, reflecting that energy, functions accordingly. The benefic or malefic potential of the Moon does not arise from any other cause than the nature of the Sun itself. The Moon being a reflecting medium, it is incapable of causing any real harm. The color of whiteness associated with it refers to the purity of its nature; the undistorted reflection of the Sun's rays is aptly symbolized by a pure, flawless pearl. The life-giving quality of the Moon makes it "born of water," for water is the element which sustains all living creatures. These qualities of the Moon emphasize its role as the universal female generative principle, capable of producing good or evil depending on its associations.

The Sun, representing the soul, is reflected by the Moon, which represents "pure intelligence." Consciousness is not related to matter; rather, it is the spiritual soul in close association with Manas, or pure intelligence. This abstract nature of the Moon imparts to it much of its mysticism and supernatural powers. Psychic awareness comes within the domain of the Moon.

The Moon is the Cosmic Mother. Solar energy incubates under her care prior to its being concretized in material form. There is a close relationship between the Moon and the growth of life-forms on earth. The procreative processes of plants, animals, birds and human beings are deeply affected by the Moon. Our emotional responses and intellectual capabilities are intimately linked with it. In fact, in the psycho-physical constitution of human beings, its influence is so great that the Sun itself is subordinate to it. The practice of casting natal charts with the Moon as the Ascendant arises from this special significance. Water is the progeny of the androgynous Moon. The Sun is the giver of life to the whole universe while the Moon is the giver of life to our globe. Energizing life on earth, the Moon shines in the borrowed robes of her master. Astrologically, the Moon strengthens any planets associated with her except Saturn, which stifles the blossoming life-energy at every level.

The Sun represents the positive or yang polarity, the father principle, whereas the Moon represents the yin polarity, the mother principle. She is passive, womb-like, protective, strengthening the growth of her progeny, taking interest in every action of her child. She is mortally afraid of the death of her child but proud of its blossoming in every aspect of life: sex, marriage, progeny, education, profession, social relations, illness, fame; nor is she interested for her own sake but for the sake of the child itself. When her attention is withdrawn or when Saturn's affliction becomes acute, we experience difficulties. The Moon is like the mind, difficult to define but essential for any kind of growth and development; it is like water, which, in association with heat from the Sun, nourishes the plants and enables them to bear fruit. Astrologically, the Moon represents the vital energy that provides the capacity for growth: it signifies the mind, mother, house, conveyances, pearls, and silver. Tranquility of mind as well as peace and harmony in human relationships and life in general are associated with a favorable disposition of the Moon.

The Moon, being associated with consciousness, has the gift of detachment even as it nourishes the emotions and strengthens the life-force and animal passions. When the Moon is strong, she radiates the sympathies of a mother: whatever the behavior of her children, she never feels humiliated by them. Individuals who are guided by the Moon encourage the growth of others and are very much concerned with the welfare and prosperity of human society as a whole. Their driving impulse comes from wisdom and love. They display the quality of self-illumination, a sense of oneness and universal brotherhood. Their philosophy is similar to Buddhism, exemplifying compassion for all. Such individuals get their principles well coordinated without much difficulty. Their problems in life arise from the more personal aspect of the mind represented by Mercury, and from sloth and lethargy as indicated by Saturn.

The most important relationship of the Moon is with Jupiter. Under Jovian influence, the Moon can express its beneficial influence easily. An association with Mars arouses enthusiasm and activity; with Venus, the Moon becomes refined, sociable and interested in a well-ordered existence. The Sun devitalizes the Moon, who is better when farthest away from the other luminary, i.e., during Full Moon. Rahu and Ketu inflict karmic impediments and much frustration.

The placement of a strong Moon in the Fourth house, which represents the heart, the depth of one's being and material comfort, is very beneficial. In other houses, its effect will be conditioned by any accompanying factors. Wherever one finds the Moon, its most important features are changeability, swiftness of motion, and an influence on the psycho-phys-iological constitution of the individual. The Moon is concerned with the pure mind (as distinct from intellectual understanding) which harnesses Divine energy for worldly use while at the same time creating the veil of illusion which is Maya. It nourishes the earth in its bosom like a mother.

The Moon has affinity with marshy places, new clothes and jewels. It is associated with the rainy season, i.e. the middle of July to the middle of September. It likes salty flavors. Permanently dwelling on the subjec-tive plane of existence, the Moon needs the influence of a concrete, practical planet to harness its energy and irrigate other levels of conscious-ness.

MERCURY ☿
The Celestial Bridge

The ageless prince of the planetary hierarchy, green like the blades of grass, Mercury is described as a mixture of the three humors, namely Vata (wind), Pitta (bile), and Kapha (phlegm). He is a skilled speech-maker, fond of fun, and possesses seven limbs. Mercury influences one's learning, eloquence, skill in fine arts, respect from the erudite, acuity in meditation, proficiency in research, and understanding of religious rituals. Mercury has affinity with oyster (pearl)-shell, places of recreation, and the Sarat season (part of autumn) which extends from mid-September to mid-November. Mercury is rajas, indicating an active temperament with an imperious disposition. Sexually Mercury is a eunuch or hermaphrodite. In predictive astrology, it is generally associated with the intellect, brain, nervous system, respiratory system, mental perception and thyroid. In day-to-day short-distance travels, the influence of Mercury is consider-able.

These characteristics of Mercury point to the stage of cosmic ideation where naada or the primeval sound is articulated. Naada is the vibration which lies at the basis of the universe. The production of such a sound assumes a primeval mind without which there cannot be any articulated sound. The mind at the root of this articulation is represented by the Sun and Moon, whose impact on the course of manifestation is described as

Mahat, the cosmic ideation. This principle is the breath of the universal mind, Manas or the human soul, a part of which casts the veil of illusion or Maya over subjective reality, distorting the true nature of manifestation. This dual nature of Mahat is represented by Mercury.

Mercury signifies duality, polarization, and intellect — which also has duality as its main characteristic. Mercury does not have a distinctive personality of its own: it imbibes the features of the planets which are associated with it. It articulates and expresses whatever is channeled through it. For this reason, brilliance of expression, adjustment and flexibility rather than originality of thought are important traits of Mercury (which makes it very suitable for the lawyers' profession). Polarization is its central quality, and its main function is to carry the messages of gods to men and of men to gods; to make abstruse ideas intelligible to human-kind and comprehend quickly what others wish to convey. Trade, transport, diplomacy, proficiency in languages, the role of an author, dramatist, critic, interpreter, logician or translator are all manifestations of Mercurial intelligence.

As a principal intelligence in the construction of reality, Mercury enables the subjectivity of an idea to be objectified. At the same time, its function is to lead the entity to grasp the *inner* reality of any phenomenon. In this sense, the scope of Mercurial action is dual. Mind is not hindered by any impediment except its own self. Mercury is the swift-footed messenger of the gods who visits heaven and earth carrying messages from one to the other.

Mercury develops an individual's intellect. It increases his compre-hension and makes him philosophical. His eagerness to understand dif-ferent phenomena is greatly activated. He can see various viewpoints simultaneously and — unless he is able to coordinate those viewpoints (which will be the contribution of other planetary influences) — he will be considered argumentative, strong-headed, inconsistent, hypercritical, and perhaps cynical. With a favorable disposition of Mercury, the person will have good reasoning powers. He will be perceptive, clever, excellent in debates, intellectual and careful of details. How the Mercurial impact is felt will depend upon various factors but will always be reflected in the *mind*.

Mercury will lead the individual toward his goals in life through a variety of tests. Under Mercury's influence, the individual is not inclined to accept advice from others. He is often overwhelmed by passions and prejudices which upset his mental balance, confusing him and obscuring his vision of his own life. With the Moon, which is pure wisdom and reflects the Divine Spirit, Mercury is not well disposed: in close association with the Moon, its power is greatly reduced. With the Sun, its power is so overwhelmed that even though the individual becomes extremely clever, the unifying capacity of Mercury between the objective and subjective worlds is greatly restrained. Mercury becomes merely a messenger of the Sun to the Earth.

Mercury and Venus are closely linked with the Sun but generally incapable of bearing its radiance. They are always close to the Sun in longitude, which implies a special relationship between these three planets. But when Mercury and Venus are well tuned to the Sun, Mercury in association with Venus might make the individual begin a tirade against spirituality (the impact of the Sun). If the horoscope is already full of spiritual potential, Mercury may enable the person to have a deep intellectual grasp of spiritual philosophy, while Venus will provide insight into spiritual laws of Nature. With Mars, Mercury is not in a favorable relationship. Mars is concerned with physical activity, unflinching devotion, and an irresistible urge towards attaining higher goals in life; Mercury, being concerned with intelligence, thought, and social relationships, is averse to physical action, devotion and idealism. Mars can exert influence on Mercury but the latter will generally be ineffective to impart its own nature in return. Perfection for Mercurian people consists of plunging into the mysterious depths of one's innermost being and wresting from it the secrets of Nature. In such an endeavor, one must be extremely pliable, free from pride, superstition, and prejudice. Under suitable circumstances, it is possible for Mercurial people to attain these qualities.

Mercury is, indeed, a planet with many contradictory characteristics. However, certain special features of it can be highlighted. Mercury channels the solar radiance and reflects it in the *wholeness* of the manifestation. It transmutes matter into universal energy and enables it to reflect the inner light pervading all forms of existence. Various allegorical references to Mercury hint at the esoteric character of the planet. The process of materializing and spiritualizing the universe and the individual is indicated by the inter-relationships of Sun, Moon and Mercury. Mercury's inner significance is revealed by the myth connecting it with Jupiter, his wife, and her abduction and seduction by Soma, the deity ruling over the Moon.[1] By relating Mercury to Saraswati, Ida, and Parvati, we stress its role as the subjective principle of cosmic intelligence. As the

---

1   See Behari, Bepin, *Myths and Symbols of Vedic Astrology,* Salt Lake City, UT: Passage Press, 1990, pp. 54-5.

mind, Mercury is a channel for serving Shiva or the Supreme Creative Principle. It is preserved and assisted by the great self-perpetuating force represented by Vishnu. Mercury the messenger reveals the hidden secrets of spiritual teaching and the deeper meanings of ritual. Mercury is ageless: it is a chalice for the downpour of the Divine.

VENUS ♀
The Cosmic Passion

The desire nature of the Cosmic Man is represented by Venus. The planet is often linked with Kama Rupa, which is the vehicle of desires and passions. The Egyptians associate the khou or animal soul with Venus and Hindu Brahmanical literature relates the planet to Vijnanamaya Kosha and Manomaya Kosha, which are the seats of egotism and avidya (illusion), but all such associations are merely indirect pointers to the cosmic principle of attraction which results in procreative activity and the unfoldment of music, harmony, appreciation, and the urge to unite. Considered a female, skilled in the art of love-making, producing the sexual and creative impulse in every human heart, Venus heightens the sensuous nature of man. The passionate urges of Venus are primarily of an intellectual kind, poetic in sensibility, artistic in expression. Belonging to the Brahmin caste and pervaded by rajas (activity), Venus is refined, cultured, sacrificing and always engaged in activities. Though Venus is classified a female, this is primarily to point out its temperamental disposition which emphasizes sensitivity, creativity, sociability, adaptability and ethics rather than the passion of lust; Venus is also considered a counselor of the planetary hierarchy and is identified with Shukracharya, the son of a Vedic sage named Bhrigu. He has the function of giving advice to the demons. The very name Shukra means semen, referring to the procreative function of the deity.

There are many mythological references to the planet which link Venus with the Divine manifestative principle on one side and the downflow of spiritual energy towards earthly relationships. In the *Shiva Purana,* mention is made of the great sexual urge aroused in Shiva at the sight of the Mohini Rupa (attractive, seductive form) of Vishnu the Preserver. This seductive vision was created by the god so as to make Shiva's semen flow downward and enable human creation to begin. The impulses produced as a result of the downward movement of human semen — consideration for others, attraction to the opposite sex, care for one's body, the desire to love and be loved — are intimately connected with Venus.

Venus can be regarded as a link with the subjective realm represented by the Sun-Moon-Mercury triad, which requires a channel to concretize the highly spiritual Divine energy for its creative function on earth. The asuras or demons, in contrast to the gods, do not reside in heaven; their teacher Venus provides desirable impulses so that life on earth can be well-harmonized. Through Venus, one receives intuitional flashes leading to unity, harmony and a sense of fulfillment. Expressed in concrete form, they result in the production of the fine arts, the intensity and perfection of which are linked with the quantity of Venusian energy absorbed by the artist.

The primary human temperament resulting from a strong Venus is harmony. Under its impact, the individual feels at-one-ness with the whole of cosmic creation. Such an ideal of perfection postulates complete annihilation of the personal self: the Lord of the Burning Ghat, Shiva, represented astrologically by the planet Saturn, has a harmonious affinity with Venus. Under Venus, the individual begins to listen to the song of life and kills all desire for personal development. His basic characteristics are the expression of inner potentialities, a fondness for the pleasures of life, giving joy and happiness to others, producing a synthesis of differing viewpoints so as to enable the fructification of Divine beauty and harmony everywhere and in every situation. Venus is a benefic planet, always trying to produce auspicious and joy-giving results.

Such a feeling of joyousness leads to several aspects of life which are differently described in astrological texts. Some of the things which man desires are closely related to Venus. Wealth, vehicles, clothes, ornaments, song, dance and music, wife, happiness, perfumes, flowers, sexual intercourse, couch, house, prosperity, poetry and the fine arts, as well as women, sports, infatuation, high status and social position, charming speech, marriage and festivities are all inferred from the disposition of Venus in a natal chart.

The position of Venus is very important for determining the type of life an individual will lead. Venus has a special influence to shed on other planets, but is greatly affected by the impact of others as well. The nature of Venus is greatly harmed by association with Saturn and Rahu: its basic impulse is soiled and made repugnant. In combination with the Sun, it is combust and unable to function on the physical, earthly level — though its spiritual potential is greatly enhanced. A harmonious relationship exists between Venus and Mercury wherein both planets operate according to their natural dispositions; with the Moon Venus bestows much tranquility, but there is always a possibility that the Moon's proximity to the Sun might destroy some of the depth of feeling that might otherwise be experienced under this influence. With Mars, Venus produces tremendous passion; the individual's sex drive and attractiveness to the opposite sex become almost irresistible.

In the Ascendant, Venus bestows responsibilities, erudition, pleasant living conditions and a well-shaped body. In the Second house, Venus will give much wealth, sweet speech, and good relations. Problems regarding eyesight, affectionate relationships with sisters and female colleagues, and much attachment to worldly illusions result from Venus in the Third house. Venus in the Fourth makes the person deeply emotional, fond of women, the pleasures of life, and a comfortable house. In the Fifth house, Venus produces great artistic sensibility. In the Sixth, unless Venus is exceptionally well placed, there are difficulties such as litigation over women and possessions, and enmity with women. Venus in the Seventh is good for gaining an attractive spouse, but there is always a possibility that extramarital relationships will rule the individual's life. Longevity is beneficially affected by Venus in the Eighth house. In the Ninth, Venus will attract the individual towards pilgrimage, religious festivities and charitable activities. In the Tenth house, the person is engaged in social activities and is well-placed in his profession. In the Eleventh house, the person may be witty, having many pleasant friends and earning substantial amounts of money. In the Twelfth house Venus makes the person extremely fond of sexual pleasure, but he always pines for a better and more comfortable life, which is often unrealized.

To sum up, Venus represents the energy that procreates. It is sensitive to the finer forces in Nature, and perceives the Divine purpose in every form of manifestation. It produces harmonious relationships, the capacity to enjoy life, and an artistic nature. In the planetary hierarchy, Venus is considered the preceptor of the asuras, and it is through Venus that one receives intuitional flashes. Venus produces unity and the desire to unite. Astrologically, Venus is connected with man's vital fluid and diseases of the reproductive system; Venus also controls and influences the attraction between male and female.

Venus radiates creativity. Its activities are rooted in the divine plan of evolution and in the realm of the spirit, but the sphere of its operation is objective existence.

MARS ♂
The Generative and Creative Principle

Mars, represented by the Hindu god Kartikeya, was born of fire and earth because Shiva was shot by Cupid's (Kamadeva's) arrow. The child born of Shiva's semen was the only one who could kill a demon whose power lay in the fact that he could only be slain by a seven-day-old child of Shiva. Another story tells of how Shiva and Parvati undertook to find brides for their two sons, Ganesh and Kartikeya. Ganesh attained the marriageable maidens by playing a trick. Disappointed, Kartikeya retired to the mountains to practice austerities. Two characteristics of Mars are emphasized here. First, Mars represents the creative fire which produces invincible power. Second, Mars has a tremendous urge for marital relationships but is denied the opportunity to consummate them.

Mars is the commander-in-chief of the planetary hierarchy. He is related to the circulation of blood which keeps the body alive, the heat which enables all forms of creation to grow. Whatever lies within is externalized under his impulse. He unveils that inner content which is intimately connected with the expression of the life-force itself. Mars is harmonious with the Sun: both radiate the life-force. The Sun operates at such a high level that its energy is unobstructed, but Mars, being an earthly planet (he was nurtured by Earth and protected by Water at birth), has to fight his adversaries — which he does invincibly. Impediments to Mars are vanquished while forces hostile to the Sun simply melt away.

The Sun provides the fire which enlivens every object, while Mars functions as the warm red blood and provides the essential heat that makes the entity live. The Sun radiates the mind, gives sparkle and vivifies the indwelling spirit; Mars invigorates the body, providing the strength and vitality which enables each individual to fight his way through the world and attain his mission. This quality of Mars is expressed by the flow of blood: the blood circulating in the veins, the menstrual flow in women, the blood spilt through accidents, the chivalry which results from passion and other such features of human life come under the influence of Mars and provide the essential warmth to human life. Mars is impulsive, valorous, and energetic. He rules accidents, fiery speech and the color red. He operates at all levels of existence from the physical to the supremely spiritual. Action is his very nature, so idleness is inimical to his spirit.

Mars is related to the Serpent Power, the Kundalini Shakti. The semen of Shiva which gave birth to Mars is the Kundalini Shakti, which in ordinary individuals is always downward-moving — the serpent remains coiled at the base of the spine and the semen flows down. In those who have attained liberation, the energy has traveled upward to unite with the Crown Chakra, the Sahasrara. When the kundalini located in the crown chakra of Shiva flowed downwards, it became such a burning fire that nothing could hold it; as an act of sacrifice, the earth consented to nurture it, for which reason Mars is known as Bhumiputra, the offspring of the earth. Mars has a cosmic as well as a human level of operation, and both of these derive from the energy inherent in the earth. Its most concrete manifestation is found in fire. If the energy of Mars can be properly absorbed, it becomes constructive, bestowing a great deal of creativity. Failing that, it destroys the person. Most of us are very uncomfortable with a Martian person, even if he is not acting offensively. The vibration emanating from Martian individuals is simply unsettling to the average person.

Mars externalizes that which lies within. It is of the nature of fire, and fire never goes within. It always burns away the dross, purifying as it moves outward. Mars destroys all impediments in the way of its externalization process and thus reaches its goal. Mars is ambitious, arrogant, fiery, impulsive, and inflexible, but this is because he is fired with a missionary zeal, and that zeal is to express his latent faculties for the good of others. He becomes an able, even ruthless military general, but only when he has a reason to fight. Mars brings to the surface the concealed powers and weaknesses of the individual, diseases as well as talents; the process of externalization may sometimes appear as aggressive behavior in the individual, but it represents the most basic quality of the planet. Surgical operations, accidents and abortions, volcanic eruptions, rebellions, wars and other such phenomena are expressions of inner turmoil coming to the surface. If Mars is well posited, its destructive attributes are modified, and only the finest masculine attributes are exhibited. Such individuals, instead of submitting to lust, may become champions of chivalry and protectors of the earth. Mars in dignity gives one a courageous and invincible disposition — impervious to fear and danger, risking his life for a cause, yet prudent in his own way.

The most stifling restrictions are imposed on Mars through association with Saturn. This planet inhibits Martian energy and inculcates depraved feelings which are radically opposed to the Martian nature. The influence of Jupiter is very strengthening. Jupiter enables all the harmonious Martian qualities to blossom. The Jovian influence regulates the impetuosity of Mars, gives it a spiritual direction and makes its efforts successful. The Sun and Mars vibrate well with each other. The association of Moon with Mars is good, because the former is energized by the latter while the latter is tempered by lunar wisdom. With Venus, Mars produces passion and irresistible lust. Mars and Mercury strengthen each other, Mars imparting active energy to Mercury while Mercury makes Mars a good strategist.

The best houses for Mars are the Ascendant, Sixth, and Tenth. The individual becomes youthful and full of energy with Mars in the First house. Personal adversaries and impediments to the fulfillment of one's mission are easily vanquished with Mars in the Sixth. Those who are preparing themselves for spiritual attainments will find that Mars in the Sixth also enables them to acquire control over Nature's finer forces. In the Tenth, the ambitious and efficient individual will become a natural leader and his contribution to human history and civilization may be noteworthy.

When this planet is significant and the individual's temperament is developing along positive Martian lines, the individual will seek Truth through material progress and scientific researches or discoveries. He will investigate the hidden laws of Nature and the powers latent in man. He is a wise man-of-the-world, filled with fiery enthusiasm for unraveling the mysteries of life and pioneering in new lands. He maintains admirable control over his organs of action and perception. Such fiery men, full of enthusiasm, without any personal prejudices and with perfect control over their physical bodies, will succeed as pure scientists and be able to wrest from Nature the secrets it holds for us. But such a disposition can arise only when Mars is not tainted by materiality, is well placed to express its fiery nature, and motivated by its spiritual ambition. Mars gives devotion, courage, and a very strong personality.

JUPITER ♃
The Grantor of God's Benediction and Limitless Expansion

Jupiter, called by the name of Brihaspati or Brahmanspati in the Vedas, intercedes with gods on behalf of men and protects mankind against the wicked. He is the preceptor or teacher of the devas (the gods). Being primarily a teacher, Jupiter always displays sympathetic consideration for mankind and tries to guide us on the path of righteousness. He has full possession of the sacred wisdom. His method of teaching is to lead students from the external to the internal, from the known or exoteric to the unknown or esoteric. Brihaspati is concerned with rituals, the perpetuation of established codes of behavior and traditional systems of relationships, imparting knowledge and wisdom rather than leading individuals to the more difficult spiritual task of release from birth and death. Venus possesses the secret of immortality which releases the individual from the cycle of incarnations; and Saturn may impart the secrets of life or guide the individual in transcending the illusory world. Surprisingly, Jupiter does not vibrate at the same wave-length as these planets. Jupiter is jiva, the personal soul, and represents the principle of life as expressed by the vital breath; Jupiter has a great influence in imparting the life, motion and sensation which increase the intensity of living. Despite his role as the preceptor of gods and the planet of religious behavior, Jupiter is a deeply earthy planet who enables his beneficiaries to live righteously in the world, bestowing on them all the conditions of affluence necessary for right living and contentment. Jupiter represents God's grace. This, however, does not imply that the devotees of Jupiter will not meet difficulties on the path or that their lives will be smooth. A Brahmin saturated with sattwic or harmonious proclivities, Jupiter is considered a first-rate benefic, but he fails to bestow the joyous conditions available under Venus or the fiery enthusiasm which, under Mars, leads to unexpected elevation in life. The Jovian impact is experienced in the quest for a better life, in receiving Divine benediction by getting opportunities which result from good karma, and in being protected against untoward incident. Jupiter is primarily concerned with wisdom and the good life, but the significance of these must be properly understood in order to fully appreciate the effect of the planet.

Expansion is a special feature of Jupiter. The energy and life essence we receive from the Sun, Moon and Mars need protection for their full development and growth before they can fulfill their missions. Jupiter protects the soul from various difficult situations, but in all these protective measures the primary objective is to enable the soul to grow and attain its final stature. Physically, Jupiter is represented as a large-bodied deity; it is connected with the Ayurvedic constitution kapha or phlegm, and wherever it aspects, that part of one's life grows big. If the aspect is on adverse areas of life such as adversaries (Sixth house) or expenditures (Twelfth house), that area grows and assumes substantial magnitude. Jupiter may not only increase the size of the physical body, it also links it with the superphysical dimension of existence through which life-energy flows to the person. Physical health is greatly affected by the disposition of this planet.

The Jovian concern with expansion arises from the fact that the planet is much more particular about externals than inner issues: if the physical health of a person is sound, he will be able to attend to his spiritual duties. Protection and nourishment of the externals are intended to turn the individual's gaze toward inner truth — which may follow as a matter of course, though not necessarily as a direct result of Jupiter's influence. The religious tendencies inculcated by Jupiter are of an exoteric nature. Under its impact, the individual may read scriptures, perform rituals, and seem deeply interested in the external manifestations of religion. He will regularly be present at temples, churches and other places of worship. To him, the various deities are personified gods rather than psychological concepts, ever ready to forgive the worshipper and remove all impediments from his path. Nevertheless, the goal is to lead the individual from the rituals to the power dwelling within.

In predictive astrology, Jupiter is related to one's knowledge, good (righteous) behavior, offspring (especially male), religious vocations or high status in an advisory capacity, the teaching profession, magnanimity of heart and generosity of disposition, the Vedas and religious scriptures, prosperity and affluence, devotion and faith, wealth, happiness in conjugal life, honor and status, and compassion. These qualities are expressions of the basic disposition of the planet. In adverse situations, Jupiter can produce cerebral congestion, abscess, dropsy, flatulence, hernia and liver complaints. Jupiterians have a tendency to be easily pleased, and even the afflictions caused by Jupiter are amenable to quick propitiation by mantras, rituals, and offerings to Brahmins.

Jupiter is very well placed in the Fifth house, connected with creativity. Whatever the person's level of functioning or sphere of activity, the Jovian influence will accentuate his creative tendencies and provide immense opportunities for creative urges to manifest. Being spiritually oriented, Jupiter in the Fifth house is not conducive to progeny, but it makes the individual spiritually inclined and averse to material bondage. In the Ninth, Jupiter is at its best; it activates the meritorious karma of the individual and enables him to reap the consequences. Status, psychological orientation, religious attitudes, health and creativity are very favorably influenced. In the Ascendant, Jupiter gives a good healthy body and a religious mind; in the Tenth house the individual is well spoken of, but one must not expect a very prosperous life unless Jupiter is supported by other planets.

The association of Jupiter with the Moon is extremely beneficial. If these two planets are conjunct, in aspect, or in kendras (angular houses) from each other, prosperity and solutions to all difficulties will result. This is one of the most auspicious relationships possible between planets; it purifies the mind of the person and guides his actions in the right direction. Such a person will hardly come to grief through any fault of his own. In association with Saturn, the nature of Jupiter is greatly cramped, and the stifling impact becomes very frustrating. The Nodes of the Moon also do not produce harmony, but they greatly destroy the nobility of Jupiter. Jupiter is very much in its element when it forms any relationship with Mars or the Sun.

Jupiter is connected with the welfare of humanity and the production of religious feelings. It does not minimize the importance of material existence. The Jovian influence includes physical welfare as well as the religious transformation of the psyche. It gives a positive approach to life.

Such a person believes in God in every form of creation. For him, working for God implies working for humanity. One can say that Jupiter represents Spirit embracing Matter. It is indeed a very vibrant energy impulse for the nourishment, expansion, and spiritual transformation of the human individual.

SATURN ♄
The Journey's End

Saturn, known as Shanishcharacharya in Sanskrit, is "the slow-moving preceptor." The journey begun under the impulse of the Sun finally comes to an end under the Saturnian veil. The long pilgrimage passes through various phases and ultimately reaches a stage wherefrom one must return. The passage is long and winding. Having been led down the garden path, one reaches the burning ghat where the physical body is consumed in fire. Saturn, represented as Yama, the god of death, is considered a son of the Sun, but under its impact the solar radiance is cast under the veil of shadow, the ethereal life-spark is encased in a material body, and the illusion is slowly destroyed. Disillusioned by life, the individual feels deceived, frustrated and miserable. Ultimately he recoils. This marks the beginning of the path of return. Saturn is often described in dreadful terms, considered the worst malefic of the planetary hierarchy. But Saturn, the initiator in spiritual wisdom as well as a significator of human miseries, is the final boundary beyond which the life-force is not permitted to cross. For those who seek the dawn of unfettered wisdom which will enable them to pass beyond the limits of material existence and attain Nirvana, Saturn is regarded as a great boon, whereas those who thirst for worldly existence experience it as heart-breaking misery.

Destruction, frustration, disillusionment, setbacks and even death are produced by Saturn. It frustrates all efforts to expand and blossom or to immerse ourselves in earthly existence. Initiative, devotion, and loyalty are not permitted to grow. Sociability, material comfort, sex, and psychic intuition are abnegated. Mind under the Saturnian impact is not free to function logically and with clarity. These frustrating experiences arise due to the great barrier Saturn imposes on the downpour of Divine energy. Depending on the intensity of the Saturnian dam, such obstructions in the expression of everyday life seem frustrating, causing great misery. That is why Saturn is the great malefic.

Saturn is generally represented as a very old man with a sickle in his hand. The Romans thought of him as a god of agriculture. He is considered both a king of the golden age and a decrepit old man. Indian seers described Saturn as dark in form, black in color, and tamasic in nature (i.e., slothful, inert), and they assigned him the places where rubbish heaps are stored. They related Saturn with rags, hillocks, mountains and forests. He is the endless and immovable duration, without beginning or end, beyond time and space. Governing timelessness and the side of life which is unattractive to worldly men, Saturn causes suffering by "adjusting" the total karma of each individual. Every action of omission and commission is accumulated in that timeless duration from which Saturn releases the force of karmic retribution. Forces which can yield material affluence may also be part of one's karmic retribution, and this is why Saturn sometimes bestows high status or worldly renown.

Saturn releases karmic forces so that the individual is free to proceed on his journey. One of the most important characteristics of Saturn is its impact on the psychological orientation of the person. Even when Saturn produces its ostensibly beneficial results, it does not enable the individual to enjoy them. It is not so much dissatisfaction as *disenchantment* which creates a feeling of detachment from life. The grapes are not actually sour but the "inner man" is no longer attracted to them. An individual may begin with greed, covetousness, and the thirst for obtaining certain things, but under Saturn's influence a kind of psychological reorientation takes place which renders the individual unable to enjoy the very things he desired. The initial reaction may be sorrow and dejection, but a detached objectivity will finally enable the individual to see the relationship between himself and the world around him.

Saturn is like a huge and intense shadow. The downpour of the creative life-spark has thus far been vivifying various aspects of life, but under the impact of Saturn that radiance is obstructed. A shadow is cast. As a result of this tendency, the individual feels restricted. A feeling of helplessness arises, and he realizes that some force is thwarting his efforts.

No house placement of Saturn is conducive to auspicious results. However, when placed in the Third or Eleventh house (the base of the Triangle of Materiality) it is not as grim. In the Third house, despite afflictions to brothers and sisters, there may be a psychological orientation which renders the individual clever in worldly matters. In the Eleventh, there can be inflow of money even if the source of income is not socially or ethically acceptable. In the Ninth house, there will be a repulsion to established religion; the individual will produce his own novel ideas and unorthodox approaches to established faith and traditions.

The impact of Saturn on the luminaries is decisively bad, creating much unhappiness in the life of the person. Any association of Saturn and the Moon will produce some kind of mental turmoil, depressive feeling, or even suicidal tendencies. Saturn is considered badly placed in the twelfth or second house from the Moon, or especially in the same house. When such afflictions take place in the case of the Sun, the individual suffers immensely. The life force seems to simply ebb out of him.

With Mars, which is ever bubbling with energy, Saturn is not well disposed. These two planets vibrate on opposite wavelengths. Mars desires action, Saturn produces sloth; Mars gives zest for life, Saturn makes the individual depressive. Mars explodes and exteriorizes, while Saturn is the cold wave which shrinks the growing life-plant and makes a person introverted. Aspects between these two planets often paralyze the person.

Saturn is so decisive and deeply active that no palliative works with it. Many methods have been suggested for propitiating Saturn. Sometimes they seem to work very well. But the real essence of propitiating Saturn lies in accepting the inevitability of its impact, surrendering oneself to God, and orienting one's life toward a spiritual path. Saturn's mill grinds slowly and surely. Any effort to deflect its impact is bound to fail. But if one can comprehend its basic nature and try to live in harmony with it, the suffering is immediately relieved. From a purely material standpoint, Saturn is impossible to appease, but if someone adopts the right spiritual approach, its adverse results are turned into valuable boons. This explains why Saturn is also associated with remedies for restoring life, rejuvenation, and the serpent wisdom.

The primary function of Saturn is to direct the evolving soul back to its source. It has immense patience. Its action is decisive. By casting a deep shadow on the radiation of the life-force, Saturn produces a psychological change under which the individual begins to recognize the inevitable influence of the Supreme Power and thus begins his homeward journey.

RAHU ☊
The Cosmic Law

There is much similarity between Rahu and Saturn: what Saturn tries to activate from the objective side, Rahu does from the subjective side. This difference radically alters the nature of their effects, though both have the aim of producing disenchantment with the materialistic side of life. Rahu and Ketu work in unison, and it is significant that together they constitute a serpent which is referred to in various scriptural texts. The most important point that students of astrology can draw from this is the elusive nature of their impact. Predictions concerning Rahu and Ketu can never be made with certainty. The only decisive judgment that can be made is that their repercussions are felt on the psychological and psychic planes of existence.

Rahu is described as immensely powerful, born of a lioness, having a huge body like a mountain of lamp-black color, snake-shaped, terrible-mouthed and a devourer of the Moon and the Sun. He is in fact more powerful than the luminaries. This special power is enjoined to Rahu because he is a messenger of the Cosmic Law under which the entire universe operates. Rahu represents the cyclic law of manifestation. Even the luminaries which provide life-giving and sustaining energy have to operate under the overall command of this Cosmic Law. The Rahu-Ketu axis should be considered as an objective personification of the subjective aspect of life; its impact is the outcome of unflinching, inevitable law. Under Rahu things happen — which may be good or bad, depending on several factors. These things produce an equilibrium that may ultimately give rise to harmony and eliminate discord. In an individual's life, Rahu operates under the Law of Karma, as a result of which its repercussions are almost impossible to escape except by paying off the debts of past lives.

Rahu is of the nature of a serpent. Rahu-Ketu took part in the churning of the ocean, wherein jewels and nectar were obtained and which the gods wanted to keep for themselves exclusively. Rahu-Ketu, one of the demon asuras, managed to partake of some of the nectar, which made him immortal. Angered, Vishnu sliced the demon into two halves — Rahu the head, and Ketu the lower half. These two forces pursue the Sun and Moon through the sky, thus causing eclipses. It is a difficult allegory to under-stand, but obviously the Nodes of the Moon are engaged in the process whereby life's experiences are churned and the nectar which sustains it is obtained. These Nodes are as eternal as the gods themselves because both of them have shared, rightly or wrongly, the nectar. In their eternal nature, the Nodes are like the cosmic law which enables individuals to realize the essence of their multifarious experiences. What lies behind all our expe-riences is revealed by the Nodes, and this realization is primarily a subjective experience which leads to radical transformation in the psyche.

Rahu is half-bodied. The completion of the effect it perpetrates must be experienced through Ketu. When Rahu begins to provoke radical changes in the psyche of the individual, that psyche must attain its original pristine nature. This cannot take place as long as there is any reliance on past forces or on anything external. This is a hard time for the individual. The troubles produced by Rahu are not only elusive in nature and beyond the help of any remedial measures, they also completely obscure one's sense of perspective. One must bear the trouble by himself and come to an understanding of its real nature.

Rahu is snake-shaped, born of a lioness, and a devourer of the Sun and Moon. These terms express some of the secret nature of Rahu. In all religions, the serpent symbol is used in esoteric allegories. In Hindu mythology, references are made which only become comprehensible when esoteric keys are applied to them. Generally speaking, the serpent symbol stands for spiritual knowledge, the Serpent Fire. Rahu stands for secret wisdom as well as for the initiator. When an individual passes through initiation, he undergoes immense pain; his whole life seems to melt away. All guidance disappears during such an initiation, and the whole existence of the person seems empty of Divine assistance. Rahu stands for the guide as well as the initiation itself. The significance of Rahu devouring the Sun and Moon refers to another condition that occurs during the initiatory process. The individual's psyche, represented by the Moon and soiled by the shadow of materialism, completely vanishes. In the final level of initiation, the Moon becomes invisible, enters the bosom of the Sun (i.e., a solar eclipse always occurs on a Full Moon), and finally comes out rejuvenated. While the rejuvenation process takes place, the physical man is severed from the sustenance of the Sun and Moon. Once the ritual is complete, his psychic nature is completely renewed. The fact that Rahu is the offspring of a lioness points to his special status as an inner guide who enables the individual to obtain new powers and the blossoming of his latent faculties as represented by the Serpent Fire. Through the trials and afflictions caused by Rahu, the individual unfolds some of these latent faculties and begins to understand the mysteries of life.

Rahu's association with any planet is bad. With the Sun and Moon, it cuts off the sources of life and illumination. With Jupiter, it destroys the very nature of the planet and almost makes him a malefic; Jupiter emphasizes religious rituals and traditional philosophy while Rahu destroys the past to arouse a radically different kind of illumination. Unless the person is prepared for this downpour, he acts in an unpleasant and socially unapproved manner. Mars will accentuate the tendencies of Rahu in its malefic as well as its spiritualizing process, but it will intensify the process so acutely it becomes unbearable. With Saturn, Rahu will make one's life miserable both at the objective and subjective levels.

Rahu's placement in the Third, Sixth, Tenth and Eleventh houses is supposed to be better than others. Bad for siblings, Rahu in the Third will give much courage for enduring injustices done to the individual. Rahu posited in the Sixth house overcomes impediments in regard to health, service conditions, food, litigations, debts, theft, and even the ill-fame caused by other planets: Rahu in the Sixth makes smooth sailing for the individual. In the Tenth house, Rahu can conquer the world, either with physical prowess, intellectual power, or with spiritual devotion. Rahu in the Eleventh house is highly propitious for acquiring renown; a favorable Rahu in the Eleventh will help the individual in attaining his aspirations, whether those aspirations are material or spiritual. Rahu, who gained the nectar despite the watchfulness of the gods, must somehow or other satisfy the desires of the individual.

Rahu has a great affinity with material forms of existence and Ketu with spiritual. Together they churn the life of the individual with a view to manifesting the Divine Plan meant for him and the powers latent in him. The eternal law which regulates life on earth is expressed as the Law of Karma. It enables the individual to enjoy the gifts of life as much as his destiny permits. The individual is denied these gifts only when his karma so ordains. The two Nodes of the Moon function like two sentinels of the Lords of Karma, restricting or granting gifts according to law. The two Nodes, therefore, form the axis around which the entire life of the individual revolves. Rahu first immerses man in affluence, then leads him into frustration, while Ketu gives the humiliation which arouses spirituality. Both lead the individual to contemplation of life's experiences, and, through the deeper experience of the life-force, one acquires the secret of heaven.

KETU ☋

The Eternal Wisdom

Ketu represents the lower portion of the Rahu-Ketu axis, symbolized by a serpent Naga. It is always placed in the opposite house from Rahu. Both planets, which are primarily shadowy in character, create an impact which must be considered as a unit, though they also have distinct and separate features of their own. Both are agents for spiritualization, but the manner in which each produces this effect is quite different. Ketu creates turmoil and impels the mind toward deep thinking which finally induces enlightening results. It assimilates experience and, activating the intellect, leads the individual to contemplation. It is not necessary that a cataclysm should occur prior to the beginning of the thought process. Even precocious children are sometimes under the influence of Ketu. However, generally speaking, some experience of dissatisfaction precedes the thinking activities. What is important is one's feeling of helplessness in attaining any specific goal in life. The individual feels small in relation to what the world expects of him, as a result of which the world seems to conspire to make him feel smaller still. This at first is *humiliating*; in time it develops into genuine *humility*. Thus the individual achieves a firm base for the moral and spiritual foundations of life. Ketu aims at creating a way of life radically different from the worldly game.

Some outstanding features of the Rahu-Ketu axis are that it has greater power than the Sun and Moon, which are obscured by the shadow of Rahu and Ketu, and that it may lead the individual toward liberation. Ketu in particular has much influence on the spiritual side of an individual's life; it has control over the psyche. It arranges events in the life of a person in such a way that the psyche is cut off from its material attachments, which are consequently perceived objectively. At best, this process makes the individual more spiritual in the true sense of the word and enables him to come face to face with his own inner teachers.

Ketu's influence is more pronounced when it is placed in sensitive houses or under conditions where paranormal faculties may be easily developed. Ketu with the Moon in the Twelfth will provide such favorable conditions for the development of psychic faculties. Conjunct with the Sun in the Eighth house — especially in Sagittarius, Capricorn, Aquarius, or Pisces — Ketu brings the individual into contact with evolved souls and the deeper mysteries of Nature. But if the influences are less favorable, Ketu may produce certain kinds of perversity. With Venus, for example, and especially in Taurus, Cancer, Virgo, or Libra, sexual and psychological abnormality cannot be ruled out. The important point is that Ketu heightens the paranormal sense-perception, which, if not properly controlled, can make the individual psychologically unbalanced, while under spiritually oriented forces Ketu provides the best conditions for psychic unfoldment. With favorable conditions in the Sixth house, for instance, Ketu could make the unfoldment of clairvoyance, clairaudience, and other such faculties possible. But with more materialistic planets, Ketu in the Sixth would bestow worries, mental anguish, and unmitigated difficulties in everyday life.

Ketu is a mendicant. Toward material property and attainments, its attitude is rather indifferent. Those who are under the influence of Ketu are seldom attracted to objects of a worldly nature: wine, women and wealth will not satisfy them. Ketu prefers to wander from one place to another; it does not wish to hold onto anything for long. It is very much akin to Mars in the sense that it causes the kind of psychological explosion which allows us to break through our limitations. Staying in one place and in one situation fossilizes our energy. But Mars and Ketu perform their liberating roles in different ways. The physical force fired by ambition, aspiration, and devotion enables Mars to break through the outer crust so that the energy within gushes out and conquers new worlds of experience. Ketu, on the other hand, moves with the impulse of inquiry and is fueled by disenchantment with the external outside world. It delves deep into the realities of life. In both cases, the outer crust is destroyed, but the liberating effect of Ketu is of a radically different nature. A new understanding, a new way of life is achieved. While one may consider Mars the commander of an army, Ketu is more like a mystic inquiring into the secrets of nature.

The ancient seers gave to Ketu such epithets as Tamas and Dwajah, which reveal the basic character of the planet. Tamas is one of the three basic attributes ordinarily means darkness, but the darkness produced by Ketu is the Great Illusion, Maya, which makes all manifestation possible. Ketu is like a serpent with a luminous star at its head; it shines in the darkness so as to illuminate the true reality. Dwajah ordinarily means a flag or emblem, but it has other connotations too. It may symbolize an eminent person, the organ of generation, or a house situated in the east. These indications reveal the inner significance of Ketu and point out certain traits which are marked in its working. An individual under the influence of Ketu gives the impression of being emotionally involved (as in the case of Mars) in the results of his efforts. But this is not so. The individual undoubtedly works with tremendous zeal, like a beast of burden, but he does so in order to carry out the orders given to him by higher consciousness, a higher spiritual authority. A flag is also an emblem of some higher force in whose name and under whose authority the person operates. Similarly, the generative organ does not by itself procreate — it merely carries the germ or seed of procreation from the male to the female. Ketu merely functions as a channel for creative energy. It does not involve itself in the physical realm of creativity because it is fully aware of the transient nature of existence on this plane. It functions on the mental plane. Ketu is a catalytic agent linking manifestation with inner reality.

Rahu and Ketu have great importance in the manifestation of the universe at large as well as in the life history of the individual. On their disposition depends, to a great extent, the course of life's unfoldment. Rahu operates like the very embodiment of matter, while Ketu is the mysterious illumination of Spirit. The Nodes of the Moon together spin the web which produces the universe. This is the function of the Rahu-Ketu axis. In this assignment, Rahu is given the task of materialization and Ketu that of mentation and spiritual regeneration. Rahu has a scimitar and spear in his hands, while Ketu is associated with an arrow; Rahu works from without while Ketu looks out from within the veil of ignorance. But both bestow riches and wealth and both face south, taking their orders from the Divine Intelligence which guides the destiny of the universe. Taken together, they personify the Great Law on which the cosmic order rests and which preserves the cohesion and equilibrium of all.

PART II

INFORMATION BASE

IMPORTANT PLANETARY CHARACTERISTICS

Planets	Benefic/ Malefic	Aspect of Cosmic Man	Color	Direction	Element	Body Humor
Sun	Malefic	Soul	Red (Reddish-White)	East	Fire	Bone, Bile
Moon	Depends upon its distance from the Sun*	Con-scious-ness	White	North-West	Water	Cough, Phlegm, Blood
Mercury	Depends upon as-sociating planet	Voice	Dark Green	North	Earth	Skin, Bile, Phlegm, Wind
Venus	Benefic	Sex-urge	Varie-gated in Color	South-East	Water	Semen, Phlegm, Wind
Mars	Malefic	Valor, Fortitude	Deep-Red	South	Fire	Bile, Bone Marrow
Jupiter	Benefic	Comfort & Wisdom	Golden Yellow	North-East	Ether	Fat, Phlegm
Saturn	Malefic	Sorrow	Dark	West	Air	Sinews, Wind, Phlegm
Rahu	Malefic		Dark	South-West		Wind
Ketu	Malefic		Dark			

* The Moon is benefic from the 8th day of its waxing phase to the 8th day of its waning phase and a malefic the rest of the time.

ASPECTS: All planets aspect the 7th house from themselves, but Mars also aspects the 4th and 8th house; Saturn also aspects the 3rd and 10th house; and Jupiter also aspects the 5th and 9th. Some astrologers have given the additional aspects of the 5th and 9th to Rahu and Ketu.

1
THE NATAL
CHART

The natal chart or horoscope is a diagram of the sky showing the relative positions of the planets and signs at a given moment (typically the birth of an individual). On the basis of this chart, predictions of future events in the person's life are made and the various traits of character are discovered. In India, we commonly find three kinds of diagrams, though as we shall see, a rectangular format is most often used. In Western countries, circular representation of the chart is standard. Essentially, all horoscope diagrams are comprised of three basic elements —

1. The eastern horizon line and the astronomical zenith point or meridian line which together form the prime axes of the birth chart.
2. The signs of the zodiac depicted with reference to the horizon (i.e., the Ascendant or rising sign represents the zodiacal constellation which is rising on the eastern horizon at the time of birth).
3. The longitudinal position of the planets in various zodiacal signs.

In South India, the horoscope diagram shown in Fig. 1 is prevalent. Each box represents one sign of the zodiac. The second box from the left on the top row represents Aries, and the signs move clockwise around the diagram. The eastern horizon is indicated by placing a diagonal line indicating the Lagna or Ascendant in the appropriate box. The planets are also placed in the box or sector representing the sign they occupied at the time of birth.

In Eastern India, the same data is depicted differently. The basic diagram is constructed by the intersection of two vertical and two horizontal lines, the four corners of which are again divided by four diagonal lines. The top box in this diagram (Fig. 2) also pertains to Aries or the first sign of the zodiac, but the subsequent signs move in a counterclockwise direction. The Ascendant and the planetary positions are indicated as before. The third diagram (Fig. 3) is the popular North Indian form of horoscope. Here, it is the Ascendant which is always fixed. The different

Methods of Representing the Birth Chart

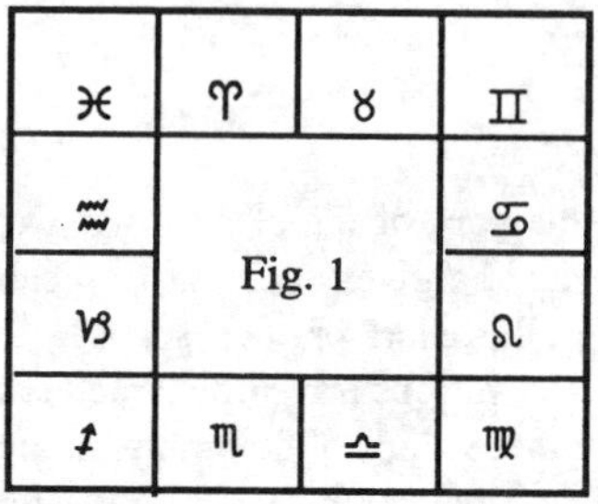

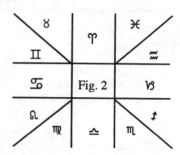

Fig. 1

The South Indian chart is sign-oriented. The Ascendant is indicated by a diagonal line (/) superimposed from the lower left corner to the upper right corner over the appropriate sign.

Fig. 2

The Eastern Indian chart is also sign-oriented. The Ascendant and planets are superimposed over the signs.

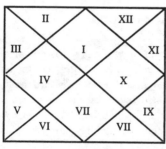

Fig. 3

The North Indian chart is house-oriented. The signs are superimposed on the chart with the numerals 1 for Aries, 2 for Taurus, and so on.

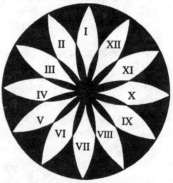

Fig. 4

A circular North Indian chart. The signs and planets are superimposed as in Fig. 3.

signs follow in serial order. An important circular type of representation is in the form of petals (Fig. 4). In this case, the topmost petal is the First house and the other petals in counterclockwise direction represent the following houses. The houses are fixed, and the signs are superimposed.

The Western type of horoscope (Fig. 6) places the eastern horizon or Ascendant on the left-hand side, while the topmost point depicts the Midheaven (M.C.) or Tenth house. The right-hand side represents the Descendant or Seventh house and the bottom the Nadir or Fourth house. These points are the "cusps" of the houses. One important difference between Western and Hindu astrology is that Western astrology defines a cusp as the beginning of a house division, while Hindu astrologers define it as the midpoint of a house.

Another important difference between Western and Hindu astrology lies in the use of the tropical zodiac by Western astrologers and the sidereal zodiac by Hindus.

Over the course of many centuries, the earth changes it polar orientation to the stars and constellations. This change occurs due to a slight wobble in the earth's axis, and the motion thus created is called the precession of the equinoxes. The zodiac "begins" at 0° Aries because the earth's polar axis once pointed to that degree during the vernal equinox, or first day of spring. To be more precise, it pointed to that degree when the present zodiacal calendar was established (according to Hindu calculations, this would have been in 285 AD). Now, however, the precession of the equinoxes has altered our polar orientation. The earth's axis is no longer pointing toward Aries at the vernal equinox.

Western astrologers have preferred to arbitrarily name the Sun's position at the equinox as 0° Aries. Therefore, the tropical zodiac is also called movable, because it moves the true vernal point in order to keep Aries correlated with the first day of spring. Hindu astrologers allow for the precession of the equinoxes. Their sidereal zodiac is called fixed, because it is constant against the background of the fixed stars and constellations (i.e., the vernal point may move, but the zodiac itself does not, since it is a collection of stars and constellations).

Another important point is that the precession of the equinoxes moves in retrograde motion (i.e., backward). Therefore the true vernal point is somewhere in Pisces. It is, in fact, about to pass over into Aquarius. This is what Western astrologers mean when they say that we are entering the Age of Aquarius.

In order to convert a standard Western horoscope to a Hindu one, therefore, we must subtract the difference in precessional motion from the tropical planetary positions given in Western charts.

Methods of Representing the Birth Chart

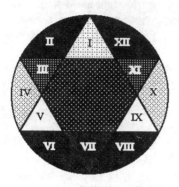

Fig. 5

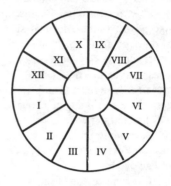

Fig. 6

A house-oriented chart for analysis. **Quadrants:** I (Asc.), IV (Hiranyagrabha or Bythos), VII (Descendant), X; **Sea of Immutability, the Mysterious Depth:** II, VI, VIII, XIII; **Triangle of Materiality:** III, VII, XI; **Spiritual Triangle:** I, V, IX.

The Western chart is house-oriented. The signs and planets are superimposed on the chart. Here the housecusp begins at 0°.

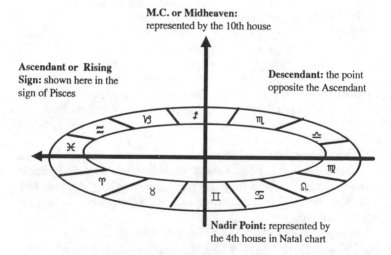

M.C. or Midheaven: represented by the 10th house

Ascendant or Rising Sign: shown here in the sign of Pisces

Descendant: the point opposite the Ascendant

Nadir Point: represented by the 4th house in Natal chart

Fig. 7
The Path of the Signs

But exactly how many degrees will have to be subtracted? This is an important but vexing question. From a scientific point of view, it is not possible to measure the precessional movement exactly. We know that the vernal point has moved almost one sign (30°) back from the first degree of Aries. Among Hindu astrologers, the precise number of degrees to be subtracted from the tropical positions is a matter of lively debate. There are numerous opinions.

The difference between the tropical and sidereal position (i.e., the precession correction) of any planet or house cusp is called the ayanamsha. When we speak of converting a Western chart into its Hindu equivalent, we speak of subtracting the ayanamsha. Since we are measuring motion in time, it is obvious that the ayanamsha will vary from year to year. For a birth date in 1986, it will be necessary to subtract a larger number of degrees and minutes than for a birth date in 1924.

Western sidereal astrologers use an ayanamsha developed by Cyril Fagan and Donald Bradley. In India, the two best-known ayanamshas are those of B.V. Raman and N. C. Lahiri. In this text we shall make use of the Lahiri ayanamsha.

AYANAMSHAS			
Date	Raman	Fagan Bradley	Lahiri
1/01/1900	21° 00' 50"	23° 20' 56"	22° 27' 43"
1/01/1910	21° 09' 14"	23° 28' 46"	22° 36' 06"
1/01/1920	21° 17' 37"	23° 37' 38"	22° 44' 28"
1/01/1930	21° 26' 00"	23° 45' 36"	22° 52' 51"
1/01/1940	21° 34' 24"	23° 54' 17"	23° 01' 14"
1/01/1950	21° 42' 47"	24° 02' 28"	23° 09' 34"
1/01/1960	21° 51' 10"	24° 10' 54"	23° 17' 53"
1/01/1970	21° 59' 34"	24° 19' 21"	23° 26' 21"
1/01/1980	22° 07' 57"	24° 27' 32"	23° 34' 31"
1/01/1990	22° 16' 20"	24° 23' 46"	23° 43' 14"
1/01/2000	22° 24' 44"	24° 44' 11"	23° 51' 11"

CASTING THE HOROSCOPE

Most Hindu astrologers, like their Western counterparts of an earlier era, erect a birth chart "from the ground up." Western students of the Hindu system, however, typically begin with a birth chart which has already been cast in the Western style.[1] (In the United States or Europe, where Lahiri's sidereal ephemeris is not readily available, there is really nowhere else to begin.) The procedure, then, is to convert the tropical longitudes of the Western chart into sidereal longitudes.

The easiest way to make this conversion by hand is to consider all zodiacal positions as portions of the 360° circle. This allows us to render any longitudinal position into numbers.

0°	=	0° Aries	180°	=	0° Libra
30°	=	0° Taurus	210°	=	0° Scorpio
60°	=	0° Gemini	240°	=	0° Sagittarius
90°	=	0° Cancer	270°	=	0° Capricorn
120°	=	0° Leo	300°	=	0° Aquarius
150°	=	0° Virgo	330°	=	0° Pisces

Let us take, as an example, the following birth data: February 19, 1940, at 6:45 p.m. in Jersey City, New Jersey (74W04, 40N44). The Western or tropical version of this horoscope, whether calculated by hand or by computer, will look like this (Fig. 8):

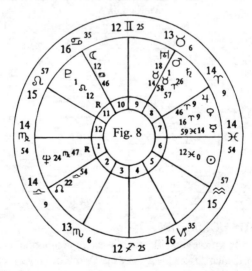

Fig. 8

---

1   For the benefit of readers living in India, or for the few Westerners lucky
     enought to possess Lahiri's Emphemeris, the complete system of Vedic
     horoscope calculations is included in the Appendix.

Let us begin with the Ascendant, which is 14° 54′ Virgo. This longitudinal position may be expressed numerically as 164° 54′.

Now refer to the ayanamsha tables on p. 119. At the beginning of 1940, the ayanamsha was 23° 01′ 21″. For purposes of calculation, this may be simplified to 23° 01′ from 164° 54′. This yields a sum of 141° 53′, which we re-translate back into zodiacal longitude as 21° 53′ of Leo. This, then, is the sidereal Ascendant.

The next thing we need is a horoscope diagram. Using the one shown in Fig. 1 (p. 116), we simply find the box that corresponds to Leo and place a slash through it to indicate the Ascendant. This is the First house. The other houses, as we have seen, simply follow sign by sign, box by box, around the zodiac.

Now we need to find the positions of the planets. The procedure is exactly the same. Simply subtract the ayanamsha from the tropical positions, then re-express the figures in terms of zodiacal longitude. This yields the following positions for our sample horoscope:

Sun	7° 11′ Aquarius	Jupiter	16° 45′ Pisces
Moon	19° 45′ Gemini	Saturn	3° 56′ Aries
Mercury	21° 58′ Aquarius	Rahu (N. Node)	29° 53′ Virgo
Venus	16° 15′ Pisces	Ketu (S. Node)	29° 53′ Pisces
Mars	8° 57′ Aries	Lagna	21° 53′ Leo

Note that we have omitted the positions of the outer planets. As we have explained, they are not used in Hindu astrology.

Now place the planets in the boxes which correspond to their positions by sign. We have constructed our initial birth chart or basic document.

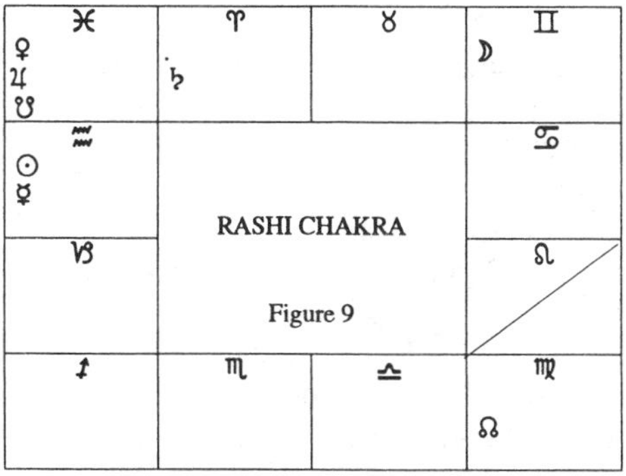

RASHI CHAKRA

Figure 9

BHAVA KUNDALI

We have constructed the basic birth chart. Each of the boxes in the diagram equals one sign of the zodiac; hence this chart is called the rashi kundali or "sign chart."

The rashi kundali works quite well for most of the fundamentals of astrological interpretation. Hindu astrologers regard it as perfectly valid to interpret the chart as if one sign (rashi) were equal to one house (bhava). This may be confusing to those trained in Western astrology, where the houses are seldom equal. Nevertheless, it works. But Hindu astrologers also use charts with unequal houses. In fact, there are as many methods of dividing the houses in Hindu astrology as there are in Western astrology. In this text we shall make use of a method called the bhava kundali or house chart.

We shall illustrate the process by using our sample chart. The two points of reference for constructing the bhava kundali are the Ascendant and the Midheaven. We have noted that the sidereal Ascendant is 21° 53' Leo. (This implies that the opposite point, or cusp of the Seventh house, will be 21° 53' Aquarius, a distance of 180°). Referring back to the Western or tropical version of the horoscope, we note that the Midheaven or zenith point (the beginning of the Tenth house in Western terms) is 12° 25' Gemini. Subtracting the ayanamsha of 23° 01', we get a sidereal Midheaven of 19° 24' Taurus.

Our next step is to find the distance between the Midheaven and Ascendant. The distance (in degrees) between 19° 24' Taurus and 21° 53' Leo is 92° 29'.

Next, divide the distance between Ascendant and Midheaven by 3. The answer is 30° 49' 40".

In order to find the house cusps, we keep counting from the Midheaven in 30° 50' increments. The cusp of the Eleventh house will be 20° 14' Gemini; the cusp of the Twelfth will be 21° 04' Cancer. Thus we reach the Ascendant or First house cusp again at 21° 53' Leo.

This entire operation is repeated for the distance between the Ascendant and 4th house cusp (the Nadir), the distance between the Nadir and Seventh house cusp (Descendant), and the distance from the descendant back to the Midheaven.

If you have a table of houses which includes the Porphyry house system, you can obtain these quantities at a glance. However, a Porphyry Table of Houses is not easy to come by. You are far more likely to possess a computer program which includes a Porphyry Houses.

Even when you have obtained these house cusps, however, you are only halfway there. In Hindu astrology, a house cusp refers to the center or midpoint of a house, not to its boundary or beginning. We must still ascertain the boundary (bhava sandhi) for each house.

The process is perhaps best illustrated using a Western-style diagram or horoscope wheel. (Remember, all diagrammatic representations of a birth chart simply describe the same factors in different ways.) Having ascertained our house cusps, we have a diagram that looks like this: (Fig. 10).

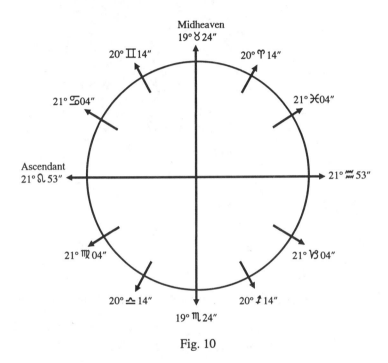

Fig. 10

To find our house boundaries, we simply divide the distance (in degrees) between each cusp.

For instance, our sample Midheaven is 19° 24' Taurus, while our 11th house cusp is 20° 14' Gemini. When the distance (30° 50') is divided by 2, we get 15° 25', which equals 4° 49' Gemini. This process is simply repeated all the way around the chart for each cusp. Our final result will look like this: (Fig. 11).

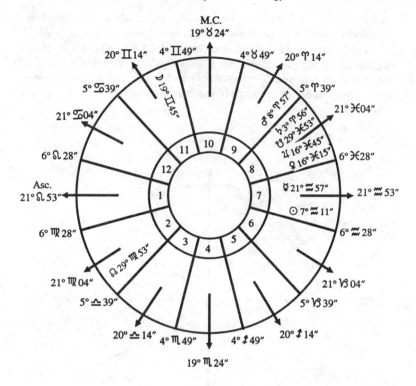

Fig. 11

The bhava kundali is important for fine tuning one's predictions. In the rashi kundali the sign of the Ascendant is regarded as the First house, regardless of the degrees involved. The sign following the Ascendant sign becomes the Second house, and so on. The bhava kundali and rashi kundali do not have the same house boundaries. In the bhava kundali, a house may be comprised of portions of two different signs. It is not impossible for parts of three signs to constitute a single house.[2] From this, it follows that the full spectrum of signs in a specific house will have to be evaluated properly. For example, if Aries covers the entire First house, the effect will be quite different than if Taurus and Aries, or Pisces and

---

2　Western astrologers will be familiar with this phenomenon, which is called "interception."

Aries share the First house together. In our sample chart, Saturn appears in the Eighth house of the bhava kundali, while in the rashi it appears in the Ninth. Thus the interpretation of Saturn in the chart should represent a blend of Eighth and Ninth house factors.

Secondly, in predictive astrology, the changes occurring due to a planet lying on house boundary lines will also require careful examination. If only the rashi kundali is taken into account, a planet lying at the boundary of two signs is paralyzed and unable to make any satisfactory impact.[3] When a planet lies on the bhava sandhi in the bhava kundali chart, its inability to make an impact on either house is quite pronounced.

There are many other considerations which we shall note later; the placement of a planet in different bhavas in the rashi kundali or bhava kundali forms an important foundation of Hindu predictive astrology.

THE STRENGTH OF THE HOROSCOPE

Three kinds of strength are evaluated in grading a horoscope. This assessment is made on the basis of the strength of different signs, the disposition of the planets, and the quality of the different bhavas. In the final analysis, the judgment of a horoscope is based on calculations assessing the relationships between signs, planets, and houses. Precise astrological predictions will require a careful examination of these factors, not merely in their broad general features but in terms of almost microscopic relationships which yield the most finely-tuned results. This branch of Hindu astrology is very advanced. The classical texts are full of so much detail that their esoteric implications cannot be deciphered on the basis of mere exoteric astrological rules. We shall, however, try to give below some of the calculations which are helpful to the beginner.

The ancient seers indicated six steps in the judgment of a horoscope:

1. Determination of the exact time of birth.

2. Fixing of the longitudes of the different planets and the rising sign.

3. Rectification of horoscopes according to various established practices.[4]

---

3   In Hindu astrology, a planet which occupies 0° or 29° of any sign is considered powerless or debilitated.

4   Rectification is the art of determining an exact birth-time from inexact data.

4. Determination of the strength of the bhavas.

5. Determination of the strength of planetary aspects.

6. The aggregation of various kinds of strength derived from the inter-relationship of the different astrological factors.

In examining the strength of different planets, six main types of potency are recognized:

1. Positional strength.

2. Directional strength

3. Temporal strength.

4. Motional strength.

5. Inherent strength of the planet.

6. Aspects.

Positional strength refers to the specific point in a sign where the planet is located. Certain planets are strong in certain directions, which also need to be taken into account. Similarly, the time of birth, i.e., day or night, also influences planetary strength; this must be considered in relation to the various seasons and so on. Motional strength refers to retrogradation or otherwise of the planet. Under these conditions, the normal influence of a planet is subtly altered. The natural strength of each planet depends upon its inherent quality. The value assigned to each planet depends upon its luminosity, which has been assigned differently for different planets. The aspects depend upon the angular positions of planets as well as the affinity existing between them. We shall examine all these factors before we attempt to show how they are evaluated.

Zodiacal signs are zones of influence. The symbolism of the various signs, described earlier, is merely the tip of the iceberg. In order to assess the true strength of the horoscope, one must discover the inner harmonics of each sign. Like the layers of an onion, each sign is peeled away to reveal other levels. Sixteen such levels are traditional in Hindu astrology. Collectively, they are known as the sixteen vargas. At each level or varga, several different planets will activate certain portions of a sign. At each level, different deities will be associated with certain portions of a sign. As each layer is removed, different planets energizing different signs working under different deities will be found. The uppermost level of a sign is markedly altered on the inner levels. As we go deeper, astrology merges with metaphysics. We shall not endeavor to go to that full depth, but merely summarize the different vargas, their planetary rulerships and guiding deities, and the particular aspects of life which each varga influences. Since this material is very technical, it may seem a bit forbidding to the beginning student. Do not worry if everything is not clear at first. The section on the vargas deserves careful study; take your time. A table will be provided to aid in the actual calculations involved.

Though there are sixteen vargas in all, a basic assessment can be made with only six. The six divisions of the zodiac are:

1. RASHI, the basic birth chart which considers each sign as a complete unit.

2. HORA, which divides each sign into two parts, each consisting of 15°.

3. DREKKANA, dividing each sign into three parts of 10° each.

4. CHATURTAMSHA, division in four parts of 7° 30' each.

5. SAPTAMSHA, which divides each sign into 4° 17', making seven equal parts to a sign.

6. NAVAMSHA, or division into nine parts, each of 3° 20'.

In addition, there are other vargas:

7. DASHAMSHA, one-tenth division of a sign, each part equaling 3°.

8. DWADASHAMSHA, dividing each sign into twelve parts, each of which is 2° 30'.

9. SHODASHAMSHA, division into sixteen parts, each containing 1° 52' 30".

10. VIMSHAMSHA, one-twentieth of a zodiacal sign, each part having 1° 30'.

11. SIDDHAMSHA, division into 24 parts of 1° 15' each.

12. SAPTAVIMSHAMSHA, division into 27 parts of 1° 06' each.

13. TRIMSHAMSHA, a specialized division in five parts of 6°.

14. SWADEVAMSHA, division into 40 parts of 45' each.

15. AKSHAVEDAMSHA, division by 45 with 40' for each division.

16. SHASTIAMSHA, consisting of 60 divisions with 30' for each division.

DEITY'S RULING THE DIVISIONS (VARGAS) OF THE SIGNS OF THE ZODIAC

DIVISIONS	
2	
3	
4	
7	
9	
10	
12	
16	
20	ODD / EVEN
24	
27	
30	
40	
45	MOVABLE / FIXED / COMMON
60	

The table cross-references the zodiacal divisions (vargas) — 2, 3, 4, 7, 9, 10, 12, 16, 20, 24, 27, 30, 40, 45, 60 — against their ruling deities.

Principal deity groups listed across the columns include: DEVAS (SANAKA, SANANDANA, KSHARA, KSHIRA, NARADA, AGNI, INDRA, GANESHA, BRAHMA, VISHNU, SHIVA, YAMA, SURYA, RAKSHASA, SARPA, ASHWINI, VARUNA, VAYU, NARA, DEVA), PITRIS, RASHI, AGASTYA, KUMAR, IKSHURAS, KUBERA, EESHANA, GANESHA, DURVASHA, SANATANA, SUDHAJALA, ANANTA, PADMAJA, etc.

Left-hand degree column (d m s):

30°00'00"	1
15°00'00"	2
10°00'00"	3
07°30'00"	4
04°17'8.6"	7
03°20'00"	9
03°00'00"	10
02°30'00"	12
01°52'30"	16
01°30'00"	20
01°15'00"	24
01°06'40"	27
01°00'00"	30
00°45'00"	40
See 1 below / 00°40'00"	45
See 2 below / 00°30'30"	60

Notes:
1. B = Brahma, V = Vishnu, M = Mahesh
2. = Reverse order for even signs

When the quantitative strength of these divisions is estimated for each planet, the natal chart assumes a radical significance. New predictive possibilities open up. We shall presently see how these divisions are identified with their planetary rulers and guiding deities.

For assessing the strength of the planets, generally speaking, only six zodiacal divisions, namely the birth chart or Rashi, Hora, Drekkana, Navamsha, Dwadashamsha, and Trimshamsha are taken into consideration, while the others are employed for very specialized purposes. For these six divisions of the zodiacal signs, we shall briefly indicate the method of calculating them and a table is provided which will allow the student to work them out easily. Later on, we shall deal with the other divisions for those who are more metaphysically inclined.

1. RASHI

The various factors associated with the Rashi or birth chart will be considered in detail later in the text. In the present context, only the planetary rulers of the different zodiacal signs are being taken into account.

2. HORA

Each particle of manifestation contains within itself a positive and negative, or masculine and feminine aspect. The concept of Ardhanareshwara, the Supreme Deity as male and female together in the same body, is represented by the Hora division of the zodiac.

In the Hora division, each sign is divided in two equal parts, the first extending from 0° to 15°, and the next from 15° to 30°. The masculine or yang part is the Sun's Hora, and the feminine or yin part is the Moon's Hora. In even signs such as Taurus, Cancer, etc., the first half is ruled by the Moon and the second by the Sun. In odd signs, it is the other way around.[5]

The Moon's Hora is guided by Pitris and the Sun's Hora by Devas. The Pitris are the ancestors of the humankind, spirits which preceded the races of men and were physically and spiritually superior to us. They are even now related to lunar influence. The Devas are resplendent beings specially charged with the task of carrying out the Divine mission of manifestation at various levels, overcoming difficulties confronted in its

---

5   The "even" or feminine (earth or water) signs are : Taurus, Cancer, Virgo, Scorpio, Capricorn, and Pisces. The "odd" or masculine (fire or air) signs are Aries, Gemini, Leo, Libra, Sagittarius and Aquarius.

implementation. At other times they rest in heaven, enjoying everlasting harmony as they are not bound by any personal karma.

3. DREKKANA

This is the one-third division of the zodiac. The first third of any sign is ruled by the lord of the sign itself, while the second Drekkana is under the rulership of the planet ruling over the fifth sign from it and the third Drekkana is under the lordship of the planet ruling over the ninth sign.

The presiding deities of the various Drekkanas are Narada, Agastya, and Durvasha. When the Drekkana sign is a movable or cardinal sign such as Aries, Cancer, Libra or Capricorn, it is guided by Narada; if it is fixed, such as Taurus, Leo, Scorpio or Aquarius, the guiding deity is Agastya; but for the common signs, namely Gemini, Virgo, Sagittarius, and Pisces, the presiding deity is Durvasha. Narada is the name of the divine sage celebrated as a mind-born son of Brahma, the celestial creator. He is a messenger from the gods to men and vice versa. He is said to have invented lute-playing. He travels to all the lokas (divisions of the universe), establishing harmony. He is the celestial bard who unceasingly and uninterruptedly sings and proclaims the code of divine law. Agastya is a Vedic deity, allegorically said to be born of a pitcher. He is a sage working for the right development and unfoldment of different cultures. He taught science, religion and philosophy to the early races of humanity. Durvasha was a very irascible sage who performed severe penance and acquired much spiritual power, but was so quickly enraged by disobedience or the nonfulfillment of his demands that he often cursed people to suffer immense misery.[6]

4. NAVAMSHA

Under this division, each sign is divided into nine parts, each consisting of 3° 20'. If the sign under consideration is a cardinal sign, then the nine divisions will be ruled by the planets which rule the nine consecutive signs of the zodiac beginning with that sign itself. In the case of fixed signs, the planetary ruler of the nine consecutive signs begins with the ninth sign from the (fixed) sign under consideration. For the common signs, count fifth from the sign concerned. The deities presiding over different navamshas are the Devas, Nara and the Rakshasas, who control the various divisions in cyclic order. Devas are celestial beings, but Nara

6   Readers may enjoy the classical Sanskrit drama *Shakuntala,* readily available in English. The plot hinges on one of Durvasha's curses.

represents the Supreme spirit as well as human beings en masse. The term also refers to humanity struggling to attain perfection. Rakshasas are the demonic forces always trying to hinder the divine plan of evolution, in which process they arouse the latent faculties of the struggling entity.

5. DWADASHAMSHA

Dwadashamsha refers to the twelfth division of the zodiac. The rulers are fixed on the basis of the planetary ruler of the sign itself, and the lords of succeeding signs are assigned rulership of the following divisions of the sign of the zodiac. Thus the first Dwadashamsha ruler in the case of Aries will be Mars, followed by the lord of Taurus, namely Venus. The first Dwadashamsha lord of Taurus will be Venus, the lord of Taurus, followed by the lord of Gemini and so on.

The deities guiding the various divisions of the Dwadashamsha are Sri Ganesha, the Ashwini Kumars, Yama, and Sarpa. Beginning with the first division in Aries, they follow in cyclic order, taking three turns in each sign. Sri Ganesh, presiding over the first 2° 30' of Aries, is followed by the Ashwini Kumars up to 5° 00', after which Yama takes his turn up to 7° 30', succeeded by Sarpa until 10° 00'. Once these four deities have completed their rulership (in the first Drekkana of the sign), they again follow the same order in the second Drekkana and the third. Ganesha is the deity worshipped at the beginning of every arduous but auspicious undertaking; he was born mysteriously and has an elephant's head with enormous wisdom contained in it. The Ashwini Kumars have tremendous courage and the initiative to begin a new cycle of creation. Twin sons of the Sun, they were also born mysteriously and have unfathomable healing and rejuvenating power. Yama is the death god; the burial ground is connected with him and he rides a black buffalo; he has a rope in his hand to hang the dead. In spiritual philosophy, however, he is related to the destruction of the old decrepit body which enables the soul to take on a new body and gain new experience. Sarpa is related to wisdom, which dawns upon the individual unheralded and silently. As these deities will work in each Drekkana division with Narada, Agastya, and Durvasha, one will have to recognize that the various subsections of a sign obtain the guidance of different sets of deities working at different levels.

6. TRIMSHAMSHA

Trimshamsha refers to the one-thirtieth division of a sign, but its assessment is done differently. In these zodiacal divisions, the Nodes of the Moon are not taken into account, and only those planets which have rulership over various signs of the zodiac are assigned rulership of the different divisions. In the present case even the two luminaries, the Sun and Moon, are excluded. Moreover, all divisions so far have been made proportionately, but Trimshamsha divisions are based on a different principle.

In the case of odd signs such as Aries, Gemini, Leo, etc., the first division consists of the first five degrees ruled by Mars. The second five degrees (5° 00' to 10° 00' of the sign) is ruled by Saturn; the third division consists of eight degrees covering 10° 00' to 18° 00' and ruled by Jupiter; while the next seven degrees (18° 00' to 25° 00') are under Mercury. The last five degrees of the sign will be ruled by Venus.

In even signs such as Taurus, Cancer, Virgo, etc., the order is reversed. Here, one may be reminded of the Hora, where a similar reversal between odd and even signs was made. The first five degrees in even signs are ruled by Venus, the second seven degrees (0° 00' to 12° 00') by Mercury, the third division of eight degrees (12° 00' to 20° 00') by Jupiter, the fourth division (20° 00' to 25° 00') by Saturn, and the last five degrees (25° 00' to 30° 00') by Mars.

The deities related to the Trimshamsha are Jalada, Dhanada, Shakra, Vayu, and Vahni. This is the order of deities assigned to the different divisions, but the sequence is opposite in odd and even signs. In even signs the first division is ruled by Jalada, while in odd signs, the sequence begins with Vahni. Vahni is fire; Vayu is wind; Shakra is a name for Indra as well as meaning "fourteen," which stands for the fourteen divisions of the universe; Dhanada refers to a generous or munificent individual; and Jalada stands for moisture-filled clouds. These qualities associated with different divisions of the odd and even signs point to the natural forces which are engaged in concretizing the ideational principle.

7. SAPTAMSHA

Besides these divisions or vargas, the Saptamsha is used when working out the Sapthavarga or sevenfold strength. This method of determining planetary strength is considered just as important as the Shadavarga or sixfold strength.

Saptamsha is the sevenfold division of a sign. Each division extends for 4° 17' 8.5", which for simplicity's sake is considered as 4° 17' only, and the last one is given an additional degree to make the division end with the final degree of the sign.

The deities presiding over the different divisions are Kshara, Kshira, Dahi, Aajya, Ikshuras, Madya, and Sudhajala. They are not gods as such, but represent the spirit of certain objects which we use for sustaining ourselves. Kshara means salinity, and refers to the essence of an object which makes it desirable; Kshira is milk or the milky juice of a tree or its sap; Dahi is prepared by thickening milk, putting a little curd in it, and preserving the mixture at a certain temperature for the preparation of coagulated milk; Aajya is clarified butter or ghee which is often used in sacrificial fire; Ikshuras is sugarcane juice; Madya is any intoxicating drink, but in spiritual literature the word enotes that which takes away earthly pains and directs the thinking principle to the realization of cosmic unity, the experience of which has an intoxicating impact whose culmination is experienced as Divine ecstasy. Sudhajala is pure water, but in this case also the significance of the word lies in its esoteric meaning. Water is the concretization of elements in a form which becomes essential for life; in a way it stands for the very essence of the life-force, the energy which enables the ego to flow in the life-current. The reference here is not to ordinary water, but to the potential fluid contained in boundless space. In the second sense, especially when the qualifying term "pure" is used, water becomes an object which is poured on the statues of deities while worshipping them; thus water becomes a channel for one's dedication to the Supreme, making the soul fit enough to perform its spiritual task.

OTHER ZODIACAL DIVISIONS
1. Chaturtamsha
Chaturtamsha is a fourfold division of the zodiac. Each division consists of 7° 30'. The planetary rulership of these four divisions is assigned to the planets ruling the First, Fourth, Seventh and Tenth houses counted from the sign whose divisions have been made. It implies that the four divisions of Aries will be ruled by Mars, Moon, Venus and Saturn while the four divisions of Taurus will be ruled by Venus, Sun, Mars and Saturn.

The deities presiding over the four divisions are Sanaka, Sanandana, Kumar and Sanatana. The legends tell us that these entities came to earth from some other planet to guide human evolution. In them also is vested the authority to permit anyone to be initiated into the inner mysteries of the world.

2. Dashamsha
Dashamsha refers to the one-tenth division of the zodiac, each of which consists of 3° 00'. For odd signs, one begins with the planet ruling that sign and for every succeeding division the next sign's ruling planet is assigned. That is, for Aries the ten divisions will be ruled by Mars, Venus, Mercury, Moon and so on. For even signs, this sequence of planetary rulership begins with the planet ruling the ninth house from it.

Thus, from Taurus, which is an even sign, the ninth sign is Capricorn, ruled by Saturn, so the first division of Taurus will be ruled by Saturn, the second by Saturn as lord of Aquarius, the third by Jupiter, and so on.

For odd signs, the presiding deities of the various divisions in order are Indra (the god of gods), Agni (the god of fire), Yama (the god of death), Rakshasa (demon), Varuna (the god of water), Vayu (the god of air), Kubera (the god of wealth), Eeshana (a ruler: Sun as a representation of Lord Shiva), Padmaja (lotus-born Brahma), and Ananta (the deity of Infinitude). For even signs, the order is reversed, but the sequence is the same, that is, the first division of an even sign will be ruled by Ananta, followed by Padmaja, followed by Eeshana, and so on.

3. Shodashamsha

Shodashamsha divides each sign into sixteen equal parts, each division being 1° 52' 30". Under this division, the signs of the zodiac must first be classified as movable, fixed or common. Movable signs begin with rulership by the planet which owns the First house; fixed ones begin with the planet ruling the Fifth house; and the common signs begin with the planet ruling the Ninth house. Successive rulerships are assigned in special order. For cardinal signs, the first sign will begin with the ruler of Aries (Mars) followed by that of Taurus (Venus), of the third by Mercury and so on, while for Taurus, a fixed sign, the first division will be ruled by the Sun, the lord of the fifth sign from the first, and for Gemini, a common sign, the first division will be ruled by Jupiter, lord of the ninth sign.

The deities associated with these divisions are: Brahma, Vishnu, Shiva and Surya. This sequence holds good for odd signs and is reversed for even signs. Having completed the first four divisions, the order is repeated again. There will be three cycles of this order in every sign.

4. Vimshamsha

Vimshamsha, the one-twentieth division of the zodiac, each of which is equal to 1° 30', gives planetary ownership to the lords of the first, ninth and fifth signs of the zodiac. The twenty divisions of the movable signs begin with the ruler of the First sign, namely Aries. The usual order is followed until Pisces is reached. Then the same order repeats again ending with Scorpio, ruled by Mars. The next series, starting with a fixed sign such as Taurus, will begin rulership with the sign following the last sign in the previous series, which ended with Scorpio. Thus the series of fixed signs will begin with Sagittarius, whose lord is Jupiter. Following the same cyclic order, its twentieth division will be under the planetary ruler of Cancer, the Moon. The common signs begin with their first division's lord the Sun, and follow the sequential order.

5. Siddhamsha or Chaturvishamsha

These names refer to the one-twenty-fourth division of the zodiac, each division consisting of 1° 15'. The planetary rulership of the different divisions follows a sequential order similar to the previous one. In the case of odd signs, the first division is owned by the planet ruling Leo, the Sun, after which the planetary lord of each successive sign is assigned every succeeding division. Thus all odd signs end with Cancer, ruled by the Moon. All even signs begin with the Moon, lord of Cancer, as ruler of the first division; the second division is ruled by the lord of Leo and the final division is ruled by Mercury (Gemini).

As far as deities are concerned, the divisions are assigned to masculine deities who are personifications of different elements and qualities. The order of rulership existing in the odd signs is reversed in even signs.

6. Saptavimshamsha

Saptavimshamsha divides each sign into twenty-seven divisions. Each division consists of 1° 6' 40". In this case, the twelve signs are classified in three groups: the first four signs in the first group, the second four in the second group, and the last four in the third group. Beginning with the first group, the planetary rulership of the various divisions will begin with the lord of the first sign (Mars), who will be followed by the lord of the next sign (Venus), and so on. On completion of one set of rulers, the cyclic order for the next twelve divisions will follow in the same order. On completion of the first sign of the zodiac, the last division will be ruled by Mercury, the ruler of Gemini. The planetary rulership for the next sign will begin with the ruler of the sign succeeding Gemini, i.e., Cancer. The Moon will rule the first division of Taurus and the last will be ruled once again by Mercury, lord of Virgo. The third series of divisions, starting with Libra, will end with Sagittarius in its twenty-seventh division, indicating Jupiter as ruler of that division. The fourth set of twenty-seven divisions (of the sign Cancer) will begin with Capricorn, ruled by Saturn; this set will have Pisces in its last division. The same sequence will be repeated in the group of the next two sets of four zodiacal signs each.

The deities associated with each of the twenty-seven divisions in this classification are the same as those of the nakshatras or lunar mansions. This emphasizes the fact that the primeval forces energizing the asterisms are present in every twenty-seven divisions of a sign.

7. Swadevamsha

This division of the zodiac comprises 45'; there are forty such divisions. In this division, the odd signs such as Aries, Gemini, etc., begin with Aries, whose lord owns the first division. In the case of even signs, the first division is assigned to Libra, whose lord Venus rules it. Following the normal cyclic order of zodiacal signs, the odd zodiac will have Cancer as its last division. In the case of even signs, the last division (Capricorn) will be ruled by Saturn.

The deities presiding over the various divisions in this case are twelve, who follow a cyclic order ruling 3⅓ divisions of the forty. In odd as well as in even signs, the cyclic order of presiding deities is the same. The twelve deities are: (1) Vishnu (the preserver of the universe), (2), Chandra (the Moon as the sustainer of life on earth), (3) Marichi (one of the ten patriarchs created by the first Manu), (4) Tvashta Vishwakarma or the celestial architect), (5) Dhata Saptarishi, the seven celestial rishis represented by the seven stars of Ursa Major who maintain the balance of the earth, (6) Shiva (the Supreme Lord of Harmony), (7) Ravi (Sun), (8) Yama (the god of death), (9) Yakshesh (the lord of the Prajapatis, Kubera), (10) Gandharva (the celestial musician), (11) Kala (Time and Duration), (12) Varuna (the regent of the ocean). These deities point to the great upholding and sustaining radiation emanating from such minute divisions of each sign.

8. Akshavedamsha

Akshavedamsha divides the zodiac into forty-five equal divisions of forty minutes. The movable signs begin with Mars, the planetary lord of Aries, fixed signs begin with the ruler of Leo (Sun), and the common signs begin with the lord of Sagittarius (Jupiter). Following the cyclic order of zodiacal signs and their planetary rulership, the last division of movable signs will have Sagittarius, ruled by Jupiter, fixed signs will have Aries, ruled by Mars, and common signs will end with Leo, ruled by the Sun.

The deities associated with this classification are Brahma (the creator), Vishnu (the preserver) and Mahesh (the destroyer). These three deities follow a cyclic order appearing fifteen times in each division. But in movable signs, the cyclic order will be Brahma, followed by Mahesh and Vishnu; in fixed signs the order will be Mahesh, followed by Vishnu and Brahma. In common signs the sequence is Vishnu, Brahma, and Mahesh.

9. Shastiamsha

Shastiamsha, implying one-sixtieth part of a sign and consisting of only 30′ extension, begins in the first division with the planetary lordship of the sign itself followed by the planet ruling the sign next to it. Thus in Aries, the first division will be ruled by Mars, the second division by Venus, the third by Mercury and so on. In Taurus, the first division will be ruled by Venus followed by Mercury and so on. Thus every division begins with the sign itself and completes five cycles in each division.

There are sixty different personifications of the powers of nature representing different qualities. The order of these deities for rulership of the different divisions in odd signs is reversed in even signs. The names of some of these natural powers are Dhira (fortitude), Rakshasa (demonic qualities), Deva (helpful beneficence), Kubera (generosity), Yaksha (guardians of the spiritual world), Kinnar (celestial entertainer), Bhrastha (fallen), Kulaghna (inauspicious), Garal (poison), Agni (fire), Maya (illusion), etc. This order, pertaining to odd signs, is reversed in even signs.

✳ ✳ ✳

These divisions of the zodiacal signs are important in many ways. Some of these classifications, as we shall see, are important for determining the strength of planets and of different house divisions in a natal chart. If a planet appears again and again in its sign of rulership or exaltation throughout the vargas, it is considered more and more auspicious. The different classifications also have specialized meanings as indicated below.

Rashi (birth chart)	the physical body
Hora	property, assets
Drekkana	brothers and other relatives
Chaturtamsha	luck
Saptamsha	fortunate situations connected with children and grandchildren
Navamsha	fortune arising from one's spouse or other partners in life
Dashamsha	attainment of any specific goal or mission in life
Dwadashamsha	fortune from parents
Shodashamsha	transport and vehicles
Vimshamsha	fruitfulness of religious penance
Siddhamsha	acquisition of esoteric knowledge
Saptavimshamsha	status
Trimshamsha	difficulties and impediments in life

Swavedamsha	good and bad conditions (i.e., opportunities)
Akshavedamsha	divine forces operating on the individual
Shastiamsha	detailed information relating to the spiritual forces which guide the course of the individual

PLANETARY RULERSHIP OF SAPTAVARGA
THE SEVENFOLD SIGN DIVISION

Sign	Beg. Degree	Hora	Drek kana	Sap- tamsha	Navam- sha	Dwada- shamsha	Trim- shamasha
♈	00° 00′ 00″	☉ ♌	♂ ♈	♂ ♈	♂ ♈	♂ ♈	♂ ♈
♈	02° 30′ 00″	☉ ♌	♂ ♈	♂ ♈	♂ ♈	♀ ♉	♂ ♈
♈	03° 20′ 00″	☉ ♌	♂ ♈	♂ ♈	♀ ♉	♀ ♉	♂ ♈
♈	04° 17′ 09″	☉ ♌	♂ ♈	♀ ♉	♀ ♉	♀ ♉	♂ ♈
♈	05° 00′ 00″	☉ ♌	♂ ♈	♀ ♉	♀ ♉	☿ ♊	♄ ♒
♈	06° 40′ 00″	☉ ♌	♂ ♈	♀ ♉	☿ ♊	☿ ♊	♄ ♒
♈	07° 30′ 00″	☉ ♌	♂ ♈	♀ ♉	☿ ♊	☽ ♋	♄ ♒
♈	08° 34′ 17″	☉ ♌	♂ ♈	☿ ♊	☿ ♊	☽ ♋	♄ ♒
♈	10° 00′ 00″	☉ ♌	☉ ♌	☿ ♊	☽ ♋	☉ ♌	♃ ♐
♈	12° 30′ 00″	☉ ♌	☉ ♌	☿ ♊	☽ ♋	☿ ♍	♃ ♐
♈	12° 51′ 26″	☉ ♌	☉ ♌	☽ ♋	☽ ♋	☿ ♍	♃ ♐
♈	13° 20′ 00″	☉ ♌	☉ ♌	☽ ♋	☉ ♌	☿ ♍	♃ ♐
♈	15° 00′ 00″	☽ ♋	☉ ♌	☽ ♋	☉ ♌	♀ ♎	♃ ♐
♈	16° 40′ 00″	☽ ♋	☉ ♌	☽ ♋	☿ ♍	♀ ♎	♃ ♐
♈	17° 08′ 34″	☽ ♋	☉ ♌	☉ ♌	☿ ♍	♀ ♎	♃ ♐
♈	17° 30′ 00″	☽ ♋	☉ ♌	☉ ♌	☿ ♍	♂ ♏	♃ ♐
♈	18° 00′ 00″	☽ ♋	☉ ♌	☉ ♌	☿ ♍	♂ ♏	☿ ♊
♈	20° 00′ 00″	☽ ♋	♃ ♐	☉ ♌	♀ ♎	♃ ♐	☿ ♊
♈	21° 25′ 43″	☽ ♋	♃ ♐	☿ ♍	♀ ♎	♃ ♐	☿ ♊
♈	22° 30′ 00″	☽ ♋	♃ ♐	☿ ♍	♀ ♎	♄ ♑	☿ ♊
♈	23° 20′ 00″	☽ ♋	♃ ♐	☿ ♍	♂ ♏	♄ ♑	☿ ♊
♈	25° 00′ 00″	☽ ♋	♃ ♐	☿ ♍	♂ ♏	♄ ♒	♀ ♎
♈	25° 42′ 52″	☽ ♋	♃ ♐	♀ ♎	♂ ♏	♄ ♒	♀ ♎
♈	26° 40′ 00″	☽ ♋	♃ ♐	♀ ♎	♃ ♐	♄ ♒	♀ ♎
♈	27° 30′ 00″	☽ ♋	♃ ♐	♀ ♎	♃ ♐	♃ ♓	♀ ♎
♉	00° 00′ 00″	☽ ♋	♀ ♉	♂ ♏	♄ ♑	♀ ♉	♀ ♉
♉	02° 30′ 00″	☽ ♋	♀ ♉	♂ ♏	♄ ♑	☿ ♊	♀ ♉
♉	03° 20′ 00″	☽ ♋	♀ ♉	♂ ♏	♄ ♒	☿ ♊	♀ ♉
♉	04° 17′ 09″	☽ ♋	♀ ♉	♃ ♐	♄ ♒	☿ ♊	♀ ♉
♉	05° 00′ 00″	☽ ♋	♀ ♉	♃ ♐	♄ ♒	☽ ♋	☿ ♍
♉	06° 40′ 00″	☽ ♋	♀ ♉	♃ ♐	♃ ♓	☽ ♋	☿ ♍
♉	07° 30′ 00″	☽ ♋	♀ ♉	♃ ♐	♃ ♓	☉ ♌	☿ ♍
♉	08° 34′ 17″	☽ ♋	♀ ♉	♄ ♑	♃ ♓	☉ ♌	☿ ♍
♉	10° 00′ 00″	☽ ♋	☿ ♍	♄ ♑	♂ ♈	☿ ♍	☿ ♍
♉	12° 00′ 00″	☽ ♋	☿ ♍	♄ ♑	♂ ♈	☿ ♍	♃ ♓

PLANETARY RULERSHIP OF SAPTAVARGA
THE SEVENFOLD SIGN DIVISION

Sign	Beg. Degree	Hora	Drek kana	Sap- tamsha	Navam- sha	Dwada- shamsha	Trim- shamasha
♉	12° 30′ 00″	☽ ♋	☿ ♍	♄ ♑	♂ ♈	♀ ♎	♃ ♓
♉	12° 51′ 26″	☽ ♋	☿ ♍	♄ ♒	♂ ♈	♀ ♎	♃ ♓
♉	13° 20′ 00″	☽ ♋	☿ ♍	♄ ♒	♀ ♉	♀ ♎	♃ ♓
♉	15° 00′ 00″	☉ ♌	☿ ♍	♄ ♒	♀ ♉	♂ ♏	♃ ♓
♉	16° 40′ 00″	☉ ♌	☿ ♍	♄ ♒	☿ ♊	♂ ♏	♃ ♓
♉	17° 08′ 34″	☉ ♌	☿ ♍	♃ ♓	☿ ♊	♂ ♏	♃ ♓
♉	17° 30′ 00″	☉ ♌	☿ ♍	♃ ♓	☿ ♊	♃ ♐	♃ ♓
♉	20° 00′ 00″	☉ ♌	♄ ♑	♃ ♓	☽ ♋	♄ ♑	♄ ♑
♉	21° 25′ 43″	☉ ♌	♄ ♑	♂ ♈	☽ ♋	♄ ♑	♄ ♑
♉	22° 30′ 00″	☉ ♌	♄ ♑	♂ ♈	☽ ♋	♄ ♒	♄ ♑
♉	23° 20′ 00″	☉ ♌	♄ ♑	♂ ♈	☉ ♌	♄ ♒	♄ ♑
♉	25° 00′ 00″	☉ ♌	♄ ♑	♂ ♈	☉ ♌	♃ ♓	♂ ♏
♉	25° 42′ 52″	☉ ♌	♄ ♑	♀ ♉	☉ ♌	♃ ♓	♂ ♏
♉	26° 40′ 00″	☉ ♌	♄ ♑	♀ ♉	☿ ♍	♃ ♓	♂ ♏
♉	27° 30′ 00″	☉ ♌	♄ ♑	♀ ♉	☿ ♍	♂ ♈	♂ ♏
♊	00° 00′ 00″	☉ ♌	☿ ♊	☿ ♊	♀ ♎	☿ ♊	♂ ♈
♊	02° 30′ 00″	☉ ♌	☿ ♊	☿ ♊	♀ ♎	☽ ♋	♂ ♈
♊	03° 20′ 00″	☉ ♌	☿ ♊	☿ ♊	♂ ♏	☽ ♋	♂ ♈
♊	04° 17′ 09″	☉ ♌	☿ ♊	☽ ♋	♂ ♏	☽ ♋	♂ ♈
♊	05° 00′ 00″	☉ ♌	☿ ♊	☽ ♋	♂ ♏	☉ ♌	♄ ♒
♊	06° 40′ 00″	☉ ♌	☿ ♊	☽ ♋	♃ ♐	☉ ♌	♄ ♒
♊	07° 30′ 00″	☉ ♌	☿ ♊	☽ ♋	♃ ♐	☿ ♍	♄ ♒
♊	08° 34′ 17″	☉ ♌	☿ ♊	☉ ♌	♃ ♐	☿ ♍	♄ ♒
♊	10° 00′ 00″	☉ ♌	♀ ♎	☉ ♌	♄ ♑	♀ ♎	♃ ♐
♊	12° 30′ 00″	☉ ♌	♀ ♎	☉ ♌	♄ ♑	♂ ♏	♃ ♐
♊	12° 51′ 26″	☉ ♌	♀ ♎	☿ ♍	♄ ♑	♂ ♏	♃ ♐
♊	13° 20′ 00″	☉ ♌	♀ ♎	☿ ♍	♄ ♒	♂ ♏	♃ ♐
♊	15° 00′ 00″	☽ ♋	♀ ♎	☿ ♍	♄ ♒	♃ ♐	♃ ♐
♊	16° 40′ 00″	☽ ♋	♀ ♎	☿ ♍	♃ ♓	♃ ♐	♃ ♐
♊	17° 08′ 34″	☽ ♋	♀ ♎	♀ ♎	♃ ♓	♃ ♐	♃ ♐
♊	17° 30′ 00″	☽ ♋	♀ ♎	♀ ♎	♃ ♓	♄ ♑	♃ ♐
♊	18° 00′ 00″	☽ ♋	♀ ♎	♀ ♎	♃ ♓	♄ ♑	☿ ♊
♊	20° 00′ 00″	☽ ♋	♄ ♒	♀ ♎	♂ ♈	♄ ♒	☿ ♊
♊	21° 25′ 43″	☽ ♋	♄ ♒	♂ ♏	♂ ♈	♄ ♒	☿ ♊
♊	22° 30′ 00″	☽ ♋	♄ ♒	♂ ♏	♂ ♈	♃ ♓	☿ ♊

PLANETARY RULERSHIP OF SAPTAVARGA
THE SEVENFOLD SIGN DIVISION

Sign	Beg. Degree	Hora	Drek kana	Sap- tamsha	Navam- sha	Dwada- shamsha	Trim- shamasha
♊	23° 20′ 00″	☽ ♋	♄ ♒	♂ ♏	♀ ♉	♃ ♓	☿ ♊
♊	25° 00′ 00″	☽ ♋	♄ ♒	♂ ♏	♀ ♉	♂ ♈	♀ ♎
♊	25° 42′ 52″	☽ ♋	♄ ♒	♃ ♐	♀ ♉	♂ ♈	♀ ♎
♊	26° 40′ 00″	☽ ♋	♄ ♒	♃ ♐	☿ ♊	♂ ♈	♀ ♎
♊	27° 30′ 00″	☽ ♋	♄ ♒	♃ ♐	☿ ♊	♀ ♉	♀ ♎
♋	00° 00′ 00″	☽ ♋	☽ ♋	♄ ♑	☽ ♋	☽ ♋	♀ ♉
♋	02° 30′ 00″	☽ ♋	☽ ♋	♄ ♑	☽ ♋	☉ ♌	♀ ♉
♋	03° 20′ 00″	☽ ♋	☽ ♋	♄ ♑	☉ ♌	☉ ♌	♀ ♉
♋	04° 17′ 09″	☽ ♋	☽ ♋	♄ ♒	☉ ♌	☉ ♌	♀ ♉
♋	05° 00′ 00″	☽ ♋	☽ ♋	♄ ♒	☉ ♌	☿ ♍	☿ ♍
♋	06° 40′ 00″	☽ ♋	☽ ♋	♄ ♒	☿ ♍	☿ ♍	☿ ♍
♋	07° 30′ 00″	☽ ♋	☽ ♋	♄ ♒	☿ ♍	♀ ♎	☿ ♍
♋	08° 34′ 17″	☽ ♋	☽ ♋	♃ ♓	☿ ♍	♀ ♎	☿ ♍
♋	10° 00′ 00″	☽ ♋	♂ ♏	♃ ♓	♀ ♎	♂ ♏	☿ ♍
♋	12° 00′ 00″	☽ ♋	♂ ♏	♃ ♓	♀ ♎	♂ ♏	♃ ♓
♋	12° 30′ 00″	☽ ♋	♂ ♏	♃ ♓	♀ ♎	♃ ♐	♃ ♓
♋	12° 51′ 26″	☽ ♋	♂ ♏	♂ ♈	♀ ♎	♃ ♐	♃ ♓
♋	13° 20′ 00″	☽ ♋	♂ ♏	♂ ♈	♂ ♏	♃ ♐	♃ ♓
♋	15° 00′ 00″	☉ ♌	♂ ♏	♂ ♈	♂ ♏	♄ ♑	♃ ♓
♋	16° 40′ 00″	☉ ♌	♂ ♏	♂ ♈	♃ ♐	♄ ♑	♃ ♓
♋	17° 08′ 34″	☉ ♌	♂ ♏	♀ ♉	♃ ♐	♄ ♑	♃ ♓
♋	17° 30′ 00″	☉ ♌	♂ ♏	♀ ♉	♃ ♐	♄ ♒	♃ ♓
♋	20° 00′ 00″	☉ ♌	♃ ♓	♀ ♉	♄ ♑	♃ ♓	♄ ♑
♋	21° 25′ 43″	☉ ♌	♃ ♓	☿ ♊	♄ ♑	♃ ♓	♄ ♑
♋	22° 30′ 00″	☉ ♌	♃ ♓	☿ ♊	♄ ♑	♂ ♈	♄ ♑
♋	23° 20′ 00″	☉ ♌	♃ ♓	☿ ♊	♄ ♒	♂ ♈	♄ ♑
♋	25° 00′ 00″	☉ ♌	♃ ♓	☿ ♊	♄ ♒	♀ ♉	♂ ♏
♋	25° 42′ 52″	☉ ♌	♃ ♓	☽ ♋	♄ ♒	♀ ♉	♂ ♏
♋	26° 40′ 00″	☉ ♌	♃ ♓	☽ ♋	♃ ♓	♀ ♉	♂ ♏
♋	27° 30′ 00″	☉ ♌	♃ ♓	☽ ♋	♃ ♓	☿ ♊	♂ ♏
♌	00° 00′ 00″	☉ ♌	☉ ♌	☉ ♌	♂ ♈	☉ ♌	♂ ♈
♌	02° 30′ 00″	☉ ♌	☉ ♌	☉ ♌	♂ ♈	☿ ♍	♂ ♈
♌	03° 20′ 00″	☉ ♌	☉ ♌	☉ ♌	♀ ♉	☿ ♍	♂ ♈
♌	04° 17′ 09″	☉ ♌	☉ ♌	☿ ♍	♀ ♉	☿ ♍	♂ ♈
♌	05° 00′ 00″	☉ ♌	☉ ♌	☿ ♍	♀ ♉	♀ ♎	♄ ♒

PLANETARY RULERSHIP OF SAPTAVARGA
THE SEVENFOLD SIGN DIVISION

Sign	Beg. Degree	Hora	Drekkana	Saptamsha	Navamsha	Dwadashamsha	Trimshamasha
♌	06° 40' 00"	☉♌	☉♌	☿♍	☿♊	♀♎	♄♒
♌	07° 30' 00"	☉♌	☉♌	☿♍	☿♊	♂♏	♄♒
♌	08° 34' 17"	☉♌	☉♌	♀♎	☿♊	♂♏	♄♒
♌	10° 00' 00"	☉♌	♃♐	♀♎	☽♋	♃♐	♃♐
♌	12° 30' 00"	☉♌	♃♐	♀♎	☽♋	♄♑	♃♐
♌	12° 51' 26"	☉♌	♃♐	♂♏	☽♋	♄♑	♃♐
♌	13° 20' 00"	☉♌	♃♐	♂♏	☉♌	♄♑	♃♐
♌	15° 00' 00"	☽♋	♃♐	♂♏	☉♌	♄♒	♃♐
♌	16° 40' 00"	☽♋	♃♐	♂♏	☿♍	♄♒	♃♐
♌	17° 08' 34"	☽♋	♃♐	♃♐	☿♍	♄♒	♃♐
♌	17° 30' 00"	☽♋	♃♐	♃♐	☿♍	♃♓	♃♐
♌	18° 00' 00"	☽♋	♃♐	♃♐	☿♍	♃♓	☿♊
♌	20° 00' 00"	☽♋	♂♈	♃♐	♀♎	♂♈	☿♊
♌	21° 25' 43"	☽♋	♂♈	♄♑	♀♎	♂♈	☿♊
♌	22° 30' 00"	☽♋	♂♈	♄♑	♀♎	♀♉	☿♊
♌	23° 20' 00"	☽♋	♂♈	♄♑	♂♏	♀♉	☿♊
♌	25° 00' 00"	☽♋	♂♈	♄♑	♂♏	☿♊	♀♎
♌	25° 42' 52"	☽♋	♂♈	♄♒	♂♏	☿♊	♀♎
♌	26° 40' 00"	☽♋	♂♈	♄♒	♃♐	☿♊	♀♎
♌	27° 30' 00"	☽♋	♂♈	♄♒	♃♐	☽♋	♀♎
♍	00° 00' 00"	☽♋	☿♍	♃♓	♄♑	☿♍	♀♉
♍	02° 30' 00"	☽♋	☿♍	♃♓	♄♑	♀♎	♀♉
♍	03° 20' 00"	☽♋	☿♍	♃♓	♄♒	♀♎	♀♉
♍	04° 17' 09"	☽♋	☿♍	♂♈	♄♒	♀♎	♀♉
♍	05° 00' 00"	☽♋	☿♍	♂♈	♄♒	♂♏	☿♍
♍	06° 40' 00"	☽♋	☿♍	♂♈	♃♓	♂♏	☿♍
♍	07° 30' 00"	☽♋	☿♍	♂♈	♃♓	♃♐	☿♍
♍	08° 34' 17"	☽♋	☿♍	♀♉	♃♓	♃♐	☿♍
♍	10° 00' 00"	☽♋	♄♑	♀♉	♂♈	♄♑	☿♍
♍	12° 00' 00"	☽♋	♄♑	♀♉	♂♈	♄♑	♃♓
♍	12° 30' 00"	☽♋	♄♑	♀♉	♂♈	♄♒	♃♓
♍	12° 51' 26"	☽♋	♄♑	☿♊	♂♈	♄♒	♃♓
♍	13° 20' 00"	☽♋	♄♑	☿♊	♀♉	♄♒	♃♓
♍	15° 00' 00"	☉♌	♄♑	☿♊	♀♉	♃♓	♃♓
♍	16° 40' 00"	☉♌	♄♑	☿♊	☿♊	♃♓	♃♓

PLANETARY RULERSHIP OF SAPTAVARGA
THE SEVENFOLD SIGN DIVISION

Sign	Beg. Degree	Hora	Drek kana	Sap- tamsha	Navam- sha	Dwada- shamsha	Trim- shamasha
♍	17° 08' 34"	☉ ♌	♄ ♑	☽ ♋	☿ ♊	♃ ♓	♃ ♓
♍	17° 30' 00"	☉ ♌	♄ ♑	☽ ♋	☿ ♊	♂ ♈	♃ ♓
♍	20° 00' 00"	☉ ♌	♀ ♉	☽ ♋	☽ ♋	♀ ♉	♄ ♑
♍	21° 25' 43"	☉ ♌	♀ ♉	☉ ♌	☽ ♋	♀ ♉	♄ ♑
♍	22° 30' 00"	☉ ♌	♀ ♉	☉ ♌	☽ ♋	☿ ♊	♄ ♑
♍	23° 20' 00"	☉ ♌	♀ ♉	☉ ♌	☉ ♌	☿ ♊	♄ ♑
♍	25° 00' 00"	☉ ♌	♀ ♉	☉ ♌	☉ ♌	☽ ♋	♂ ♏
♍	25° 42' 52"	☉ ♌	♀ ♉	☿ ♍	☉ ♌	☽ ♋	♂ ♏
♍	26° 40' 00"	☉ ♌	♀ ♉	☿ ♍	☿ ♍	☽ ♋	♂ ♏
♍	27° 30' 00"	☉ ♌	♀ ♉	☿ ♍	☿ ♍	☉ ♌	♂ ♏
♎	00° 00' 00"	☉ ♌	♀ ♎	♀ ♎	♀ ♎	♀ ♎	♂ ♈
♎	02° 30' 00"	☉ ♌	♀ ♎	♀ ♎	♀ ♎	♂ ♏	♂ ♈
♎	03° 20' 00"	☉ ♌	♀ ♎	♀ ♎	♂ ♏	♂ ♏	♂ ♈
♎	04° 17' 09"	☉ ♌	♀ ♎	♂ ♏	♂ ♏	♂ ♏	♂ ♈
♎	05° 00' 00"	☉ ♌	♀ ♎	♂ ♏	♂ ♏	♃ ♐	♄ ♒
♎	06° 40' 00"	☉ ♌	♀ ♎	♂ ♏	♃ ♐	♃ ♐	♄ ♒
♎	07° 30' 00"	☉ ♌	♀ ♎	♂ ♏	♃ ♐	♄ ♑	♄ ♒
♎	08° 34' 17"	☉ ♌	♀ ♎	♃ ♐	♃ ♐	♄ ♑	♄ ♒
♎	10° 00' 00"	☉ ♌	♄ ♒	♃ ♐	♄ ♑	♄ ♒	♃ ♐
♎	12° 30' 00"	☉ ♌	♄ ♒	♃ ♐	♄ ♑	♃ ♓	♃ ♐
♎	12° 51' 26"	☉ ♌	♄ ♒	♄ ♑	♄ ♑	♃ ♓	♃ ♐
♎	13° 20' 00"	☉ ♌	♄ ♒	♄ ♑	♄ ♒	♃ ♓	♃ ♐
♎	15° 00' 00"	☽ ♋	♄ ♒	♄ ♑	♄ ♒	♂ ♈	♃ ♐
♎	16° 40' 00"	☽ ♋	♄ ♒	♄ ♑	♃ ♓	♂ ♈	♃ ♐
♎	17° 08' 34"	☽ ♋	♄ ♒	♄ ♒	♃ ♓	♂ ♈	♃ ♐
♎	17° 30' 00"	☽ ♋	♄ ♒	♄ ♒	♃ ♓	♀ ♉	♃ ♐
♎	18° 00' 00"	☽ ♋	♄ ♒	♄ ♒	♃ ♓	♀ ♉	☿ ♊
♎	20° 00' 00"	☽ ♋	☿ ♊	♄ ♒	♂ ♈	☿ ♊	☿ ♊
♎	21° 25' 43"	☽ ♋	☿ ♊	♃ ♓	♂ ♈	☿ ♊	☿ ♊
♎	22° 30' 00"	☽ ♋	☿ ♊	♃ ♓	♂ ♈	☽ ♋	☿ ♊
♎	23° 20' 00"	☽ ♋	☿ ♊	♃ ♓	♀ ♉	☽ ♋	☿ ♊
♎	25° 00' 00"	☽ ♋	☿ ♊	♃ ♓	♀ ♉	☉ ♌	♀ ♎
♎	25° 42' 52"	☽ ♋	☿ ♊	♂ ♈	♀ ♉	☉ ♌	♀ ♎
♎	26° 40' 00"	☽ ♋	☿ ♊	♂ ♈	☿ ♊	☉ ♌	♀ ♎
♎	27° 30' 00"	☽ ♋	☿ ♊	♂ ♈	☿ ♊	☿ ♍	♀ ♎

PLANETARY RULERSHIP OF SAPTAVARGA
THE SEVENFOLD SIGN DIVISION

Sign	Beg. Degree	Hora	Drek kana	Sap- tamsha	Navam- sha	Dwada- shamsha	Trim- shamasha
♏	00° 00' 00"	☽♋	♂♏	♀♉	☽♋	♂♏	♀♉
♏	02° 30' 00"	☽♋	♂♏	♀♉	☽♋	♃♐	♀♉
♏	03° 20' 00"	☽♋	♂♏	♀♉	☉♌	♃♐	♀♉
♏	04° 17' 09"	☽♋	♂♏	☿♊	☉♌	♃♐	♀♉
♏	05° 00' 00"	☽♋	♂♏	☿♊	☉♌	♄♑	☿♍
♏	06° 40' 00"	☽♋	♂♏	☿♊	☿♍	♄♑	☿♍
♏	07° 30' 00"	☽♋	♂♏	☿♊	☿♍	♄♒	☿♍
♏	08° 34' 17"	☽♋	♂♏	☽♋	☿♍	♄♒	☿♍
♏	10° 00' 00"	☽♋	♃♓	☽♋	♀♎	♃♓	☿♍
♏	12° 00' 00"	☽♋	♃♓	☽♋	♀♎	♃♓	♃♓
♏	12° 30' 00"	☽♋	♃♓	☽♋	♀♎	♂♈	♃♓
♏	12° 51' 26"	☽♋	♃♓	☉♌	♀♎	♂♈	♃♓
♏	13° 20' 00"	☽♋	♃♓	☉♌	♂♏	♂♈	♃♓
♏	15° 00' 00"	☉♌	♃♓	☉♌	♂♏	♀♉	♃♓
♏	16° 40' 00"	☉♌	♃♓	☉♌	♃♐	♀♉	♃♓
♏	17° 08' 34"	☉♌	♃♓	☿♍	♃♐	♀♉	♃♓
♏	17° 30' 00"	☉♌	♃♓	☿♍	♃♐	☿♊	♃♓
♏	20° 00' 00"	☉♌	☽♋	☿♍	♄♑	☽♋	♄♑
♏	21° 25' 43"	☉♌	☽♋	♀♎	♄♑	☽♋	♄♑
♏	22° 30' 00"	☉♌	☽♋	♀♎	♄♑	☉♌	♄♑
♏	23° 20' 00"	☉♌	☽♋	♀♎	♄♒	☉♌	♄♑
♏	25° 00' 00"	☉♌	☽♋	♀♎	♄♒	☿♍	♂♏
♏	25° 42' 52"	☉♌	☽♋	♂♏	♄♒	☿♍	♂♏
♏	26° 40' 00"	☉♌	☽♋	♂♏	♃♓	☿♍	♂♏
♏	27° 30' 00"	☉♌	☽♋	♂♏	♃♓	♀♎	♂♏
♐	00° 00' 00"	☉♌	♃♐	♃♐	♂♈	♃♐	♂♈
♐	02° 30' 00"	☉♌	♃♐	♃♐	♂♈	♄♑	♂♈
♐	03° 20' 00"	☉♌	♃♐	♃♐	♀♉	♄♑	♂♈
♐	04° 17' 09"	☉♌	♃♐	♄♑	♀♉	♄♑	♂♈
♐	05° 00' 00"	☉♌	♃♐	♄♑	♀♉	♄♒	♄♒
♐	06° 40' 00"	☉♌	♃♐	♄♑	☿♊	♄♒	♄♒
♐	07° 30' 00"	☉♌	♃♐	♄♑	☿♊	♃♓	♄♒
♐	08° 34' 17"	☉♌	♃♐	♄♒	☿♊	♃♓	♄♒
♐	10° 00' 00"	☉♌	♂♈	♄♒	☽♋	♂♈	♃♐
♐	12° 30' 00"	☉♌	♂♈	♄♒	☽♋	♀♉	♃♐

PLANETARY RULERSHIP OF SAPTAVARGA
THE SEVENFOLD SIGN DIVISION

Sign	Beg. Degree	Hora	Drek kana	Sap- tamsha	Navam- sha	Dwada- shamsha	Trim- shamasha
♐	12° 51′ 26″	☉ ♌	♂ ♈	♃ ♓	☽ ♋	♀ ♉	♃ ♐
♐	13° 20′ 00″	☉ ♌	♂ ♈	♃ ♓	☉ ♌	♀ ♉	♃ ♐
♐	15° 00′ 00″	☽ ♋	♂ ♈	♃ ♓	☉ ♌	☿ ♊	♃ ♐
♐	16° 40′ 00″	☽ ♋	♂ ♈	♃ ♓	☿ ♍	☿ ♊	♃ ♐
♐	17° 08′ 34″	☽ ♋	♂ ♈	♂ ♈	☿ ♍	☿ ♊	♃ ♐
♐	17° 30′ 00″	☽ ♋	♂ ♈	♂ ♈	☿ ♍	☽ ♋	♃ ♐
♐	18° 00′ 00″	☽ ♋	♂ ♈	♂ ♈	☿ ♍	☽ ♋	☿ ♊
♐	20° 00′ 00″	☽ ♋	☉ ♌	♂ ♈	♀ ♎	☉ ♌	☿ ♊
♐	21° 25′ 43″	☽ ♋	☉ ♌	♀ ♉	♀ ♎	☉ ♌	☿ ♊
♐	22° 30′ 00″	☽ ♋	☉ ♌	♀ ♉	♀ ♎	☿ ♍	☿ ♊
♐	23° 20′ 00″	☽ ♋	☉ ♌	♀ ♉	♂ ♏	☿ ♍	☿ ♊
♐	25° 00′ 00″	☽ ♋	☉ ♌	♀ ♉	♂ ♏	♀ ♎	♀ ♎
♐	25° 42′ 52″	☽ ♋	☉ ♌	☿ ♊	♂ ♏	♀ ♎	♀ ♎
♐	26° 40′ 00″	☽ ♋	☉ ♌	☿ ♊	♃ ♐	♀ ♎	♀ ♎
♐	27° 30′ 00″	☽ ♋	☉ ♌	☿ ♊	♃ ♐	♂ ♏	♀ ♎
♑	00° 00′ 00″	☽ ♋	♄ ♑	☽ ♋	♄ ♑	♄ ♑	♀ ♉
♑	02° 30′ 00″	☽ ♋	♄ ♑	☽ ♋	♄ ♑	♄ ♒	♀ ♉
♑	03° 20′ 00″	☽ ♋	♄ ♑	☽ ♋	♄ ♒	♄ ♒	♀ ♉
♑	04° 17′ 09″	☽ ♋	♄ ♑	☉ ♌	♄ ♒	♄ ♒	♀ ♉
♑	05° 00′ 00″	☽ ♋	♄ ♑	☉ ♌	♄ ♒	♃ ♓	☿ ♍
♑	06° 40′ 00″	☽ ♋	♄ ♑	☉ ♌	♃ ♓	♃ ♓	☿ ♍
♑	07° 30′ 00″	☽ ♋	♄ ♑	☉ ♌	♃ ♓	♂ ♈	☿ ♍
♑	08° 34′ 17″	☽ ♋	♄ ♑	☿ ♍	♃ ♓	♂ ♈	☿ ♍
♑	10° 00′ 00″	☽ ♋	♀ ♉	☿ ♍	♂ ♈	♀ ♉	☿ ♍
♑	12° 00′ 00″	☽ ♋	♀ ♉	☿ ♍	♂ ♈	♀ ♉	♃ ♓
♑	12° 30′ 00″	☽ ♋	♀ ♉	☿ ♍	♂ ♈	☿ ♊	♃ ♓
♑	12° 51′ 26″	☽ ♋	♀ ♉	♀ ♎	♂ ♈	☿ ♊	♃ ♓
♑	13° 20′ 00″	☽ ♋	♀ ♉	♀ ♎	♀ ♉	☿ ♊	♃ ♓
♑	15° 00′ 00″	☉ ♌	♀ ♉	♀ ♎	♀ ♉	☽ ♋	♃ ♓
♑	16° 40′ 00″	☉ ♌	♀ ♉	♀ ♎	☿ ♊	☽ ♋	♃ ♓
♑	17° 08′ 34″	☉ ♌	♀ ♉	♂ ♏	☿ ♊	☽ ♋	♃ ♓
♑	17° 30′ 00″	☉ ♌	♀ ♉	♂ ♏	☿ ♊	☉ ♌	♃ ♓
♑	20° 00′ 00″	☉ ♌	☿ ♍	♂ ♏	☽ ♋	☿ ♍	♄ ♑
♑	21° 25′ 43″	☉ ♌	☿ ♍	♃ ♐	☽ ♋	☿ ♍	♄ ♑
♑	22° 30′ 00″	☉ ♌	☿ ♍	♃ ♐	☽ ♋	♀ ♎	♄ ♑

PLANETARY RULERSHIP OF SAPTAVARGA THE SEVENFOLD SIGN DIVISION

Sign	Beg. Degree	Hora	Drek kana	Sap-tamsha	Navam-sha	Dwada-shamsha	Trim-shamasha
♑	23° 20′ 00″	☉ ♌	☿ ♍	♃ ♐	☉ ♌	♀ ♎	♄ ♑
♑	25° 00′ 00″	☉ ♌	☿ ♍	♃ ♐	☉ ♌	♂ ♏	♂ ♏
♑	25° 42′ 52″	☉ ♌	☿ ♍	♄ ♑	☉ ♌	♂ ♏	♂ ♏
♑	26° 40′ 00″	☉ ♌	☿ ♍	♄ ♑	☿ ♍	♂ ♏	♂ ♏
♑	27° 30′ 00″	☉ ♌	☿ ♍	♄ ♑	☿ ♍	♃ ♐	♂ ♏
♒	00° 00′ 00″	☉ ♌	♄ ♒	♄ ♒	♀ ♎	♄ ♒	♂ ♈
♒	02° 30′ 00″	☉ ♌	♄ ♒	♄ ♒	♀ ♎	♃ ♓	♂ ♈
♒	03° 20′ 00″	☉ ♌	♄ ♒	♄ ♒	♂ ♏	♃ ♓	♂ ♈
♒	04° 17′ 09″	☉ ♌	♄ ♒	♃ ♓	♂ ♏	♃ ♓	♂ ♈
♒	05° 00′ 00″	☉ ♌	♄ ♒	♃ ♓	♂ ♏	♂ ♈	♄ ♒
♒	06° 40′ 00″	☉ ♌	♄ ♒	♃ ♓	♃ ♐	♂ ♈	♄ ♒
♒	07° 30′ 00″	☉ ♌	♄ ♒	♃ ♓	♃ ♐	♀ ♉	♄ ♒
♒	08° 34′ 17″	☉ ♌	♄ ♒	♂ ♈	♃ ♐	♀ ♉	♄ ♒
♒	10° 00′ 00″	☉ ♌	☿ ♊	♂ ♈	♄ ♑	☿ ♊	♃ ♐
♒	12° 30′ 00″	☉ ♌	☿ ♊	♂ ♈	♄ ♑	☽ ♋	♃ ♐
♒	12° 51′ 26″	☉ ♌	☿ ♊	♀ ♉	♄ ♑	☽ ♋	♃ ♐
♒	13° 20′ 00″	☉ ♌	☿ ♊	♀ ♉	♄ ♒	☽ ♋	♃ ♐
♒	15° 00′ 00″	☽ ♋	☿ ♊	♀ ♉	♄ ♒	☉ ♌	♃ ♐
♒	16° 40′ 00″	☽ ♋	☿ ♊	♀ ♉	♃ ♓	☉ ♌	♃ ♐
♒	17° 08′ 34″	☽ ♋	☿ ♊	☿ ♊	♃ ♓	☉ ♌	♃ ♐
♒	17° 30′ 00″	☽ ♋	☿ ♊	☿ ♊	♃ ♓	☿ ♍	♃ ♐
♒	18° 00′ 00″	☽ ♋	☿ ♊	☿ ♊	♃ ♓	☿ ♍	☿ ♊
♒	20° 00′ 00″	☽ ♋	♀ ♎	☿ ♊	♂ ♈	♀ ♎	☿ ♊
♒	21° 25′ 43″	☽ ♋	♀ ♎	☽ ♋	♂ ♈	♀ ♎	☿ ♊
♒	22° 30′ 00″	☽ ♋	♀ ♎	☽ ♋	♂ ♈	♂ ♏	☿ ♊
♒	23° 20′ 00″	☽ ♋	♀ ♎	☽ ♋	♀ ♉	♂ ♏	☿ ♊
♒	25° 00′ 00″	☽ ♋	♀ ♎	☽ ♋	♀ ♉	♃ ♐	♀ ♎
♒	25° 42′ 52″	☽ ♋	♀ ♎	☉ ♌	♀ ♉	♃ ♐	♀ ♎
♒	26° 40′ 00″	☽ ♋	♀ ♎	☉ ♌	☿ ♊	♃ ♐	♀ ♎
♒	27° 30′ 00″	☽ ♋	♀ ♎	☉ ♌	☿ ♊	♄ ♑	♀ ♎
♓	00° 00′ 00″	☽ ♋	♃ ♓	☿ ♍	☽ ♋	♃ ♓	♀ ♉
♓	02° 30′ 00″	☽ ♋	♃ ♓	☿ ♍	☽ ♋	♂ ♈	♀ ♉
♓	03° 20′ 00″	☽ ♋	♃ ♓	☿ ♍	☉ ♌	♂ ♈	♀ ♉
♓	04° 17′ 09″	☽ ♋	♃ ♓	♀ ♎	☉ ♌	♂ ♈	♀ ♉
♓	05° 00′ 00″	☽ ♋	♃ ♓	♀ ♎	☉ ♌	♀ ♉	☿ ♍

PLANETARY RULERSHIP OF SAPTAVARGA
THE SEVENFOLD SIGN DIVISION

Sign	Beg. Degree	Hora	Drekana	Sap-tamsha	Navam-sha	Dwada-shamsha	Trim-shamasha
♓	06° 40' 00"	☽ ♋	♃ ♓	♀ ♎	☿ ♍	♀ ♉	☿ ♍
♓	07° 30' 00"	☽ ♋	♃ ♓	♀ ♎	☿ ♍	☿ ♊	☿ ♍
♓	08° 34' 17"	☽ ♋	♃ ♓	♂ ♏	☿ ♍	☿ ♊	☿ ♍
♓	10° 00' 00"	☽ ♋	☽ ♋	♂ ♏	♀ ♎	☽ ♋	☿ ♍
♓	12° 00' 00"	☽ ♋	☽ ♋	♂ ♏	♀ ♎	☽ ♋	♃ ♓
♓	12° 30' 00"	☽ ♋	☽ ♋	♂ ♏	♀ ♎	⊙ ♌	♃ ♓
♓	12° 51' 26"	☽ ♋	☽ ♋	♃ ♐	♀ ♎	⊙ ♌	♃ ♓
♓	13° 20' 00"	☽ ♋	☽ ♋	♃ ♐	♂ ♏	⊙ ♌	♃ ♓
♓	15° 00' 00"	⊙ ♌	☽ ♋	♃ ♐	♂ ♏	☿ ♍	♃ ♓
♓	16° 40' 00"	⊙ ♌	☽ ♋	♃ ♐	♃ ♐	☿ ♍	♃ ♓
♓	17° 08' 34"	⊙ ♌	☽ ♋	♄ ♑	♃ ♐	☿ ♍	♃ ♓
♓	17° 30' 00"	⊙ ♌	☽ ♋	♄ ♑	♃ ♐	♀ ♎	♃ ♓
♓	20° 00' 00"	⊙ ♌	♂ ♏	♄ ♑	♄ ♑	♂ ♏	♄ ♑
♓	21° 25' 43"	⊙ ♌	♂ ♏	♄ ♒	♄ ♑	♂ ♏	♄ ♑
♓	22° 30' 00"	⊙ ♌	♂ ♏	♄ ♒	♄ ♑	♃ ♐	♄ ♑
♓	23° 20' 00"	⊙ ♌	♂ ♏	♄ ♒	♄ ♒	♃ ♐	♄ ♑
♓	25° 00' 00"	⊙ ♌	♂ ♏	♄ ♒	♄ ♒	♄ ♑	♂ ♏
♓	25° 42' 52"	⊙ ♌	♂ ♏	♃ ♓	♄ ♒	♄ ♑	♂ ♏
♓	26° 40' 00"	⊙ ♌	♂ ♏	♃ ♓	♃ ♓	♄ ♑	♂ ♏
♓	27° 30' 00"	⊙ ♌	♂ ♏	♃ ♓	♃ ♓	♄ ♒	♂ ♏

PLANETARY DISPOSITION

In certain signs of the zodiac, planets are considered exalted. Their nature and disposition are radically altered. The intensity of their impact differs according to exaltation, rulership and other such relationships between planets and signs of the zodiac. We shall deal with three such relationships which are generally known as (1) the exaltation sign of the planet, (2) the sign where the planet is in its mulatrikona, which can be translated as basic trine, and (3) rulership or ownership of the sign.

Exaltation

Exaltation changes the nature and disposition of a planet, but the rationale of the relationship between the sign of the zodiac and the planet exalted therein is not indicated in astrological tradition. The relationship is simply assumed as given.

The Sun exalts in Aries, the Moon in Taurus. Virgo is the exaltation sign for Mercury, Venus is exalted in Pisces, Mars in Capricorn, Jupiter in Cancer, and Saturn in Libra. These are not necessarily the signs ruled by planets friendly to the exalted planets; neither do planets necessarily become exalted in the signs owned by their enemies. Saturn and the Sun are exalted in the signs owned by their friends, but Mars exalts in Capricorn, which is owned by its arch-enemy Saturn.

The specific longitude at which the planets receive their exaltation is given as follows: The Sun is exalted at 10° Aries; the Moon at 3° Taurus; Mercury at 15° Virgo; Venus at 27° Pisces; Mars at 28° Capricorn; Jupiter at 5° Cancer, and Saturn at 20° Libra. There is no unanimity regarding the exaltation points of Rahu and Ketu; generally Taurus is accepted as the exaltation sign for Rahu and Scorpio for Ketu, but some ancient seers considered Gemini as the sign in which Rahu receives exaltation. Depending upon their inclinations, astrologers have chosen the exaltation points for the Nodes of the Moon based on their personal understanding and experience. The specific degrees of exaltation for Rahu and Ketu are not mentioned. A planet is considered debilitated or weakened when it occupies the sign or degree opposite its exaltation position.

In certain cases, a range is assigned to a planet which is considered "the zone of exaltation." For example, though the Moon is exalted at 3° Taurus, it is considered to be in its zone of exaltation anywhere in the first three degrees of that sign. Exact specifications of the planetary position become much more important in the case of mulatrikona positions.

Mulatrikona, or Basic Trine Positions

Exaltation is the most powerful position for a planet. Rulership of the sign in which it is posited also gives a planet special strength, but less than exaltation. In between these two positions there is a situation known as mulatrikona. Here the planets get less power than in their exaltation signs but more than in their own signs. It is said that the Sun has its mulatrikona position in Leo, which is also its own sign. The Moon's mulatrikona is in Taurus, which is also its exaltation sign. Virgo provides exaltation, mulatrikona, and ownership to Mercury. Venus has its mulatrikona position in Libra which is also its own sign. Sagittarius provides mulatrikona as well as ownership to Jupiter. The same is true of Saturn with regard to Aquarius, where it has mulatrikona as well as ownership. Rahu has Taurus for exaltation, Cancer for mulatrikona and Aries for ownership, while Ketu has Scorpio for exaltation, Capricorn for mulatrikona and Libra for rulership. Some authorities list Gemini as the exaltation sign for Rahu and Virgo for ownership, while the opposite is the case for Ketu.

Rulership of Zodiac Signs

It has already been indicated earlier that the Sun rules Leo, the Moon Cancer, Mercury Gemini and Virgo, Venus Libra and Taurus, Mars Aries and Scorpio, Jupiter Sagittarius and Pisces, and Saturn Capricorn and Aquarius. In the light of the above, confusion is bound to arise, and in order to assess the strength of different planets in a natal chart it will be necessary to base calculations on some agreed specifications. We give below the generally accepted views on exaltation, debilitation, mulatrikona positions, and rulership positions of the different planets.

Planet	Exaltation	Debilitation	Mulatrikona	Own Sign
Sun	10° ♈	10° ♎	01°-10° ♌	20°-30° ♌
Moon	03° ♉	03° ♏	04°-30° ♉	
	0°-03° ♉	00°-03° ♏		♋
Mercury	15° ♍	15° ♓	16°-20° ♍	20°-30° ♍
	0°-15° ♍	00°-15° ♓		♊
Venus	27° ♓	27° ♍	00°-10° ♎	10°-30° ♎
				♉
Mars	28° ♑	28° ♋	00°-18° ♈	18°-30° ♈
				♏
Jupiter	5° ♋	5° ♑	00°-13° ♐	13°-30° ♐
				♓
Saturn	20° ♎	20° ♈	00°-20° ♒	20°-30° ♒
				♑
Rahu	♉	♏	♋	♈
Ketu	♏	♉	♑	♎

INTERPLANETARY FRIENDSHIPS

Three types of friendly relations exist between the planets; inherent, temporary, and aggregative. The first category depends upon the basic qualities of the planets, the second on their mutual relationships in a specific horoscope, and the resulting relationships of these two factors determine the aggregative interplanetary friendship pertaining to the case in hand.

Planets are inherently friendly with the lords of 2nd, 4th, 5th, 8th, 9th and 12th sign lords from their mulatrikona houses, besides the lords of the signs in which they become exalted. Based on this consideration, if a planet becomes friendly on two counts, it is truly friendly. If the friendly relationship emerges only once, the planet is considered neutral, while those which do not come within the scope of this relationship are considered unfriendly or inimical. The Sun and Moon become friendly even if they come within the scope of friendly relationships only once.

For example, the Sun has its mulatrikona position in Leo. The second sign from Leo is Virgo, owned by Mercury; the fourth is Scorpio, ruled by Mars; the fifth is Sagittarius, ruled by Jupiter; the eighth is Pisces, also owned by Jupiter; the ninth from Leo is Aries which is a sign of Mars; and the twelfth is Cancer, owned by the Moon. The Sun is exalted in Aries, which is ruled by Mars. Mars and Jupiter appear twice (or more than twice), so they are the Sun's friends. The Moon occurs in the above counts, so it also becomes the Sun's friend. Mercury has occurred in the list but once, so it is considered just a neutral planet to the Sun. As Venus and

Saturn do not appear even once, they are not considered friendly with the Sun and are therefore treated as enemies.

Considered in this way, the inherent friendly relationships can be represented as follows:

INHERENT FRIENDSHIP BETWEEN PLANETS			
Planet	Friends	Neutrals	Enemies
Sun	Moon, Mars, Jupiter	Mercury	Saturn, Venus
Moon	Sun, Mercury	Mars, Jupiter, Venus, Saturn	
Mercury	Sun, Venus	Mars, Jupiter, Saturn	Moon
Venus	Mercury, Saturn	Mars, Jupiter	Sun, Moon
Mars	Sun, Moon, Jupiter	Venus, Saturn	Mercury
Jupiter	Moon, Mars, Sun	Saturn	Mercury
Saturn	Mercury, Venus	Jupiter	Sun, Moon, Mars

The friendly relations of Rahu and Ketu are not included in the present analysis. However, in some texts, Jupiter, Venus and Saturn are considered their friends.

Temporary Friendship

The inherent friendship existing between various planets is, to some extent, modified as a result of their placements in any specific horoscope. All planets situated in the 2nd, 3rd, 4th, 10th, 11th and 12th signs from a planet are reckoned as its friends. But if a planet is situated along with another in any house, or in the 5th, 6th, 7th, 8th or 9th houses from it, such planets are treated as an enemy. Under such conditions, it is possible that some planets which are inherent friends or enemies alter their temporary relationships as a result of their placements in a specific horoscope. These temporary relationships superimposed on the inherent planetary relationships provide the special interplanetary relationships for a specific horoscope. The resulting relationships are considered under aggregative relationship.

Aggregative Friendly Relationships

The aggregative relationship is classified under five categories, namely: Very Friendly, Neutral, Enemy, Very Inimical. This classification takes into account the different relationships pertaining to any specific horoscope according to the above classifications. If two planets are friendly according to both methods of classification, the planets are considered Very Friendly.

If under one classification a planet is friendly to another, but in the next becomes neutral, the two will be treated as Friendly. If according to one classification they are friendly but inimical according to another, they will be treated as Neutrals.

In case two planets are neutrals according to one classification whereas under the next set of conditions they become enemies, they will be reckoned as Enemies.

If, under both sets of considerations, two planets are found to be unfriendly, they will be treated as Very Inimical.

Assessment of Planetary Strength

The categorization of various planets in their exaltation, debilitation, and friendly or unfriendly categories enables the assigning of power to the planets. We shall see later on that there are several methods by which planetary strengths are assessed. The assessment of strength on the basis of exaltation, mulatrikona position, friendly, etc. positions is as follows.

Dignities and debilities that the planets receive due to their occupancy of different signs in a horoscope, having been classified as above, enable us to treat the planets in nine types. On the basis of their placements in this order they receive dignities or a certain order of influence. The relative proportions of these dignities are as follows:

Exaltation	100	Very Friendly	37.5	Enemy	6.250
Mulatrikona	75	Friendly	25.0	Very Inimical	3.125
Rulership	50	Neutrals	12.5	Debilitation	0.000

The designations for Very Friendly, Friendly, etc., are to be treated as follows: when a planet occupies a sign ruled by a planet to which it is Very Friendly in aggregative strength, then it is in a Very Friendly sign, etc.

PLANETARY POSITIONAL STRENGTH

Positional strength of a planet depends upon five kinds of locational situations. These are: (1) the location of the planet with regard to its exaltation point; (2) the sevenfold positional situations considered under (a) Rashi, (b) Hora, (c) Drekkana, (d) Saptamsha, (e) Navamsha, (f) Dwadashamsha, and (g) Trimshamsha; (3) occupancy of a planet in odd or even signs; (4) occupancy in different groups of houses; and (5) the relationship between sex classification of planets and their location in different Drekkanas of the zodiac.

The calculations given below are, in some cases, very complicated and time-consuming. The student should not despair: these calculations are given here primarily to indicate the various considerations (i.e., exaltation, mulatrikona, etc.) which go into determining planetary strength. Most Westerners do these calculations — if they do them at all — by computer.

Strength of Exaltation

Every planet has its exaltation point; the opposite point is its debilitation. When a planet is at its exaltation point it gets its full strength, while at its debilitation point it has lost its power. On its way from debilitation to exaltation, the planet gains its strength proportionately, while on its reverse journey it loses power.

Considering one full unit of planetary power as consisting of sixty divisions (known as virupas), the planet gains one full unit of strength at its exaltation (sixty virupas). This power becomes nil at its debilitation point. The power of the planet at any specific longitude can be calculated by simple arithmetical method indicating the loss or gain of sub-units during the course of its journey over 180 degrees. A short-cut method is given below.

From the longitude of a planet subtract its debilitation point. If the difference is more than 180 degrees, it should be subtracted from 360 degrees. The result is divided by three to give the planetary strength in virupas.

For example, in the illustrative horoscope, if Saturn has the longitude of 21° 20' Libra, which gives 201° 20'. The debilitation point of Saturn is 20°, so 201° 21' – 20° = 181° 21', which is greater than 180°, so this amount has to subtracted from 360°. The resultant 178° 39', divided by 3, gives 59.55 as the exaltation strength of Saturn in virupas.

Sevenfold Planetary (Saptavargabala) Strength

For this assessment, we begin with the sign in which a planet lies. Then we must identify the *ruler* of that sign. The relationship of the planet under consideration with the planet owning the sign will be indicated as Very Friendly, Friendly, etc. A planet in its mulatrikona sign is assigned ¾ strength, which is equivalent to 45 virupas, ½ strength or 30 virupas in its own sign, ⅜ or 22.5 virupas in a sign owned by a Very Friendly planet, ¼ or 15 virupas in the sign of a Friend, ⅛ or 7.5 virupas in the case of a Neutral planet's sign, V_{16} or 3.75 virupas for an Enemy's sign, and only V_{32} or 1.875 virupas for a Very Inimical sign. Mulatrikona strength is assigned only for Rashi location, not for other vargas.

Having assigned these strengths to the Rashi, Hora, Drekkana, Saptamsha, Navamsha, Dwadashamsha, and Trimshamsha, all the powers for different planets have to be totaled. This will indicate the sevenfold strength of the planets.

Odd-Even Occupancy Strength

Sun, Mars, Jupiter, Mercury and Saturn are powerful in odd signs, whether in Rashis or Navamshas. When they are so placed, they get 1/4 strength, equal to 15 virupas. If they are so placed in *both*, they will acquire (1/4 + 1/4) or 1/2 strength, equivalent to 30 virupas.

The Moon and Venus get similar power when they are in even signs whether in Rashis or Navamshas.

Strength From Occupying Different Groups or Houses

The various houses in a natal chart are classified in different ways. The First, Fourth, Seventh and Tenth houses in a horoscope are known as angles or kendras. The Second, Fifth, Eighth, and Eleventh houses are known as panaphara (succedent), while the Third, Sixth, Ninth and Twelfth are known as apoklima (cadent).

Another set of houses, namely the First, Fifth and the Ninth, are known as konas or trines.

The Sixth, Eighth and Twelfth houses are known as cruel, wicked or spoiled houses. The Fourth and Eighth houses are known as quadrangular or four-cornered (chathurasra) houses.

The Third, Sixth, Tenth and Eleventh houses are classified as up-achaya, meaning accumulation, growth, prosperity.

Based on these classifications of different houses, the planetary occupancy of houses provides added strength to planets. Any planet occupying the angles or kendras derives full strength and thus is assigned 60 virupas, while one in panaphara gets only 1/2 or 30 virupas, and a planet in apoklima get merely 1/4 or 15 varupas. Such strengths assigned to different planets are also known as Kendra Bala.

Occupancy Strength of Drekkanas
Based on Sex Classification of Planets

The planets are classified in three sexual groups. Sun, Jupiter and Mars male planets, while the Moon and Venus are female. Mercury and Saturn are androgynous.

We have also seen that a zodiacal sign can be divided into three parts under the Drekkana division, each part comprising ten degrees. The first Drekkana, extending from 0° to 10° of a sign, provides full strength to male planets equaling 15 virupas. Female planets derive 15 virupas in the third Drekkana, while the androgynes get 15 virupas in the second Drekkana of a sign.

PLANETARY STRENGTH
Some Further Considerations

Planetary strength is partly derived from the juxtaposition of planets and signs, but considerable influence is exerted on it by more subtle celestial relationships. An assessment of these influences becomes important in many cases. For everyday predictive exercises, we may overlook some of these detailed calculations, but we should be aware of their existence nonetheless. Among this category one may include: (1) Directional Strength; (2) Temporal Strength; (3) Motional Strength; (4) Natural Strength, and (5) Aspect Strength. For a truly comprehensive determination of the importance of any aspect of life, it will be necessary to assess these influences, as well as the positional strength described above, but for general purposes the student may simply keep these subtle influences in the back of his mind without engaging in all the detailed calculations.

Directional Strength

Planets acquire a kind of strength due to their occupancy of different directions. Jupiter and Mercury acquire power when they are placed in the Ascendant. The Moon and Venus acquire such strength in the Fourth house. Saturn gets directional strength in the Seventh, while the Sun and Mars are powerful in the Tenth. These four angles represent four *directions*. The Ascendant stands for the east, the Descendant or Seventh house for the west, the Fourth house for the north and the Tenth house for the south. Opposite the house of a planet's directional strength is its house of Directional Powerlessness. The distance of the planet from its point of greatest Directional Strength, i.e., the cusp of the house concerned, will proportionately indicate the true Directional Strength of the planet.

Temporal Strength

The Temporal Strength of a planet depends upon time — the year, month, weekday, bright or dark fortnight of the lunar month, solstitial distance of the Sun, exact time of birth during any specific portion of the day, etc. The Temporal Strength of planets relates the individual to an extensive interplay of stellar forces which, in many ways, are spiritual influences. For astrological purposes the ancient texts have given detailed methods for their calculations. These calculations primarily aim at determining: (a) NATHONNATHA BALA, which relates to birth occurring during day or night. The Moon, Saturn and Mars are powerful at midnight; the Sun, Jupiter and Venus are powerful during midday. Mercury is always powerful. Opposite a the point of power is the point of powerlessness, and accordingly Nathonnatha Bala is assessed. (b) PAKSHA BALA is the strength of a fortnight. During the bright half of the lunar month the benefics are powerful, whilst the malefics are powerful during the dark half. (c) THRIBHAGA BALA depends upon which of the threefold divisions of the day-night duration the birth time occupies. (d) ABDA BALA or Varshadhipa Bala is worked out according to the planetary ownership of the year in question. (e) MASA BALA derives from the special power bestowed on the planet that owns the month of birth. (f) On the basis of VARA BALA, the planet which is the lord of the day of birth gets extra power. (g) HORA BALA is worked out by dividing the period from sunrise to sunrise into twenty-four hours or horas, each hora of which is ruled by a particular planet. The first hora of the duration is ruled by the planet owning the day, i.e., the Sun becomes the first hora-lord on Sunday, the Moon on Monday and so on. The cyclic order of planetary ownership of the hora-cycle is of the same order as the days of the week. The planet that rules the birth hour gets additional power under this reckoning. (h) AYANA BALA is the strength that a planet obtains by its situation either towards the north or south of the celestial equator. (i) YUDDHA BALA is related to two planets which are situated together. Planets are said to be at war when the distance between them is less than one degree. All planets excepting the Sun and Moon are subject to this relationship. The planet in the earlier degree of zodiacal longitude is the one considered the conquering planet. The difference between the aggregate of Directional Strength and Temporal Strength up to Hora Bala i.e., (a) to (g) above, of the warring planets should be added to the strength of the conquering planet and subtracted from that of the vanquished one. In this calculation the difference is also traditionally divided by the difference between the diameters of the discs of the two planets. This will give Yuddha Bala. The total of (a) to (i) gives the Temporal Strength of the planet.

Motional Strength

In the calculation of total planetary strength, retrograde motion is also to be taken into account. The precise magnitude of strength acquired by the planet is determined by very involved calculations, but retrogradition itself is an important aspect of predictive astrology.

Natural Strength

The Natural Strength of a planet depends upon its luminosity. The Sun is the brightest of the planets and has been assigned the highest value in that context. Saturn, being the darkest, is assigned the least value. The Natural Strength of planets is the same for every individual. The following values have been assigned to different planets as their natural strengths; the values are given in virupas, sixty of which are considered as one full unit.

PLANET	NATURAL STRENGTH	
	Virupas	Decimals
Sun	60.00	1.000
Moon	51.43	0.857
Venus	42.85	0.714
Jupiter	34.28	0.571
Mercury	25.70	0.428
Mars	17.14	0.286
Saturn	8.57	0.143

Aspect Strength

The Aspect Strength of a planet is determined on the basis of the various malefic and benefic aspects received. A planet does not aspect any planets or houses which are only one house or 30° ahead of it, or any which are two houses or 60° behind it. The center of view or Drishti Kendra gradually increases up to 90° in the forward aspect of the planet. From 90° to 120° it again diminishes till it becomes void at 150°. From 150° to 180° it increases and is at its highest at 180°. Subsequently, there is a gradual decline till the Aspect Strength becomes nil at 300°. By subtracting the longitude of the aspecting planet from the longitude of the aspected planet, one gets the *center of view* or Drishti Kendra. If the remainder exceeds six signs and is within ten signs, this remainder is subtracted from ten signs and, converting the remainder into minutes, the resultant is divided by two to obtain the Aspect Value. If the Drishti Kendra is between six signs and ten signs, the result is the same if the difference between 300° and the Drishti Kendra is divided by two. In cases where the Drishti Kendra is less than six signs, some minor adjustments are made. Over and above the value obtained, additional values for special aspects of Mars, Jupiter and Saturn are added to the results obtained earlier. These aspects are calculated separately for benefics and malefics, and malefic aspect values must be subtracted from the benefic values of the different planets. The net values thus obtained are divided by four to obtain the Aspect Strength of different planets.

SHADBALA

The total strengths or Shadbala for all planets, when tabulated, give the final planetary strength. Planets own various signs or houses in a horoscope, and the strength or weakness of these houses is assessed according to the Shadbala of the planet owning them.

PLANETARY ASPECTS

We have already mentioned that no planet casts an aspect at its own house position. Planets do not have any aspect on the second, eleventh, or twelfth signs from themselves. Nor does the sixth house obtain any aspect. But all planets aspect their opposite house or seventh house. Some planets, such as Mars, Jupiter and Saturn, have been assigned special aspects. Mars has special aspects on the fourth house (90°–120°) and eighth house (210°–240°) from itself, in addition to the seventh. Saturn has an aspect on the third (60°–90°) and tenth (270°–300°) houses additionally. Jupiter enjoys, in addition to the seventh house, an aspect on the fifth (120°–150°) and ninth (240°–270°) houses.

Besides these full aspects, Hindu astrology assigns half and quarter aspects to various planets. All planets, except Mars which already has full aspect on its fourth and eighth houses, have been assigned three-quarters or seventy-five percent aspect on *their* fourth and eighth houses. Excepting Jupiter, all other planets enjoys half or fifty percent aspect on their fifth and ninth houses. Besides Saturn, which already possesses *full* aspect on its third and tenth houses, all other planets obtain one quarter aspect or twenty-five percent to these houses. Rahu and Ketu possess special powers in regard to planetary aspects.

The following table shows the magnitude of different planetary aspects.

MAGNITUDE OF PLANETARY ASPECTS			
PLANET	100% ASPECT	75% ASPECT	50% ASPECT	25% ASPECT
SUN	7th	4th & 8th	9th & 5th	10th & 3rd
MOON	7th	4th & 8th	9th & 5th	10th & 3rd
MERCURY	7th	4th & 8th	9th & 5th	10th & 3rd
VENUS	7th	4th & 8th	9th & 5th	10th & 3rd
MARS	4th, 7th & 8th		9th & 5th	10th & 3rd
JUPITER	5th, 7th & 9th	4th & 8th		10th & 3rd
SATURN	3rd, 7th & 10th	4th & 8th	9th & 5th	
RAHU	5th, 7th, 9th & 12th	2nd & 10th	3rd, 4th, 6th & 8th	
KETU	5th, 7th, 9th & 12th	2nd & 10th	3rd, 4th, 6th & 8th	

Generally speaking, planetary aspects are considered from house to house, yet according to one school of astrology, aspects are concentrated within a more limited range. The most concentrated aspect is on the exact central point of 180°, 90°, etc. from the aspecting planet. It is also said that the Sun casts an aspect with an orb of around 10° from the central aspected point. The orb for the Moon is 5°, for Jupiter and Saturn 4½°, for Mars 4°, Mercury 3½°, and Venus 3° degrees. Only those planets and house cusps that fall within this zone obtain the full benefit of the aspect.

In some classical texts, a special rule for planetary aspects has been indicated. According to this rule, Aries, Cancer, Libra and Capricorn, the movable or cardinal signs, cast aspects on the fifth, eighth and eleventh signs from themselves. This implies that cardinal signs aspect all the fixed signs except the closest one. Aries, for example, will aspect Leo, Scorpio, and Aquarius, which are fixed signs, but not Taurus. Cancer will aspect every fixed sign except Leo; Libra will not aspect Scorpio, nor Capricorn Aquarius. The fixed signs, Taurus, Leo, Scorpio, and Aquarius, will aspect their third, sixth and ninth houses, i.e., all the movable signs except the nearest one. Thus Taurus will aspect Cancer, Libra, and Capricorn, but not Aries. Leo will aspect all the movable signs except Cancer and so on. Common or mutable signs aspect only their opposite signs. Gemini will aspect only Sagittarius, and vice versa; Virgo will exchange mutual aspects with Pisces. This rule suggests that a planet posited in any sign of the zodiac will have the aspect pertaining to the sign in which it is located. Thus, if a planet is placed in Aries, it will aspect the fifth, eighth and eleventh houses from itself, as well as any planets therein. The following diagram will illustrate this rule.

ZODICAL ASPECTS

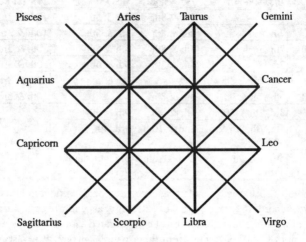

PART III

BASIC CONCEPTS

SYMBOLS OF THE ZODIAC
AND NAKSHATRAS

1
THE COSMIC
MAN

The concept of Kala Purusha, the Cosmic Man, is a very abstruse philosophical principle. All astrological predictions, in fact, are derived from the relationship existing between Kala Purusha and the individual human being whose future is under consideration. The assumptions underlying this relationship have never been spelled out, but a little imagination will reveal that the universal life-principle pervades the entire universe which, according to its own rhythm, has been externalizing all forms of creation in subjective as well as objective existence.

What the concept of Kala Purusha essentially represents has only been discussed in religio-philosophical treatises. The Cosmic Man is imagined as an entity incredibly large, but this symbol of an infinitely huge man is only an approximation of the underlying concept — the extension of the human organism in all possible psychic and temporal dimensions. Kala Purusha is an all-pervading universal reality, a stream of omniscient consciousness ever engaged in externalizing inner potentiality into actual objective reality. The finality of this process is still in the womb of universal possibility; the splendor and power of this realization transcends all human imagination: the only certainty is that an immutable law operates behind all forms of creation. One may even consider this law either as the expression of Kala Purusha or as Kala Purusha himself.

Etymologically, Kala Purusha is related to the positive creative principle operating in time. Primeval subjective potentiality externalizes Time and Duration, wherein all forms of evolving entities are produced. Nothing flows *back* to this ever active cosmic energy: it is ever in all forms of creation and at all levels of functioning. Pleasure and pain, creation and destruction, attraction and repulsion, all feelings, emotions, and thoughts, are part of this Cosmic Man who remains unaffected by the backward reflection of creation. Kala Purusha is always a *positive* influence, the personification of Eternal Time which causes the universe to revolve around itself.

The Cosmic Man is apparent in everyday phenomena — as is evident in political astrology and in the expression of human feelings and emotions, efforts and disappointments, sickness and health which make up the subject matter of natal astrology. The vibration of this universal principle, the breathing of Kala Purusha, can be felt in the rise and fall of human civilizations, the changes in the earth's vast continents, the birth and death of the universe.

Astrologically considered, the various zodiacal signs are the inward rhythmic pulses of the Cosmic Man. Operating on the universal level, these zodiacal impulses are expressed as different phases of manifestation.

ARIES represents the unity between the subjective and objective states of being. It exemplifies readiness to go forth and create, but no action has so far been taken on the objective plane; motivation has arisen for creative involvement, but actualization of the intention is yet in the womb of potential.

The process of actualization begins with TAURUS, which expresses the polarization between subjective and objective. "I" and "Thou," impulse and expression, Spirit and Matter, God and his creation, begin to crystallize at this stage.

GEMINI represents the interaction between the subjective and objective. The union between the Mother and Father principles, copulation between male and female, and the journeys of Sage Narada between the realms of gods and men are symbolic expressions of the third zodiacal impulse.

At CANCER, the Great Depth, the anima mundi or Hiranyagarbha, the store-house of human potential is identified. Time and Duration are made manifest, marking the first concretization of the subjective principle. The essence or heart of man has been formed: the blood can circulate through the body.

When the semen of the Father sinks into the Hiranyagarbha or womb of the Mother and the incarnating soul takes its first karmic steps, that stage is indicated by LEO.

With this emergence of new creative energy there is a further movement towards self-generating creative activity. A greater quantum of human potential is actualized, but such activity can never, under the existing laws of nature, go unchallenged. The dichotomies of action-reaction, effort-struggle, difficulties and trials, all with a view to obtaining something from within one's own self or displaying one's creative and sustaining capacities, come within the domain of VIRGO.

The immersion of creative energy in matter has reached its lowest depth now. The downward impulse results in frustration as the primeval spark continues to long for expansion. A sort of balance between materiality and spirituality occurs, wherein the thirst for material, sensuous experience is counterbalanced by the possibility of spiritualization of the self. This is what LIBRA represents.

When such a possibility dawns on the incarnating soul, a kind of churning process takes place. The dark and hidden counterpart of the self is activated. Revolutions, cataclysms, earthquakes and volcanic eruptions occur in the life of the individual as in the outer world. Hidden difficulties, diseases, problems with relationships all come to the surface. What was hidden is exposed, purged in order to pave the way for the awakening of the Buddhic consciousness. This is the realm of SCORPIO. It provides a new foundation for human transformation.

SAGITTARIUS is a fiery impulse which burns away the old, destroys the material, and purifies the alchemical gold which is the essential pristine nature in man. The unwanted chips are chiseled away from the scaffolding of one's emotions and goals. Smoke and dirt are cleansed so that "the image slumbering in the stone," as Nietzsche would have called it, can come to the surface.

The individual is transformed and his consciousness is merged in the universal consciousness. His pituitary gland is activated and his consciousness is established in the universal stream. This is where CAPRICORN operates.

The current now flows in a radically different direction. In AQUARIUS, the individual works under Divine inspiration; heaven descends to earth and there is social transformation. Humanity is prepared for a new kind of relationship; a new civilization dawns under this impulse. This is the stage where the *one universal life* is released. With such a new dawn, the old order ends and a new beginning takes place.

If Aquarius represents the seeds for a new cycle of manifestation, PISCES heralds the close of one cycle and the readiness to begin the next. Kala Purusha rests on his feet before taking the next step.

Such an orderly exposition of inward impulses of the Cosmic Man is not merely a well-integrated philosophical system, but strikingly reveals the celestial impact on the everyday experiences of man. One of the uses of the Kala Purusha concept is to superimpose his personified human form on the natal chart of the individual to assess the vitality of the different aspects of his life. With the personified Cosmic Man, one may associate the various yogic force-centers or chakras emanating from different parts of the human body. Depending upon which chakras are activated, different kinds of paranormal forces are energized and related faculties strengthened. On superimposing the personified representation of Kala Purusha, one will find some of the chakras lying within the zone of certain house divisions. The literature on yoga identifies seven such chakras, each with a specialized function and operating in a different part of the human body.

The Muladhara or Root Chakra is located at the base of the spinal cord where the Serpent Fire or kundalini lies coiled. The Svadhisthana or Sexual Chakra is ruled by LIBRA, while SCORPIO has dominion over the Muladhara. The vitality flowing from the Sun is absorbed by the Svadhisthana Chakra. Part of that vitality nourishes sexual urges while another portion of it is directed to the Manipura or Navel Chakra, coming under the rulership of VIRGO, which produces various sensitivities and feelings. The Anahata or Heart Chakra in the zone of CANCER, receiving its share of solar energy, enables the individual to understand the nature and feelings of other people and life forms. When the energy flows to the Vishudha or Throat Chakra in the region of GEMINI, the individual acquires the faculty of clairaudience. At the Ajna Chakra, located between the eyebrows in the region of TAURUS, the individual can maintain continuity of consciousness between dreams and waking life, as well as between different incarnations. Reaching the Sahasrara or Crown Chakra under ARIES, the individual is said to attain liberation and is free from the bondage of birth and death.

From the above, it can be observed that the last three chakras (Vishudha, Ajna and Sahasrara) are concerned with higher levels of consciousness, while Anahata (Heart Chakra) purifies human emotions and produces sympathy and compassion. The first three chakras (Muladhara, Svadhisthana and Manipura) are more concerned with the nourishment of physical and psychic faculties. On finding the relationship between these chakras with different house divisions of the horoscope, one may comprehend the deeper forces activating the various levels of one's being and the direction towards which they are channeled.

The diagrammatic representation of Kala Purusha appended shows the relationship between different parts of his body and the zodiacal signs. Aries represents the head of Kala Purusha, Taurus his face, and Gemini his neck and the upper portion of his chest and shoulders. Cancer is connected with his heart, Leo with his stomach, Virgo with his navel, Libra with his intestines, Scorpio with his generative organs, Sagittarius with his thighs, Capricorn with his knee joints, Aquarius with his calves and Pisces with his feet. The soul of Kala Purusha is represented by the Sun; the Moon is his mind, Mercury his speech, Mars his strength, Jupiter his wisdom and happiness, Venus his sexual life and Saturn his misery.

By studying the nature of the signs and planets in relation to Kala Purusha, the astrologer succeeds in predicting the strength and well-being of different aspects of the individual's life. The association of these

BASIC IMPULSES OF THE KALA PURUSHA
Represented Esoterically and Exoterically

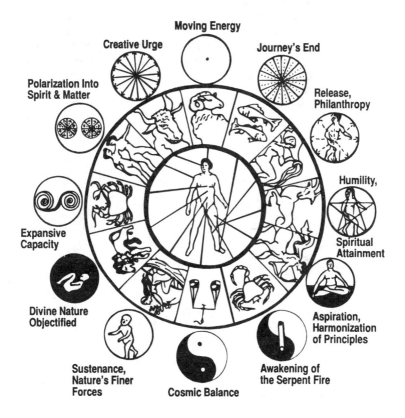

Moving Energy

Creative Urge

Journey's End

Polarization Into
Spirit & Matter

Release,
Philanthropy

Humility,

Expansive
Capacity

Spiritual
Attainment

Divine Nature
Objectified

Aspiration,
Harmonization
of Principles

Sustenance,
Nature's Finer
Forces

Awakening of
the Serpent Fire

Cosmic Balance

features with the natal chart of the individual is very useful, especially in relation to physical health. In the case of afflicted Aries, there could be head injuries, brain defects, etc; the kind of affliction depends upon the nature and strength of the afflicting planets.

Such associations lead to numerous predictive possibilities. Physical maladies, marital relationships, professional hazards, the general direction of life and its different aspects are all easily understood by superimposing the concept of Kala Purusha on the horoscope of the individual. This will show how the universal life-force wishes to direct the life of the individual; it will show the direction of his Divine pilgrimage. Astrologically, the concept is immensely productive, opening many deeper aspects of prediction which reveal the unknown depths of the individual, but also linking him with the greater source which is always close to him, assisting and directing him to his goal.

THE CARDINAL HOUSES

DIVINE SPARK
Epitome of Life; General Personality; Potential
Energy; Longevity; Honor; General Appearance

HIRANYAGARBHA: BYTHOS
Past Karmic Forces; General Prosperity;
Bio-psychological Nature; Mother;
Property; Vehicles; Travel

EXPRESSION OF PERSONALITY
Magnitude of Moral Merits; Social
Interaction; Honor; Fame; Livelihood;
Individual Destiny

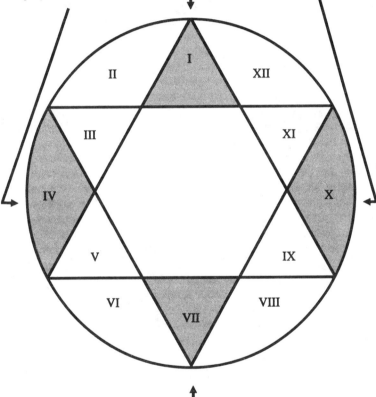

KSHETRA: THE THEATER OF LIFE
Use of One's Vital Energy; Spirituality; Trade &
Social Status; Business Partnership; Marriage;
Deviation from the Right Path; Destruction of Power

2
THE CARDINAL
HOUSES

The tremendous significance of the angles or Cardinal houses, i.e., the First, Fourth, Seventh and the Tenth, can be realized from the fact that they are a major factor in the combination called Pancha Mahapurusha Yoga, which is a significator of individual greatness that emerges when any planet (except the Sun, Moon, or Nodes) is either exalted, mulatrikona, or in its own sign while occupying one of these Cardinal houses.

If the planet producing this yoga is Mars, it is known as Ruchaka Yoga and reveals the greatness of the individual by externalizing his inherent valor and prowess. He will be renowned for his merits and will acquire much wealth but, more significantly, Mars in such a position will bestow greatness in the realm of the physical world generally, in conquering foes, exploring lands where none dare go, and scaling heights which even the imagination fails to reach.

If the yoga is caused by Mercury, features of greatness arising from the possession of wealth and renown will certainly be present, but the special uniqueness signified by this Bhadra Yoga is in the realm of intellect. Such a person will have a superb mind, will be learned and wise, recognized for his clarity of thought and perception. The world will consider him erudite and listen to his discourses with rapt attention.

Jupiter in exaltation or its own sign and positioned in a Cardinal house (Hamsa Yoga) will not only make the individual very graceful, compassionate and well-versed in traditional wisdom, but "even kings will stand before him with hands folded in deep respect." Such a commanding position arises not from the wealth and renown the individual has acquired, but from his ethical disposition and charitable actions.

Persons with Malavya Yoga, caused by Venus, will have strong limbs, will be resolute, wealthy, endowed with spouse, children and good fortune, will relish good food, enjoy the pleasures of life, possess the finest vehicles and become famous and learned. Venus will open its treasure chest and bestow all the material possessions one could hope for.

With Saturn in exaltation or owning its own house and in angles, greatness will be of an entirely different kind: this individual will be a champion of the underdog and have a vision of the future which very few others possess. Such a person will not necessarily be social, but will have such a commanding personality that even the learned and rich approach him with the greatest respect; he will have an invincible force which devastates all that is material, superficial and personal. Shasha Yoga, as this combination is known, bestows a great and unique vision. These combinations are rare and, regardless of other planetary dispositions, will make the individual singular and unique. Such a highly charged magnetic influence flows from the Cardinal houses.

The Cardinal houses have an important role to play in natal astrology, wherein the fate of an individual is assessed on the basis of the planetary positions at the time of his birth. The events of his life are inextricably linked with his past actions, generated during former lives, which must find expression in the present; the individual is also a part of the universe in its enduring or eternal nature. In a horoscope these features of human existence can be studied at three levels. The Cardinal houses indicate the involvement of the individual in everyday life.

The next level will require an examination of the Triangle of Spirituality and the Triangle of Materiality together. The Triangle of Spirituality, represented by the First, Fifth and Ninth houses, and the Triangle of Materiality by the Third, Seventh, and Eleventh, reflect together the karmic forces generated by the individual which provide those enduring impulses that transcend various births and deaths and shape the conditions of the individual's given incarnation.

Finally, the Second, Sixth, Eighth and Twelfth houses link the individual with his primeval fountain of life energy which emerges as sorrow and happiness, difficulties, acquisitions, latent capabilities and so on — waves on the surface of the sea where the churning of the life force constantly brings forth the hidden, primeval nature of being.

The proper delineation of a horoscope must recognize the relative importance of all these impulses. As the immediate is the most important aspect of one's life, the Cardinal houses must be given supreme attention. All other factors must be analyzed in relation to them. It is for these reasons that Hindu astrology has assigned to them the most important position.

The Cardinal houses are the foundation upon which the edifice of the individual's life is raised. The individual's vital energy or *elan vital*, represented by his Ascendant, sustains him through life's struggle. Upon the nature, strength and potentiality of the Ascendant depends his future unfoldment and the blossoming of his uniqueness.

His intelligence, comprehension, education and astral nature, upon which depend his responses to and ability to learn from the experiences of life, are intimately connected with his Fourth house. This house is also known as Sukhasthana, meaning the house of happiness.

The ways in which the individual comes into contact with other members of society and the nature of his partnership, whether with a spouse or in terms of social relationships and business partnerships, are indicated by the Seventh house.

The Tenth house is the individual's Karmasthana, or house of action, and it indicates the way the individual involves himself in the stream of life. Superficially it is known as the house of profession, but almost every act through which he sustains his life and works out his destiny is related to this house. The fruition of these activities is intimately linked with the Seventh house and is also conditioned by his comprehension, compassion and material assets, represented by the Fourth house. For a well-coordinated understanding of the life of an individual, it is necessary to have a deep understanding of these four houses which reveal life as it is lived in the physical world.

The welfare of one's physical well-being and constitution depend upon the strength of the head and brain (First house), heart (Fourth house), intestines (Seventh house), and knee joints (Tenth house). Unless these are in a fit condition, the body metabolism will be impaired, physical deformities and maladies will be present. Furthermore, in the life of an individual his mother (Fourth), spouse (Seventh) and father (Tenth) are as important as himself. The cyclical course of birth, love and affection, death and universalization, breaking the individual shell of isolation, is the essential pattern of life's blossoming. All these are well-integrated with the strength and quality of the Cardinal houses. For an assessment of the nature, quality and status of any individual, it is of supreme importance that these four houses be examined at the very outset of astrological analysis. On the nature and strength of these houses one can assess the dynamic involvement of the individual in his social environment.

These Cardinal houses together show the dynamic nature of the individual. A planet which fails to energize the individual may be considered inauspicious in these houses, but the factors involved in this kind of interpretation are complex. Jupiter, Venus and Mercury, as well as a strong waxing Moon, are considered benefics. These planets energize the inner principles of the individual and, on the physical plane, are very likely to make him the recipient of happy influences under which he expands, blossoms and enjoys.

But for active generation of karmic forces, benefics are not very helpful: there is a mysterious principle in their working. For this reason, it is said that the benefics as rulers of Cardinal houses are not very auspicious unless they also occupy those houses (occupancy of the trines is also included).

Malefics placed in Cardinal houses lose their adverse qualities to a large extent. This is explained by the fact that these planets strongly energize the individual. Though it is possible that there may be some adverse results due to them, yet on overall consideration they will do good to the individual.

The Sun and Mars in the Tenth house are recognized as imparting tremendous vitality to the individual's professional activities. They make him energetic, courageous, and capable of taking initiative and displaying leadership. In fact, unless these planets are somehow related to the Tenth house, the life of the individual to some extent remains in the dark and unrecognized for its merits. Saturn provides stability and enables the individual to weather the storms of life bravely and with patience. The waning Moon is problematical, but may still do some good in the Cardinal houses.

However, the malefics do become disturbing in the Seventh house, where they create marital problems. With malefics there, the individual is unable to establish a satisfactory relationship with his or her spouse. But their placement in this house enables the individual to stand on his own, though this realization comes the hard way. Benefics in the Seventh house will make the individual very indulgent.

The rule is that the ownership of Cardinal houses by benefics, unless they are located in these houses, is not auspicious, while the rulership of these houses by malefics is not considered so adverse. It is a rule which should be respected.

In fact, the Cardinal houses are so important that any planet in these houses is considered desirable. If all the Cardinal houses are occupied by planets, it produces a very auspicious combination. It is known as Chatussagar Yoga, which means "a combination concerning the four oceans." Such a combination is said to enable the individual to earn a good reputation or make him equal to a ruler or king. Under this combination, the individual has a long and prosperous life, is blessed with children and good health, and his name travels to the limits of the four oceans. When the cardinal factors of an individual's life are well-energized, his status and activities become important; his influence expands widely and he becomes greatly renowned. It is to be noted that this yoga is primarily related to personal satisfaction through receiving emotional benedictions which are not *necessarily* reflected in increased wealth. Wealth will depend upon several other conditions, but occupancy of all the Cardinal houses produces very satisfying emotional situations and the person is very influential in life.

In summary, the Cardinal houses are of supreme importance. Unless planets are posited in these houses, the life of the individual will remain at the level of mediocrity. If all four houses are filled with planets, the person becomes world-renowned. If the Cardinal houses are occupied by planets in exaltation or their own signs, it shows a highly evolved soul (Pancha Mahapurusha Yoga). If such planets are afflicted, the life may be full of struggle, but that does not change the fact that this soul is very highly evolved and has an important mission in life.

THE SPIRITUAL TRIANGLE

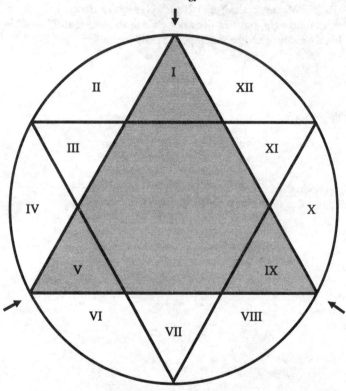

THE SOUL'S MISSION
Basic Spiritual Proclivities; The Potential
Life-Energy

**ACCUMMULATED
MERIT**
Individualisation; Profundity of
Experience; Creativity; Progeny;
Desirable Action; Mind; Intelligence;
Morals; Spiritual Urge

**MANIFESTATION OF PAST
KARMA**
Luck; Mystical Initiations; God's
Grace; DivineV isions;
Enlightenment; Dignity;
Paternal Wealth; Treasure; Travel

3
THE SPIRITUAL
TRIANGLE

The First, Fifth, and Ninth houses together constitute the Spiritual Triangle, which primarily aims at transforming the individual to a higher stage of evolution. Creativity is the guiding principle in this process. When a man is engaged in carrying forth the Divine mission of evolutionary manifestation, he produces auspicious results. The essence of all creative pursuits is to enable the blossoming of latent Divine faculties, either in oneself or in others. These three houses being related to such activities, it is understandable that their rulers can never be anything but beneficial. Whether the zodiacal signs associated with these houses are ruled by malefics or benefics, every planet which happens to influence those signs will inevitably produce favorable results leading to greater happiness. The classical texts have therefore called these houses "special treasures" — Vishesh Dhana. The benefic results of their planetary rulers are so powerful that even if one of them should also rule the Eighth house — ordinarily known as the house of death, whose association or relationship with any planet is considered very adverse — it will not suffer thereby. The rulership of the Spiritual Triangle enables planets to transcend any adverse propensity and renders them totally beneficent.

The Ascendant is always the most beneficial house and its lord the most helpful planet for an individual. The Ascendant lord is considered the king. It guides and assists the individual; his destiny is ruled by it. The lord of the Fifth house is the Minister while the lord of the Ninth is Prime Minister. Whenever these houses or their lords are linked by any kind of association or aspect, the native ascends the throne of his personal kingdom and becomes like a monarch. The houses constituting the Spiritual Triangle reveal many special features of the individual's destiny which might otherwise remain undeciphered. Many significations of these houses, however, are deeply symbolic; they seem to describe the superficial in order to suggest deeper and more spiritual characteristics.

Apart from happiness and misery, birth and old age, the Ascendant portends wisdom, dignity, pride, honor, and personal demeanor, but its real significance lies in several areas which are generally overlooked for lack of proper interest and curiosity concerning the inner workings of the human personality. The apex of the Spiritual Triangle containing the cusp of the First house reveals wisdom, creativity, detachment, premonitions and messages from the dream world, the relationship between action and the causes of action. Above all, the Ascendant shows the manner in which the individual will involve himself in creative pursuits during the course of his life.

Individual creativity attains prominence and outstanding importance in the Fifth house, which signifies the foetus and its conception, foresight, mystery, and literary activities which chronicle the trials and tribulations of the soul's quest. The soul which is concerned in spiritualizing its personal life as well as the society in which it lives will find the Fifth house conducive to the chanting of mantras and Vedic hymns; one may become a skilled craftsman, experiment in researches, or perform virtuous acts which set examples for others by embodying spiritual possibilities. The mysterious nature of the Fifth house is revealed by such significations as "embracing of courtesans," "luck through spouse," "entering the womb of one's destiny," "festivities where drum and tabor are played," "profundity of wisdom" and "intense satisfaction." Many of these indicators are symbolic expressions of the practices by which disciples prepare for initiation into the mysteries. On attaining success in such spiritual matters, the life of the individual is radically transformed; there is a great unfoldment of higher consciousness. Such an attainment is certainly very valuable and qualifies as a "special treasure," but much more valuable is the result of the Ninth house, which is called the house of luck.

The Ninth house is so important that astrologers look to it to support the entire horoscope. Even with several disquieting features in a natal chart, a well-fortified Ninth house makes the life of the person smooth sailing. In fact, the Fifth house indicates creative actions performed during the current life whose results may not necessarily be reaped in that same incarnation, but the Ninth house signifies karmic actions performed in earlier lives whose fruits are now ripe for the individual to enjoy. Under the influence of the Ninth house one receives benedictions. That is why material riches and pleasant environments which make life enjoyable are predicted from the Ninth house. The Ninth house shows the Divine benediction which has been described in classical texts in terms of paternal wealth, sons and daughters, other kinds of wealth, horses, elephants, buffaloes, the coronation hall, splendor and so on. But these are only the peripheral characteristics of the Ninth house; its deeper significance lies in its relationship with the world beyond the perception of the physical sense organs. The transforming nature of the house is indicated by travel, pilgrimages, charity, righteous living, reverence to elders, and penance.

These significators point to the other world. "Reverence to elders and the father" refers to union with the higher self; the acquisition of "the eight kinds of wealth" is a symbol of spiritual attainment against which all material wealth pales into insignificance. The expression "sprinkling of holy waters on the individual" symbolizes the benediction whereby the individual is raised to a very high status in life; whether in the realm of temporal attainments or in spiritual unfoldment is inconsequential to the metaphor.

The three house divisions constituting the Spiritual Triangle provide the basic support for the horoscope. Though their planetary rulers are always beneficial, any affliction from other planets can seriously jeopardize the strength and vitality of the chart. Weakness of the planets ruling these houses by debilitation or placement in enemy signs is undesirable. When the lords of these houses are posited in difficult houses such as the Sixth, Eighth or Twelfth, their benefic power is considerably reduced. Malefics like Mars and Saturn are inauspicious in association or aspect with them, but if these malefics are themselves the rulers of the spiritual houses the situation will be different. Generally speaking, the lords of the First, Fifth and Ninth produce immensely helpful effects unless incapacitated by adverse influences.

It is especially beneficial when the rulers of these spiritual houses establish a positive relationship with the Cardinal houses or their rulers. The angles (kendras) have been named Vishnusthana, meaning the residence of Vishnu, the preserver of the universe, whereas the trines or three houses constituting the Spiritual Triangle are called Lakshmisthana, meaning the residence of Lakshmi, the goddess of wealth and riches. Vishnu and Lakshmi are husband and wife. Their union or association is considered auspicious, capable of producing Raja Yoga, the combination for affluence and royal status. The association between them can be of many kinds: exchange of houses, mutual aspects, association together in a house and so on. When the spiritual forces producing auspicious results for the individual through trines or their ruler is also direct energy to the Cardinal houses or their planetary rulers, the individual will experience a great influx of Divine grace which will guide him successfully on his evolutionary pilgrimage, sustain him through life's trials, and provide life and light to his inner being. The individual will enjoy high status, renown, respectability and satisfaction. These results are slightly reduced if the lord of the Fifth house is in the First or the lord of the Ninth is in the Seventh.

Many auspicious combinations occur as a result of close relationship between the lords of the trines and Cardinal houses. One of them which is highly cherished is Lakshmi Yoga. When the Ascendant (which is a Cardinal house as well as a trine) is strong and the lord of the Ninth house is strong either by being in its own house, mulatrikona or exaltation and is posited in an angle, this yoga is caused. Under this combination, the native is graceful, righteous, affluent, skilled in many arts, renowned, dignified and possessing many children. There are several variations of the yoga. Lakshmi Yoga is said to arise:

1. By mutual association of the lords of the Ascendant and the Ninth,

2. By the lord of the Ninth occupying an angle, trine, or exaltation and the Ascendant lord being disposed powerfully, and

3. By the lord of the Ninth house and Venus being posited in their own or exaltation signs which also happen to be angles or trines.

Under these conditions, depending upon the strength of the planets concerned, the native will acquire wealth and attain affluence.

Another auspicious combination results when the planet ruling the sign which is occupied by the Ascendant lord is in a Cardinal house or trine as well as being in its own sign or exaltation. Under such a combination, the native will acquire a tremendous following and is capable of receiving respect from the highest powers in the land. It is said that he will be happy in the middle and later part of his life and will "receive homage from kings and rulers, be fond of war and conflict, will possess elephants, horses and many kinds of conveyances," and conform to traditions and customs while himself being honorable, generous and famous.

A relationship between the Spiritual Triangle and the Cardinal houses emphasizes close contact between the everyday life of the individual and his higher self. Unless this kind of relationship exists, the individual will have to carry on all by himself. But if such an association is present the burden of the individual is lightened by Divine benediction. As we have stated earlier, the Cardinal houses represent the everyday life of the individual. The Fifth house represents actions whose fulfillment will depend upon the intensity of the action and the time elapsing between action and its fructification, while the Ninth house results come to the individual from the karmic past. When these forces impinge upon the individual he experiences easy success, as if unexpected help were rendered to him from an unknown quarter. Such a beneficial influence always guides the individual toward the fulfillment of his destiny.

THE TRIANGLE OF MATERIALITY

INDIVIDUAL PROWESS
Materialization Urge; Desire to
Achieve & Experience Sensation;
Courage; Siblings; Colleagues; Social
Resistance; Short Travels

ACQUISITIONS
Gains; Income; Sensual Desires and
Gratifications; Extramarital Relations;
Friendship; Utilization of
One's Intelligence & Education

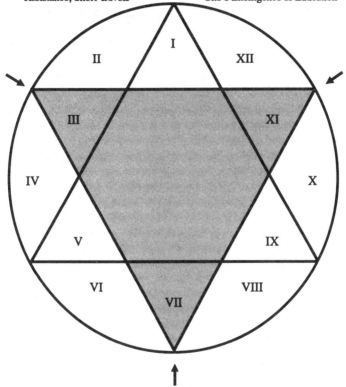

DAWN OF DARKNESS
A Break in the Journey; Deepest Immersion in
Sense Gratification; The Material Veil over the
Divine Spark; Marriage, Winning of Love; Death;
Destruction; Downfall

4
THE TRIANGLE OF
MATERIALITY

The Material Triangle represented by the Third, Eleventh and Seventh houses is not really concerned with misery, sorrow, deprivation and frustration; it indicates a way of life wherein self-indulgence is strong and attraction to the conveniences of life and sensual pleasures is great. The Spiritual Triangle reveals the quest toward moral fulfillment, while the Triangle of Materiality counters this force to establish a natural balance. The predictive principles are the same as for other houses, but the nature of the houses is radically different from others. The Cardinal houses and the Spiritual Triangle are the reservoir of forces which induce the soul toward the unfoldment of its destiny. They provide the individual with opportunities to explore the unknown dimensions of existence and involve himself actively in the evolutionary process. The Triangle of Materiality is related to the period when the soul is at rest, when the battle is not being fought, when the problems of life are relegated to the background; the individual is marking time, giving full rein to his sense organs to derive pleasure from life and enjoy himself. While describing the activities of the individual under the influence of these houses, the ancient astrological texts have not sanctioned or justified those activities; rather, they have seen them through the eyes and with the metaphors of religious philosophy.

The Third house, along with the Eleventh, forms the base of the Material Triangle. Besides brothers and sisters, courage and short travels, this house is a significator of important undertakings and the performance of one's religious duties. The Third house is "a roadside resting place, a pastime, an indicator of *bodily* growth, ornaments, partition of property, heaven and paradise." These are allegorical expressions suggesting the inner psychological state of being. To make these conditions clearer, the house is also said to represent "the confusion of the mind, daydreams, small vehicles for conveyance, and wanderings." The house does not refer to self-exertion but to "servants." At this stage, the individual is not yet completely immersed in sensual pleasures; the attraction to earthly goals has, however, begun to impinge upon his psyche and his mind has become confused. He has become more concerned with his physical growth and the pleasures of the senses than with the higher values of life.

The Eleventh house, which forms the other side of the base, shows a much deeper involvement in materiality. Representing wealth and affluence, the Eleventh house signifies a phase in which external conditions are more tempting than inner content or enduring results. Under this impulse, the individual acquires expertise in earning power. He learns the art of acquiring wealth and becomes fond of ornaments, jewels, and precious stones. He is even able to retrieve lost property. He is superbly clever, and his intellect is extremely sharp. He may be found worshipping various deities and virtuous beings, but his devotions are motivated by the craving to earn more wealth. With such an obsession, the individual under the sway of this impulse becomes a repository for all kinds of desires. He spends money on beautiful girls and involves himself in sexual liaisons. His cleverness enables him to make extremely plausible explanations for his actions and thoughts. He is in bondage to emotion and passion; he cannot extricate himself from earthly attachments and the lust for power, wealth, and sensual pleasure.

The Seventh house, representing the angle upon which the Triangle of Materiality stands, reveals the final depth of material immersion that the soul can reach. Under this influence, the individual is fond of all kinds of sensuality: alcohol, music, flowers, perfume and attractive companions. He wants to eat well, dress well, and establish sexual relationships. His spouse may be very devoted and faithful, yet the individual will be inclined to change partners frequently. Promiscuity is intensely heightened here; sowing wild oats may become second nature; and there may be involvement in scandal and sexual intrigues. The classical texts indicate that such persons will "interrupt their journey, deviate from the path, and experience destruction of power." These expressions may be taken literally as well as metaphorically to indicate that spiritual life will be difficult for persons who are very much under the spell of the Seventh house. The marital relationship that this house signifies is merely the outer expression of those material forces which might be powerful enough to waylay the individual from the path of righteousness. Not without reason is this house also known as a house of death.

No planet gives favorable results in this house. The Sun jeopardizes marital harmony; the partners are unable to bear one another's company and the marriage is often barren. The Moon makes the spouse fickle but attractive. Mars is extremely dangerous for enduring marital life; often the death of one of the partners occurs or they are separated; the wife suffers from various female diseases. With Mercury in the Seventh, the spouse is inclined to debauchery, while Jupiter therein makes the individual establish extramarital liaisons with older people (or, in a man's chart, with pregnant women). Saturn, Rahu and Ketu are never favorable here. Planets connected with this house create problems in the individual's relationships by producing karmic situations. The Seventh is a Cardinal house, but the auspicious effect of the relationship between Cardinal houses and the Spiritual Triangle is overcome when the Seventh is involved. For example, if the lord of the Seventh is posited in the Fifth, which is one of the angles of the Spiritual Triangle, the native nevertheless loses his spouse and is childless. Forming an important component of the hexagon which activates the manifestation process and enables the individual to draw karmic situations to himself, immersing him in those situations which create the cycle of births and deaths, the Material Triangle is energized by any influence upon it. One of the standing principles of Hindu astrology is the auspicious impact of all planets on the Eleventh house. Again, it is said that if the lord of any house is a malefic and is posited in the Third house, it produces a helpful impact, though benefics in the Third are not so good. But these results will only manifest for those who are oriented toward materialistic goals.

In contrast with the rule which postulates auspicious results when the lords of two trines exchange signs, such an exchange between the lords of the Third and Eleventh houses can make the native weak, diseased, and covetous of the wealth and spouse of others, but it also gives him courage and prowess. The planetary disposition of these houses requires careful examination in a world where material gains are coveted as much or more than spiritual development. Acquisition of income and wealth is as necessary for the sustenance of the individual as spiritual harmony. On a careful blending of these triangles depends the balanced growth of the individual. Planets influence the individual according to his karmic destiny, which takes into account both material and spiritual requirements for the soul's unfoldment.

The three angles of the Material Triangle represent siblings (Third), spouse (Seventh) and income (Eleventh), all of which are extremely valuable for a normal everyday existence. But they are also the houses which immerse the individual in social and material involvements which can destroy or distract his urge toward spirituality. The cravings of the heart which induce an individual to seek marriage and money to satisfy his cravings for material and emotional satisfaction also produce courage and make the individual physically strong enough to take initiative in earthly pursuits. When the individual is involved in the search for material welfare, his mind becomes confused and suffers from different kinds of obsessions. He is under the sway of illusion, Maya, unable to perceive the right values in life or make the right decisions. That is the condition produced by the Triangle of Materiality. It influences the soul to cease its efforts toward a spiritual goal and dally amid the world of pleasure.

THE MYSTERIOUS DEPTH

CHURNING OF THE OCEAN
Creativity; Sensitivity; Living Power;
Determination; Modesty, Morality;
Truth & Falsehood; Family
Relationships; Eyes; Speech; Wealth;
Diamonds; Gems; Scholarship;
Death

THE SEA OF DISSOLUTION
Awakening from Sleep; Liberation;
Renouncing One's Couch; Pain; Entry
into Heaven; Discharge of Debts;
Termination of One's Appointment;
Bodily Injury; Mental Anguish;
Travels; Expenditure

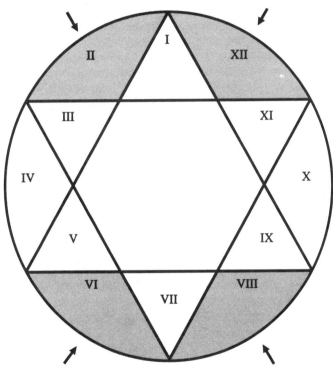

LATENT POSSIBILITIES
Great Illusion; Fear of Death; Enemy's
Satisfaction; Fighting in Combat;
Obstacles; Disease; Insanity;
Servitude; Theft; Humiliation;
Litigation; Impediments

SERPENT FIRE
Initiatory Rites; Secrecy; Grief;
Enemy's Fortress; Witchcraft; Psychic
Powers; Decapitation; Formidable
Affliction; Unexpected Events;
Suddenness

5
THE MYSTERIOUS
DEPTH

The Mysterious Depth from which every phenomenon, animate or inanimate, has arisen is indescribable, but in astrological symbolism it has been artfully represented by the Second, Sixth, Eighth and Twelfth houses. Together they represent the primeval state from which the universe, along with all that dwells within it, has been produced. Objective existence lies in the bosom of subjective consciousness. Both are linked by the laws of manifestation, of which the Law of Karma is the foundation. The Cardinal houses in a horoscope represent the field of objective existence, while the Mysterious Depth is its very foundation. It also stands for the final dissolution that occurs when the destiny of the individual is achieved and the soul has merged in the Absolute. Everything enduring is contained in this ultimate reservoir.

Time and Duration emerge from this unfathomable depth and naturally therefore all that is valuable and precious as well as mysterious and destructive originates here as well. It is the seat of all precious metals and jewels, all wisdom and learning, every form of supranormal power along with each stage of initiation into the great mysteries, and it is this Mysterious Depth that reveals the final glory of man and takes him into its bosom. Though exoteric astrology does not consider these four houses very auspicious, they play an important role in spiritual astrology as the foundation for liberation of the soul imprisoned in material bondage.

The Second house represents sensitivity, speech, and death. A Hindu myth relates how the gods and demons churned the Cosmic Ocean. Many different things emerged from the ocean as it churned, among them the nectar of immortality (amrita). The Mysterious Depth works in much the same way; through astrology we may discover precisely what is being churned up from the depths and into our everyday lives. The faculty of speech, attributed to the Second house, is not necessarily the physical vibration of sound: it is the life-giving breath of the spirit (prana) which acts as a powerful creative force. Wealth, power and possessions are related to this house — these are analogous to the jewels and precious stones which emerged from the churning of the Cosmic Ocean. Family relationships, gentle speech and scholarship are the aspects of wisdom which manifest here. But the most significant characteristic of this house is its relationship to births and deaths. The Second house represents the beginning of that crystallization of essence which produces different kinds of energies and lays bare some of its treasures for the sustenance and development of individual creativity. It provides one with speech and eyes, wealth and wisdom, and it imparts to him the secret of life and death; finally, it bestows death, suggesting the limits to which the individual may go before he is gathered back into the Mysterious Depth.

The characteristics of the Mysterious Depth become clearer on examination of the Sixth house. In exoteric astrology, this house signifies fear of death, enemies, wounds and diseases; it is also said to signify debt, arms, thieves, paternal relatives, battle, wicked acts, sin, fear, humiliation and servitude. Even in such descriptions, casual hints are given which reveal the deeper implications of the house. The Sixth house is associated with "cooked rice," intense anguish, "receiving alms," "a fall from a boat," and urinary troubles; it is also connected with the six flavors and prison. Some of these meanings are very simple and astrologers take their clues from this house when examining debts, litigation, service conditions, diseases and the like, but when we come to such attributes as urinary troubles, intense anguish, and receiving alms we are inclined to take them literally, overlooking the symbolic use of these phrases. The cooked rice, receiving of alms, six flavors and the fall from a boat are concealed references to certain stages of the initiation process. The Sixth house should in fact be considered as the Great Illusion, Maya, which veils the real nature of the Eternal: debts, diseases, and servitude are mere outer expressions of the outflow of karmic forces. The Sixth house conceals within itself the potential energy which ultimately grows into limitless splendor provided the veil of illusion is removed. During the process of removing the veil, the individual must pass through troubles and tribulations; he has to fight with himself and his limitations. His creativity is stifled and the direction of his creative energy, symbolized by semen, has to be altered (suggesting urinary trouble). When the realization dawns that individual strength and prowess are inconsequential in relation to the evolutionary course of the universe, he becomes humble and takes the begging bowl in hand — not as a result of poverty, but as a result of understanding the immense potential of nature which lies beyond the realm of human cognition. The cooked rice stands for Divine benediction; the disciple, upon being accepted as a student of the guru, partakes of cooked rice. Such a transformation changes the course of the individual's life; he no longer flows with the current but falls from the boat and must learn to swim by himself. These implications of the Sixth house establish it as the preparatory stage, when the Eternal calls the individual and begins to reveal the vast possibilities lying before him if he changes his course of life. If he is unable to hear the call, the Sixth house will continue to raise storms and difficulties on his earthly voyage until his inner consciousness is prepared to turn its center of attention from the outer world to the inner. The Sixth house stands for the latent faculties in man and the powers hidden in Nature.

The Eighth house has an intense relationship with the supra-physical realm of existence. It signifies longevity, anal diseases, and the conditions existing in previous births. It is also linked with auspicious events, "a hole or cavity," mental pain, duration of life or vital power, impurity, obstacles and servitude. Other associations of the Eighth house are "a tuft of braided hair," "an enemy's fortress," unintentional receipt of other's money, long-standing or durable property, killing of a living being, mutilation of a limb, decapitation, formidable affliction, or "a story that causes anxiety to the mind." Some of these manifestations of the Eighth house would be uncommon for most people. Their significance cannot be adequately comprehended unless one reads between the lines in order to discover their hidden suggestions. These clues are easily accepted on the assumption that astrology was an important limb of the ancient spiritual wisdom, and that various terms used in an astrological context were frequently used in a more overtly occult context to describe similar situations. Occult literature gives descriptions of the trials of initiation which are similar to what astrologers describe as the significations of the Eighth house. The reference to anus, rectum, a hole or a cavity is directly related to the Muladhara Chakra, the basic force center of which yogic literature has spoken in great detail and which is situated at the base of the spinal cord. It is also called an "enemy's fortress" because it is quite invincible and once it is attacked and its inhabitants challenged, the individual must either conquer it or lose his life. On attaining possession of the fortress, the life of the individual is radically transformed. The conquest or mastery of this inner fortress is the process of activating the Serpent Fire which entails much suffering, including several tests and trials which mystical occult literature compares to decapitation, mutilation, death, and intense mental trouble. The purpose of activating the Serpent Fire is to merge the individual in the Universal Entity. The arousal of the Serpent Fire, however, is a very difficult and dangerous process; it entails arduous preparations, intense pain and suffering. Trials and temptations are great; at every step tremendous secrecy must be observed so that the personal difficulties arising in the process cannot be shared with anyone else. The result is achieved with suddenness and, once this occurs, the life of the individual becomes vibrant with a new kind of energy. The Serpent Fire is of the same essence as the life-force ensouling each living being. This life-force flows to the individual from the primeval source of energy and remains with him till he meets his end. Its absence marks the end of one's life. The central features are secrecy, suddenness, and the provision of life-giving energy. This house has a truly unique relationship with the Mysterious Depth from which everything has arisen.

The Twelfth house is also a secret house whose nature and characteristics have not been well articulated in popular astrological texts. As a significator of outgoings, "intelligence regarding the enemy," destruction and the final ending, the house does not reveal much. Designations for the Twelfth house such as misery, leg, left eye, loss, espionage, the last phase of a drama, poverty, sin, bed, expenditure, revilement or abuse, and imprisonment are more useful, but they do not enlighten us about the *essential* influence of this house. The symbolic references, however, are more suggestive. Broken sleep, liberation from restrictions, redemption of debt, elephants and horses, ascension to heaven, renouncing one's couch, waning of one's right, an enemy's imprisonment in chains, the dawn of humility and the feeling of helplessness, bodily injury and departure for another kingdom are some of the more suggestive appellations for the Twelfth house, on the basis of which one can examine it more deeply. Life is a continuous burden, release from which is considered a redemption from debt, even though the thought of death is approached with trepidation. On release from the burden of earthly bondage, one is liberated and ascends to heaven (whatever we may understand by that term). The individual, having renounced earthly imprisonment, is without any personal power as well as without any personal resting ground; he becomes part of the universal energy. Merging with the Mysterious Depth which is the ultimate repository of everything, he paradoxically becomes the owner of everything, the elephants and horses, all the treasures of the world which are contained in that Mysterious Depth. Release from physical bondage is for those who have acquired spiritual eminence. Otherwise, for the man of the world, the influence of this house immerses him in all the troubles that the house signifies.

A curious feature of the four houses representing the Mysterious Depth is that they operate in one of two distinct ways. If an individual is ready to take the next step toward enlightenment, the spiritual features of the house which we have described will manifest, while for most people the exoteric or more negative features will predominate. A horoscope cannot describe the Cosmic Ocean or Hiranyagarbha from which all things emerge. Its proper concern is to describe the way the external features symbolized by that great ocean operate in the lives of human individuals. Thus death, speech, creative potency, the arousal of the Serpent Fire, the secret regions of one's life, and freedom from the bondage of life and death are described in popular astrological texts according to their typical manifestation in ordinary lives.

This level, however, is important for predictive purposes. Whenever these houses play an important role in a person's life, his life is unsettled. Whether they open up the spiritual possibilities or lead him to sorrow and deprivation, these houses cannot be considered auspicious on the mundane level — though we speak with some reservation as regards the Second house, since it is also related to wealth and property. Because of the destructive nature of these houses, their lords produce adverse results wherever they are located. If the lords are themselves malefics, their location in one of these houses may inflict death upon the newborn child. When energy-producing planets like the Sun and Mars are placed in the Twelfth house and the karmic planet Rahu also happens to be there, the combination is considered very inauspicious, and if the lord of this house joins them, the native is proclaimed to be destined for hell. But because the Twelfth house is not *necessarily* inauspicious, as we have indicated above, the placement of benefics in this house, while its lord is exalted and aspected by benefics, liberates the individual from the bondage of births and deaths. The disturbing influence of the Twelfth house is so great that any planet therein is dreaded, whether benefic or malefic; even while producing spiritual benefits it may lead to some kind of material deprivation and create sorrow. In such a situation the Sun, Venus, Moon and Rahu are the most dreaded occupants, but if these planets *aspect* the house their impact is radically different. They greatly mitigate the adverse results.

The determination of the effect of the planets ruling these houses is very tricky: before deciding whether they will be adverse or not, the delineation of the entire horoscope must be carefully done to ascertain the basic nature of the native, and the affinity of the different planets with the houses constituting the Mysterious Depth must be rightly assessed. It is generally advised that the Second house should be taken out of consideration in this judgment. Every general rule pertaining to these houses must be applied, keeping the disposition of the whole horoscope in the background. In general, astrologers are advised to consider the placement of benefics in the Sixth, Eighth and Twelfth houses as adverse, while outcasts or malefics bestow good results therein.

A special combination results from the rulers of these houses being posited in their own houses or exchanging positions among themselves. Planets in the Sixth, Eighth, and Twelfth in friendly, their own or exaltation signs, or aspected by benefics may prove favorable. If the lords of these houses are confined to these houses either singly or in association with one another, but *not* associated with any other planet either by conjunction or aspect, the situation produces a Raja Yoga, indicating the birth of "an emperor whose domain extends far and wide and who rules uninterruptedly in great affluence."

Jupiter's ownership of the Eighth house or its placement therein is considered favorable, while Venus is favorable in the Sixth. When these houses are recognized as the region for acquiring various siddhis whereby one attains much power, the relationship of Venus with the Sixth and Jupiter with the Eighth can produce such benefits, even though they still create adverse earthly conditions. The combination of any planet with the lords of the houses comprising the Mysterious Depth, or the placement of the lords of these houses wherever they may be in the natal chart, is a warning signal; the results, even if favorable, are not an unmitigated boon. For example, the lord of the Sixth placed in the Second will make the native fortunate in his family, a good orator, affluent, dutiful, and the resident of a foreign country, but his wealth and renown will not be acquired smoothly; there may be scandal and litigation involved. The lord of the Sixth in the Sixth will produce enmity with one's own people while others, especially foreigners, may be very friendly and helpful. The lord of the Eighth in the Second makes the individual less affluent, but also enables him to retrieve lost property. In the Sixth, the lord of the Eighth enables the native to vanquish his enemies. The lord of the Eighth in the Eighth house increases longevity but makes the native a thief and a person who is ungrateful to his teacher. Such combinations are many, which suggest that the Mysterious Depth indeed constitutes houses whose nature and disposition are mysterious; the results of different planets associated with them can only be determined after very careful consideration. The only suggestion that can be made in this context is to sound a note of warning that there may always be another side to any predictions made concerning these houses.

PART IV

PREDICTIVE GUIDELINES

1
RULES OF
INTERPRETATION

RULE 1

Planetary Strength Shows the Soul's Maturity

No individual enjoys a life of unmixed happiness. The struggles and sorrows, opportunities and failures, rewards and deprivations of life are allotted to us with the objective of developing our latent faculties. Over the years, through births and deaths, the inner man acquires skills, develops talents, and strengthens the sheaths which constitute his integrated personality. While he is assigned that portion of his accumulated karma which he is expected to work out during his present life, he receives organs, both physical and subtle, which render him capable of bearing the strain required in discharging those karmic responsibilities. The maturity of soul, the insight into life's mysteries and the emotional and mental capabilities he brings to his life's task are reflected by the disposition of the various planets. If a large number of planets are in exaltation, mulatrikona, or occupying their own signs, the incarnating soul is considered more mature.

Exaltation of planets is such an important factor that its occurrence in any chart indicates that the soul is already quite advanced on the evolutionary path. The classical texts emphasized the importance of exalted planets by stating that a person with exalted planets — even if there are less than three — when born in a royal family will become an emperor ruling over several other kings. If such a birth occurs in an ordinary family, the person becomes equal to a king in affluence and respectability. If there are four or five planets in exaltation, and they are posited in the Fifth and Ninth houses, even an individual born in a lowly family rises to the greatest position; with six planets in exaltation, the birth is considered remarkable in every way. Planets in strength signify the maturity of the soul, and anyone born with such planetary positions will find that his opportunities in life are determined by extraordinary factors; his successes and failures will make a deep impact on his psyche. If the Ascendant lord under such a condition is flanked by two benefics, or if such a situation occurs with regard to the Ascendant itself, the individual will receive unexpected help and guidance.

Planetary strength assessed in this way should be clearly distinguished from Shadbala or Saptavargabala (six or sevenfold strength). These factors show the status of an individual in his society and the impact he can make on it, while planetary strength by exaltation, mulatrikona or rulership shows the evolutionary status of his personal being.

The strength of planets in a horoscope indicates the capacities attained by the individual during his previous births, while their weaknesses reveal character flaws of an enduring nature which will require strenuous efforts to overcome. All the experiences of a person's life are transformed into various kinds of attributes, which are ingrained in the basic nature of the individual. It would be erroneous to relate the exaltation of a planet with affluence and its debilitation with poverty. Such results are produced by other factors. The strengths and weaknesses of planets should be related to personality characteristics. Neechabhanga Rajayoga, wherein certain conditions related to the debilitation of planets lead to affluence, shows that debilitation by itself is not a cause of poverty and deprivation. In the same way exaltation of planets, though highly auspicious, suggests eminence of the soul, but may not assure affluence. In combinations leading to the nullification of Raja Yoga, the exaltation of planets may seem ineffective and powerless. But even under such conditions, the impact of exalted planets on the personality will be apparent.

A powerful personality requires a special approach to the reading of the future. The general rules of astrology will have to be carefully applied in such cases, taking into cognizance an individual's special features and the destiny he is expected to fulfill.

RULE 2

The Ascendant Lord Represents the Guardian Angel. It Protects the Individual and Provides the Motive Force for his Actions.

A strong and well-aspected Ascendant lord is an asset. It guides the destiny of the individual and protects him through thick and thin. The Ascendant lord is not afflicted even when it also rules the death-inflicting Eighth house. If the Ascendant lord is in exaltation, mulatrikona or in its own sign, the individual is sure of carving a special niche for himself in society: his boat will never sink, howsoever difficult the journey or perilous the storm. Only when the Ascendant lord is weak, badly associated, or malefically aspected will the individual be overcome by his adversaries. The entire edifice of life is raised on the foundation of the Ascendant and its lord.

In Cardinal houses, the Ascendant lord provides immense vitality and makes the life of the individual very energetic and eventful. Depending upon other conditions, when the ruler of the First house is also positioned in the First, it produces sound health, great longevity, valuable assets, and makes the personality so powerful that even the lord of the land regards him with great esteem. With the Ascendant lord in the Fourth house, the native becomes the favorite of his parents, especially of his mother. This position provides so much wealth and property that he never feels deprived of any basic necessity of life. If the planet is not associated with or afflicted by malefics, his mind remains clear, his intellect sharp and undistorted: he is accorded respectability in every society. He is passionate, has strong emotions, possesses considerable wealth, and is very fond of travel. Often he likes good food, but does not eat much. In the Seventh house, the impact of the Ascendant lord is disturbing in the sense that the individual chafes to alter his way of life and feels disturbed about his spouse, who will probably be attractive, cultured and cooperative; emotions may be uncertain, often fickle. There is a great urge for movement from one place to another. Individuals under such an influence often feel restless about their social relationships and strive to change their friends and environments frequently; they feel lost and finally become indifferent to their surroundings. In the Tenth house the Ascendant lord acquires special strength, enabling the individual to acquire great respectability, wealth, and a busy life; he prefers to stand on his own without any external support. He is decisive and succeeds in achieving his objective in life and fulfilling his destiny. If the lords of the various Cardinal signs are associated with the Ascendant lord in any of the Cardinal houses or in the Trines, the individual can expect all-around success. Along with Mercury, Jupiter or Venus, the Ascendant lord in the Cardinal houses or in the Trines makes the individual a special favorite of the sovereign, affluent, intelligent and long-lived.

The Trines, i.e., the Fifth and Ninth houses, are especially auspicious places for the Ascendant lord. Such an association combines the individual's own efforts with the benedictions of the gods. Success for such an individual is easy, opportunities for acquiring merit abundant, and his contributions to society well-recognized. In the Fifth house, the Ascendant lord makes the native self-respecting, favored by the government, and acclaimed as a person of great wisdom and learning. Under such a condition, the individual generates so many karmic good deeds that his future becomes pleasant by way of consequence. In the Ninth house, the Ascendant lord enables the native to enjoy amicable society and favorable conditions for his spiritual unfoldment. It opens the floodgate of past karmic fruits, which makes him lucky in many ways. He will travel far and wide and meet diverse types of people; he will acquire much money, attain a high status, be well spoken of, and be respected for his demeanor and wisdom.

Even in the three adverse houses, the Ascendant lord does not produce bad results except in the Twelfth. In the Sixth, the planet makes the person free from diseases, vanquishes his enemies, wins in litigation, and puts him in association with good and sympathetic people. In the Eighth house sudden gains and introduction to the secret sources of natural power are possible; the individual may succeed in exhuming lost information and wealth, decipher forgotten mysteries, and receive laurels for difficult investigative studies and explorations. He accumulates much wealth. Lordship of the death-inflicting Eighth house does not make the Ascendant lord a killer for the individual. In the Twelfth house, however, the planet finds itself helpless, engaged in fruitless endeavors and often receiving unmerited ignominy. The individual is misunderstood, frustrated, deprived of good things in life, and resides among strangers. But even these conditions are produced in order to enable the individual to experience the futility of earthly endeavors so that his interest in the spiritual life is enkindled.

The strength to influence the life of the individual is greatly increased for the Ascendant lord if the yogakaraka, i.e., the planet which is the prime benefic for the individual, and the atmakaraka, i.e. his guiding planet, are harmoniously related to it. The astrological texts give many methods to determine the atmakaraka, but the easiest method is to consider the planet with the most advanced position in any sign as the atmakaraka: the planet which has attained the highest degree of longitude in any sign. Yogakaraka planets vary for each sign of the zodiac. Thus, the Ascendant lord for each sign has special affinities with some planets while having adverse relationships with others.

For Aries Ascendant, Saturn, Mercury and Venus are adverse planets; the Sun and Jupiter are auspicious. Jupiter produces mixed results due to its ownership of the Twelfth house but the Sun is altogether helpful. Association, aspect or exchange of signs between these two planets is propitious. If the Sun also becomes the atmakaraka, the benefic strength of the Ascendant lord in company with the Sun is immensely increased. Jupiter's association with Saturn, though resulting in a kendra-trikona combination, does not produce Raja Yoga. Jupiter is fairly auspicious nevertheless.

For Taurus Ascendant, Jupiter, Venus and the Moon are adverse, but the malefic content of Venus which it acquires as ruler of the Eighth house is reduced and to a great extent even nullified by its rulership of the Ascendant. The Sun and Saturn are generally malefics, but for Taurus rising they are extremely helpful. The effect of Mercury depends upon its position and aspects. Jupiter, Moon and Mars are death-inflicting planets for this Ascendant. Even otherwise, the Ascendant lord is not friendly with these planets. Whatever the atmakaraka, it is plausible to infer that Taurus people can live harmoniously only when immersed in materialistic pursuits; any spiritual stirring will produce turmoil in their lives.

For Gemini Ascendant, a special situation arises due to the fact that no planet is very auspicious for it. Mars owns the Sixth and Eleventh houses. Jupiter is a benefic which is rendered malefic because it owns two Cardinal houses; the Sun has an inherently adverse relationship with Mercury and Venus due to its ownership of the Twelfth house, though its malefic influence is greatly reduced due to its rulership of the Fifth. All these planets create problems for Mercury, the Ascendant lord. Even Saturn, which should be favorable due to its friendly relationship with Mercury and lordship of the Ninth house, is spoiled by its ownership of the Eighth. Though the Moon, due to its lordship of the Second house, is a death-inflicting planet for this Ascendant, it bestows wealth in association with Mercury.

Venus, as a benefic ruling the Cardinal Fourth house for Cancer Ascendant, is not favorable; its malefic nature is further strengthened due to its rulership of the Eleventh. Mercury becomes adverse due to its rulership of the Twelfth house as well as the Third. Mars is favorable to the Ascendant lord Moon, and so is Jupiter, though its benefic nature is somewhat reduced by rulership of the Sixth house. Saturn is a death-inflicting planet for this rising sign. The Sun, though lord of the Second house, may produce much wealth if associated with a First house Moon, but it will isolate the person from his family relations.

The Sun, as Ascendant lord for Leo, does not vibrate harmoniously with Mercury, Venus or Saturn but has affinity with Mars and Jupiter. Venus and Jupiter are lords of the Tenth and Fifth houses, but their ownership of the Third and Eighth greatly reduces their benefic impact. Saturn inflicts death. The Moon in the Ascendant is capable of producing mental composure, but if associated with a First house Sun it will create problems: unless the individual is interested in spiritual attainments and the development of psychic powers, the association of Sun and Moon in the First house may lead to mental imbalance.

Mysterious relationships exist between Virgo and different planets. Jupiter, Mars and the Moon are adverse to this sign, so their association with the Ascendant lord Mercury does not lead to a smooth life. Venus is yogakaraka for the sign and its association with Mercury is harmonious, but it is death-inflicting as well. The Sun's association with Mercury in the Ascendant is very auspicious, making the life of the individual unusually bright.

Libra vibrates unharmoniously with Jupiter, Sun and Mars, but Saturn and Mercury are favorable to it. Association between Mercury and the Moon leads to Raja Yoga. Mars inflicts death while Jupiter creates "death-like" situations. The Ascendant lord Venus is restricted in its positive effects due to its ownership of the Eighth house; nevertheless its association with Mercury, Moon or Saturn can yield auspicious results.

Saturn, Mercury and Venus, friendly among themselves, are adverse to the Ascendant lord Mars for Scorpio rising. The Moon and Jupiter are favorable to it. A combination of the Moon and Sun can lead to Raja Yoga, but the Moon suffers when too close to the Sun, so for Scorpio Ascendant a condition of extreme affluence is never possible. Since the Ascendant lord is lord of the Sixth house as well, it is not powerful enough to produce its best impact. Venus inflicts death for this Ascendant.

Sagittarius, owned by Jupiter, vibrates unharmoniously only with Venus, which owns the Sixth and Eleventh houses; the adverse effect of Mercury due to its ownership of angles almost disappears if it is posited in Cardinal houses. Mars and the Sun, lords of the Trines and friendly to Jupiter, are very auspicious. The association of Mercury and the Sun produces Raja Yoga and these planets are yogakaraka also. Saturn inflicts death, Venus produces "death-like symptoms," while the Ascendant lord Jupiter can be very powerful if posited in Cardinal houses. Jupiter's association with Mercury or the Sun in a Cardinal house greatly enhances the auspicious nature of the Ascendant lord.

Capricorn relates adversely with Mars, Jupiter and the Moon and Saturn's association with these planets creates many problems. The Ascendant lord Saturn is a deep-acting planet with strong inherent tendencies of its own; the individual with Saturn as Ascendant lord finds it difficult to modify his personality patterns. Planets like Mercury and Venus, which are friendly to Saturn, are harmoniously related to it. Mars, Moon and Jupiter can be fatal for Capricorn Ascendant; Saturn also has the potential to kill, but ownership of the Ascendant generally persuades it not to be quite so malefic. Venus is yoga karaka for this sign, and a favorable relationship between Saturn and Venus leads to money and general prosperity.

The principle of inherent affinity between planets operates effectively in the case of Aquarius rising. Under this sign, Jupiter, Moon and Mars, which are adverse to the Ascendant lord Saturn, create problems related to health, money, profession and family relations. Unless the individual intends to live a life of sacrifice and philanthropy, only the association of

Venus with the Ascendant lord can produce favorable results. Venus is yogakaraka for Aquarius and relates harmoniously with Saturn. Mercury is neutral while Jupiter, the Sun and Mars are killers for this sign.

Pisces as the sign of the Ascendant vibrates unharmoniously with Saturn, Venus, Sun and Mercury. The Ascendant lord Jupiter is very favorably related to the life-sustaining Moon, and energy-producing Mars is extremely auspicious: their relationship with Jupiter will lead to rapid intellectual advancement, as well as acquisition of property and valuable assets. Mars is yogakaraka for Pisces Ascendant. Its association or any relationship with the Ascendant lord is conducive to great material prosperity. The individual is renowned for integrity of character, ethical behavior, and for intelligence and understanding. Mars owns the Second house, which ordinarily should bestow death-inflicting power. But in deference to its friendship with the Ascendant lord it has relinquished that power and has accentuated the benefic propensities arising due to its ownership of the Ninth house. Mercury and Saturn inflict death to the person.

The Ascendant lord has tremendous power in providing stability to the individual and enabling him to rise high in life. Such functions, however, must be supported by other planets. Aspects from benefic planets on the Ascendant and its lord are immensely helpful in this regard. If these are flanked by benefics on either side, the auspicious nature of the Ascendant and its lord is greatly enhanced. A strong Ascendant lord, even unsupported by such factors, can still fortify the life of the individual. Only when its strength is reduced by malefic influences or adverse placements will the Ascendant lord become a liability. One who wishes to make a mark on society, rise high in life, and fulfill his destiny must have a strong Ascendant lord.

RULE 3
An Integrated Self is Revealed by Harmonious Relationships between the Sun, Moon and Ascendant

The astrological approach to the human individual is not restricted to his physical existence. We have seen that the various portions of the zodiacal divisions (vargas) are linked with different deities. We did not discuss the details of these relationships, but it was recognized that they play a role in human development. While dealing with the relationship between the Cardinal houses and the Spiritual Triangle, mention was made of the karmic forces influencing favorable opportunities, as well as adverse conditions. Here we wish to highlight the fact that man is a very complex organism and functions through several vehicles of consciousness. In relation to the exaltation of planets, we hinted that the maturity of these vehicles is linked with planetary strength in the natal chart; debilitation shows that the related vehicle is in a poor state of health and needs extra care. The consciousness of the individual human being is rooted in and is a part of the greater being which we call the Cosmic Man, Kala Purusha. The Sun represents the soul or atman of Kala Purusha. From it flows a current of energy in the form of a ray of light which, passing through the various sheaths or vehicles of the individual's consciousness, energizes them with this light; on reaching the physical body the ray of light activates the physical entity which we call the man. In fact, this "man" whom astrology attempts to study is multi-dimensional. An integrated self implies that the flow of the atmic ray of light from the central core of one's being (represented by the Sun) is unhindered till it reaches the physical brain, and that his actions are harmoniously blended with this central motivating impulse. The uninterrupted flow of consciousness through the various vehicles is the touchstone of an integrated self. In the examination of such a relationship, the harmonious blending of the forces represented by the Sun, Moon, Ascendant and Ascendant lord is of utmost importance.

So far we have focused our attention primarily on the physical life of the person concerned. In order to study his non-physical counterpart, it will be necessary to examine once again the luminaries as well as the Ascendant in order to determine their signification in the present context. Then we shall examine how their harmonious blending can be expressed.

The Ascendant undoubtedly represents the physical self, but the ancient seers attached much more significance to it than that. The various synonyms used for Lagna (Ascendant) provide some clues. In Sanskrit, Lagna means a point of contact, a ray of light on the eastern horizon, dawn, a beginning. It also means health, body, appearance and the head. Popular astrology concerned itself only with these latter meanings and overlooked the earlier suggestions. The First house represents birth and the present living conditions. According to astrological philosophy, life is a continuity, the present being merely a link in the chain of births and deaths of which the current Ascendant is one of the innumerable beads. The Ascendant is merely a point of contact; the physical appearance is the outer fringe of the bigger self which has many dimensions extending from the grossest to the subtlest plane. The scope of astrological influence is restricted if we use it to examine only the physical. The integrated self of a person consists of many vital components, subtler sheaths and finer principles enlivening them. An inquiry into this complex structure of the self is made possible by taking cognizance of the relationship between the

Ascendant, Sun and Moon. It is not without significance that all the astrological considerations made in relation to the Ascendant also apply to the Sun and Moon.

The Ascendant stands for the body. The planets and lunar asterisms represent the different limbs of that body. The Moon symbolizes the life-breath, prana. Upon withdrawal of the life-breath, the body falls apart and is destroyed. The Moon provides the life-sustaining energy; it nourishes the body. It acts primarily as a bridge between the body and that primary source from which the vital energy originates. The Sun is the source of that energy. The Moon receives it from the Sun and imparts it to the physical vehicles of consciousness. Thus various vehicles of consciousness receive their strength and motivation from the Moon, which represents human emotions, passion, motivation, sensitivity, and the medium through which subtler forces are channeled and directed to the physical entity for its nourishment and growth. The Moon represents the human consciousness. The human essence or atman is the core of the being. It is the soul of the individual. This permanent essence of the Self always maintains a link with the incarnating self, and the Moon operates as the bridge between the two. The rays of the Sun, falling on the seeds scattered around the world by the Moon, give birth to flowers of different kinds which are represented by the different Ascendants; the Navamsha and other divisions of the zodiac symbolize the colors and fragrance of the individual flower.

We have mentioned that the Moon represents intelligence, feelings and emotions, the core of the being, dreams and other characteristics which point to the astro-mental counterpart of the human being. More importantly, the Moon is symbolized as "a flower," "going to a fortress," "westward-facing," "strength at night," "going to distant countries," "an umbrella or the royal insignia," "fish and other water-born creatures," "serpent," "silk garments" and other features which are open to esoteric interpretation. To overlook these characteristics of the Moon belittles the significance of the planet. These characteristics refer to the Moon as the stage of consciousness in which the individual is prepared for the initiation process: the various references such as "going to a fortress," "westward-facing," "going to a distant country," "umbrella," "silk garment," and "strength at night" directly allude to such a process. Success in such processes of spiritual unfoldment bestows power comparable to the umbrella or other royal insignia, and the individual becomes as wise as the serpent. The Moon, representing water, is comparable to the stream of consciousness which flows from the hilltops, representing the height of aspiration, to the ocean, where the individual stream merges in the cosmos and man attains his liberation. The appellations of the Moon suggest that human consciousness has a dual role; apart from governing the individual's daily life, it also provides the channel whereby one can ascend to a spiritual pinnacle.

That spiritual pinnacle is represented by the Sun. We have already mentioned some of the characteristics of this planet, but there are many other features of it which are important in the present context. Knowledge of the subtler nature of the Sun and the role assigned to it in human integration and growth enable us to examine its role in producing an integrated Self. The power, strength and vitality that we receive in our everyday life from the Sun are well-known. But its unifying role, whereby all our activities are centralized and directed toward the primary goal of life, is seldom realized. In the early stages of human growth and development, the solar energy permits the individual a great deal of latitude. Under such conditions, the problem of integration is not so important. Only at a later stage, when the individual has gathered experience and acquired strength and karmic merit, does the question of unifying his various sheaths arise. Having appreciated the need for control of the mind and emotions, the task of cleansing the astro-mental sheaths becomes acute. This raises the issue of the Moon in its obvious as well as its esoteric implications. Then arises the urge for knowledge of the secrets of Nature, the desire for initiation, and the attraction to spiritual studies which indicate that the solar radiance has begun its operation: the unifying process has begun.

The astrological seers described the Sun in terms such as "fortress," "worship of Shiva," "thorn trees," "self-realization," "skyward look," "roaming over mountains," "circular shape," "a red cloth," "harmony," "blood," "sandal paste," and "thick cord." These are meaningless unless understood in a symbolic context. Regarding the Moon, mention was made of "going to a fortress," and in relation to the Sun the fortress itself is referred to; the Moon was "going to a distant land" while the Sun stands for "roaming the forest." The Moon prepares the aspirant for the initiation process while initiation itself depends upon the solar disposition. The Sun is the hierophant. The worship of Shiva represents obeisance to the Supreme Lord. When the strenuous path of initiation is ended, the aspirant is anointed with sandal and red blood. He becomes self-realized; he is no longer merely looking skyward, but has been bound with a thick cord and has thereby become part of the solar core. The task of integration is complete.

There are several astrological indications to assess the degree of integration of the Self. The physical life of the individual can be studied by the various features of the Ascendant and its lord. This study can be extended to cover the impact of the Moon and Sun. Treating them as different Ascendants as far as the astro-mental body and atmic core are concerned, one can get an idea of the nature and disposition of these vehicles. These studies will indicate the basic impulse reflected by the Sun and the vitalizing and protective force imparted by the Moon. The physical health of the person, the important features of his day-to-day life as evident from the Ascendant and its lord, and several other horoscopic considerations, will represent the external appearance of his permanent Self or atman.

An important aspect of our present task is to find out whether the individual is primarily under the impact of pravritti marg, the path of involution, or of nvritti marg, the path of withdrawal or evolution. The chart shows the operation of these forces in relation to various signs and nakshatras. Attention must be paid to the operation of the three basic attributes or gunas, namely sattwa (harmony), rajas (activity), and tamas (inertia, sloth). Each nakshatra can be categorized according to its basic attribute, and we must therefore assess which guna predominates in the individual by studying the nakshatras operative in his chart. The different houses or bhavas, as well as the nakshatras, each relate to one of the four motivational forces which energize human activities at different levels of their operation. These are artha, meaningful or goal-oriented activities; kama, passional direction of activities; dharma, action motivated by righteousness; and moksha or liberation. When all four components of the integrated self, namely the Ascendant, Ascendant lord, Sun and Moon are fixed on the map according to their gunas and motivations, a synthetic view will emerge as to how well they are coordinated among themselves. In the cases of evolved seers, one gets highly integrated occult forces impinging on the individual; as far as people at large are concerned, this assessment will reveal personality weaknesses and strong points which will be helpful for their efforts towards self-growth.

If the Ascendant lord, Sun and Moon, being in angles or trines, occupy their exaltation, own or friendly houses, the combination is named Shrikanta. The result of this yoga is that the individual will be "decked with rudraksha rosaries, with his body made white by the smearing of sacred ashes." He will be magnanimous and will always be meditating on Shiva. He will rigidly observe religious rites and will help the virtuous. He will be free from malice towards the creeds and religious beliefs of others. He will become powerful and his heart will become delighted by the worship of Shiva. The discerning reader will have recognized that this planetary combination produces personalities which are oriented toward receiving the flow from the central core of being and offering themselves up to the fulfillment of their central mission in life.

The integration of the Self requires a close relationship between the physical effort and the prompting of the inner self. This coordination requires that the Ascendant and the Moon should be harmoniously placed in relation to each other. Ideally, the Ascendant lord and Moon should be either in the same zodiacal sign or in angles from each other. Temporary friendship between the two, formed when the Ascendant lord and Moon are two, three, four, ten, eleven or twelve houses from each other, is conducive to harmony. Trine relationship between the two also leads to close coordination of their actions. The Sun and Moon should be in trines or angles to each other, but close association of the two should be avoided. In very exceptional cases the conjunction of Sun and Moon may produce a higher order of occult initiation: generally speaking, however, such combinations very much reduce the clarity of mind. The Sun in the Ascendant is permissible, but not with the Sun conjunct the Ascendant lord. If the Ascendant lord, Moon and Sun are powerful as a result of exaltation, mulatrikona or ownership position (and sevenfold strength), and they have angular or trine relationships to one another, the combination produces a highly integrated personality. If the Moon is debilitated, it must attain cancellation of debilitation (Neechabhanga Yoga) and the birth should be on a full moon day, in order to produce an integrated Self. There are certain signs such as Leo, Scorpio, Sagittarius, Capricorn, Aquarius and Pisces, as well as asterisms such as Krittika, Rohini, Vishakha, Anuradha, Jyeshta, Shravana, Dhanishta and Revati which, when emphasized, are also propitious for producing highly evolved individuals with integrated self-functioning at different levels of their existence.

RULE 4
Opportunities and Impediments in Life are Shown by the Distribution of Benefics and Malefics in the Different Bhavas of the Natal Chart.

An individual may consider himself lucky if he receives many opportunities in life to exercise his talents; his life is frustrating when such conditions are denied him. A person with capabilities for serving his society in different ways will be unable to prove his salt if there are no takers for his efforts. Absence of such favorable conditions also denies him the performance of good karmas so that he may be assured of better conditions in future lives. The presence of benefics in the different houses of the horoscope indicates opportunities for the individual, while the distribution of malefics portends handicaps.

The natural benefics are Jupiter, Venus and a strong Moon; the nature of Mercury depends upon its associations. The Sun, Mars, and Saturn are malefics. Rahu and Ketu produce karmic results, particularly those carried over from past lives. Generally speaking, they are considered malefics. The basic rules, however, are modified by planetary strength, location, aspect, and rulership of different houses. Only on the basis of a synthetic view can the benefic or malefic nature of a planet be determined. There are guidelines in this regard which we must consider carefully.

When natural benefics own Cardinal houses, they become malefics unless they are also in the angles; malefics owning the angles relinquish their malefic nature. The lords of the Second and Twelfth houses do not acquire the malefic nature of these houses merely through ownership. In order to spoil their inherent nature, other factors must be present. But the lords of the Third, Sixth and Eleventh houses invariably create problems for the individual. The lord of the Eighth house, if lord of the Ascendant as well, loses its malefic nature — at least as far as its death-inflicting potential is concerned. The lords of the Sixth, Eighth and Twelfth, if located in these same houses, whether alone or with other rulers of these houses, will produce much wealth and their malefic nature is lost. But in this condition they should not be associated with or aspected by other planets. All debilitated planets, unless they acquire debilitation cancellation (Neechabhanga Yoga), are malefic in nature; so are the planets in an enemy's sign.

With this understanding, we should be able to approach the examination of opportunities in life. There are certain houses such as the Fourth, Fifth, Seventh, Ninth, Tenth and Eleventh which produce conditions we consider as opportunities. We have already seen the significance of these houses. On this basis, we should be able to determine the areas of their benefic influence. A favorable maternal relationship, property, a house and car (Fourth house) are generally considered auspicious conditions. An absence of heart disease and emotional crises combined with clarity of mind are favorable factors indeed. An exalted Jupiter will augur well in the Fourth, but its aspect on the Eighth creates unexpected problems. In the Fifth house, from which educational prospects and the chances for children are examined, Jupiter is considered bad for progeny but good for education. In the Seventh house, even Jupiter is not desirable: it makes the individual pine for extra-marital relationships; it provides opportunities for earning money, but increases enmity from brothers and colleagues. In the Tenth house, there is considerable professional success with Jupiter there, but financial and health problems also arise. Benefics provide good opportunities in various ways, but their impact is not always a completely unmitigated blessing.

Similarly, malefics are not always adverse. For example when Mars, a malefic, is posited in the Sixth, which is a favorable house for it, it enables the individual to conquer his enemies, overcome impediments and reduce health problems. But the same Mars makes the person vulnerable to accidents. In the Eighth house Mars is good for longevity but there may be occasion for surgery as well as financial losses.

Almost any planet, malefic as well as benefic, provides good professional opportunities in the Tenth house, consonant with its special nature and disposition. For instance, Jupiter is good for all professional prospects and financial benefits, *but* health hazards and service conditions may at times become intolerable and difficult to bear. The Moon can make one's job very changeable. Mars, while giving a meteoric rise, will make the person emotionally restless and prone to educational setbacks. Even the Sun, which is generally excellent in the Tenth house, makes the individual face trouble regarding property matters.

A safe rule for determining one's opportunities is to see whether benefics are related to a specific house and whether its ruler is favorably placed, i.e., in a trine or angle from the house under consideration. Aspects from malefics should be absent. But having decided the specific result of a house, one should also examine whether the influence of these results on *other* aspects of the individual's life is also good. When adverse effects are foreseen, contacts with protective Jupiter and the inherent strength of the house lord will determine how much or how little damage can be expected. Life is never an unmixed blessing or curse.

RULE 5
Fruit-gathering Souls (Bhog Yonis) and Action-Oriented Individuals (Karma Yonis) are Identified on the Basis of Planets Being Above or Below the Horizon in the Natal Chart.

Only when a soul begins to mature do patterns begin to emerge in planetary configurations. At an advanced stage of evolution, the individual has a great deal of karma to work out, but much to generate as well. Those who must bear the results of past karma plow through life until they finally receive the opportunities which allow them to create the future. Astrologically, those who have planets concentrated below the horizon (i.e., between the Ascendant and the Seventh house) have incarnated primarily to reap the consequences of past actions. Such horoscopes are not necessarily good or bad with regard to providing comfortable and pleasant conditions of life. They merely show that the individual is very much a pawn in the hands of his own destiny. On the other hand, those with planets concentrated between the Seventh and the Ascendant will confront situations wherein their decisions and actions give a new and momentous direction to the soul's journey. With planets both above and below the horizon, the individual will be a beneficiary of both past actions and opportunities for generating fresh actions.

A glance at the different houses will make the point clear. The Ascendant can be divided at its cusp with one portion above the horizon and the other below. The former represents the individual's possibilities for generating fresh karma, while the latter refers to the karma that he already brings with him into this life. The First house represents the very essence of his life-force which is under evolution. This essence is his potential, his treasure, upon the careful use of which his future will very much depend. But it also signifies various other aspects of life, such as face, appearance, personality, environment and the early part of life over which he has little control. The impact of different planets on these aspects of life merely carries forward past conditions which the individual has to bear.

That portion of the horoscope comprised of the Second to the Sixth houses inclusive signifies those aspects of life over which the individual has no control. The Second is concerned with sensitivity, creative potential, eyesight and speech, family relations, capital assets or accumulated wealth, and death. None of these is subject to the will of the person concerned; the auspicious or inauspicious conditions pertaining to them must simply be accepted.

The Third house primarily represents one's prowess; it also signifies helpful suggestions, impediments, injuries, short journeys, and ears. Any planets affecting this house can only increase or reduce the possibilities of receiving such opportunities. Mars may strengthen courage and valor, but the *goals* to which these qualities are directed are not offered by this house; for that, one must look to the Ninth or some other house. When brothers, friends and relatives are signified by this house, the presence of Mercury may give the individual pleasant relations, while Saturn may restrict this aspect of life. None of these attributes by themselves activate the individual in any definite way; all are mere capacities which, by themselves, lack specific direction. They are the individual's possessions; one may receive them, but he cannot do anything *about* them, except try to use them for some purpose — the impulse for which must come from other houses.

This situation becomes very marked in the case of the Fourth house. It represents the home life, mother, houses and cars, landed property, the heart, intelligence and false allegations. All of these may upset the individual; they can disturb his mental composure and peace of mind. A favorable Moon provides harmony here, while Rahu or Saturn damage one's equanimity. Mars can make one impulsive, while the Sun may make him a matter-of-fact person. These factors will go to build up his emotional and mental constitution. The individual will have to accept these conditions and can hope to alter them only marginally. One cannot change one's mother, howsoever hard he may try. Such is the situation for fruit-gathering souls.

Even the Fifth and Sixth houses, which are very important in deciding the fortune and ease of a person's life, also produce conditions over which the individual has no control. Any planetary activation of these houses indicates the environment in which the individual must survive and the favorable or adverse circumstances under which he must carry out his life's journey. The Fifth house indicates offspring, technical and general intelligence, psychic faculties, artistic talents, love affairs, virtuous acts done by the person's father, ethics, recreation and so on. It would seem that one has much freedom in using his creative intelligence and utilizing his artistic talents. But in fact, the house does not signify the *utilization* of these faculties so much as their *possession*. Sex does not insure offspring; the mere fact of a love affair does not indicate which partner takes the initiative. Challenging situations concerning intelligence, sex, and morality are not always amenable to one's conscious efforts. In the Fifth house, situations are imposed on the individual from which he cannot always extricate himself.

In the Sixth house the malefics are expected to produce favorable results, but this rule is liable to much misunderstanding. From this house predictions regarding physical and mental suffering, enemies, theft and litigation, fear of death, ill health and servitude are made. No one really wants these aspects of life to flourish. If some planetary influence restricts their development and increase, it is considered helpful. The Sixth is a very mysterious house, whose results come to the surface from those primeval levels of the soul wherein lie causes accumulated aeons ago. Such karmic impediments arise for special reasons which cannot be avoided. When malefics influence this house, as when Mars, the Sun or Rahu are posited here, the expansion of this house is impeded. For this reason the malefics are considered desirable. This, however, does not nullify the fact that the individual is helpless to do anything to mitigate the effects of this house except bear them courageously and with perseverance.

Individual freedom becomes a possibility in the Seventh house. From this point onward, celestial influence operates on the individual's free will. The Seventh house signifies marriage and sexual relations, partnership in business, trade and commerce, functioning and diseases of the genitals, death, pride, and status in life. Many of these factors are beyond the control of the individual. But at this point, the individual is also exposed to conditions which produce in his mind the urge to *do* something about them. At this stage, conditions arise which may induce him to dissipate his energy. It is important to note that at the junction of night and day, psychic forces fill the horizon. Dawn and dusk are moments of great spiritual power. The individual must be very alert in order to ward off the adverse influences emanating at this time and absorb those which can take him to higher levels of consciousness. These special forces very much affect this house, the symbolic point of dusk. Very fine judgment will be needed to decide how the balance will be tilted. Planets in the Seventh house, especially the portion of it which is above the cusp or horizon, throw open the possibilities for the exercise of free will.

The possibilities for such independent action become pronounced in the Eighth house. From this house onward, there are two currents of celestial force. On the one hand, there will be certain factors which, as in previous houses, will have to be borne without any possibility of change. The second type of influence shows the areas in which there is wide scope for individual initiative, involvement, and acquisition of further capabilities. The individual may be led to take action of some kind which will influence the future conditions of life. He generates fresh conditions which will reach fruition in times to come. This is the main difference between lives under these two conditions.

The Eighth house influences longevity, secret diseases, legacies, secret pleasures, the rectum, the place and nature of death; everything secret is connected with this house. These conditions, which include scandals, secret enemies, and undiagnosed diseases, are the fruits of past actions — even though activated by planets above the horizon — and will have to be borne. The individual will have very little control over them. But these factors exist along with others which the individual will perform in the present, the results of which he will have to bear later. Actions connected with the Eighth house are a preparation for the initiatory process, murder, and involvement in black magic or some form of cruelty. When Mars activates this house, there is the possibility of externalizing inner urges. If other factors suggest cruelty, this may lead to bloodshed, but spiritualizing influences will produce urges towards unraveling the secrets of Nature. Under such compulsions, the individual will move toward preparing himself for the secret trials wherein the mysteries of Nature are unfolded before him. The Sun will heighten this influence and the individual may attain high levels of occult status. Saturn may activate karmic diseases which are difficult to diagnose or encourage illicit sexual relationships, but under spiritual impulse there will be immense endurance for undertaking the arduous task of exploring Nature's secrets. What is important is that planets in the Eighth will energize the individual to take action, work, make decisions, and involve himself in situations which will produce future karmic conditions. The special features of this house will merely show the kinds of action that can be expected.

The Ninth house forms part of the Spiritual Triangle. It involves the individual in action, not merely in fruit gathering. Under the impulse of the Ninth house, the individual will receive those results of past karmas which are made available to him so that he may involve himself in new spiritual activities. The house is related to preceptors and gods, from whom he receives benedictions surrounding him with a spiritual atmosphere. The Ninth house gives a philosophical attitude, long travels, and grace. It provides suitable conditions for penance, mantra and meditation. One begins a new career and makes an effort toward realizing the nature of God. A radical transformation begins at this stage. The Ninth house generates deep karmic causes which may have a long gestation period. These actions radically *change* the course of one's life. Favorable planets in this house will add benedictions, thereby generating forces which finally produce auspicious results. Even the impact of malefics like the Sun, Mars, Saturn, a waning Moon or the Moon's Nodes will be greatly significant in *changing* one's attitudes, capabilities, and conditions in life.

The Tenth house is concerned with the manner of one's involvement in the outside world. It is generally regarded as the house of profession and livelihood, the father, and honor from the state. As far as these factors are concerned, one has little control. But other aspects of this house energize the individual's life so that his potentialities come to the fore. Under the impact of the Tenth house, the individual comes in contact with different persons and circumstances where his *contribution* is important. In this sense, the Tenth house signifies involvement in social activities, the accomplishment of certain spells (mantra siddhis), teaching, counseling and commanding, the adoption of sons, renown and dedication to work and ideals. Unless some agent is present to activate these impulses, they will remain dormant. For this reason, the presence of any planet in this house is considered favorable. The future course of life greatly depends upon the forces generated by this house. The presence of planets is therefore very vital. The Tenth house represents the midheaven, and planets near the zenith at the time of birth are indicators of the height to which the individual may legitimately hope to attain.

The Eleventh house is a very popular house, an important base of the Triangle of Materiality. Under the influence of this house things, opportunities, benedictions and material wealth flow to the individual. Primarily it is a house of gains. Income, friendship, wealth, and many other things begin in this house. These are some of the aspects of life which are greatly valued by men of the world. The presence of planets here is therefore desired; such planets are treated as profitable in a limited worldly sense. But this house has another side to it. It signifies the socialization process, friendship, love-making, and the acquisition of power; under the impact of this house one may also join a religious order and devote himself to worshiping the deities. Though the house is often condemned for its excessive materialism, it has a positive influence in orienting the individual toward philanthropic and social action. The presence of planets in this house enables the individual to break through his isolation and personal(self-centered) considerations in order to become socially conscious. Planets in this house, though they may be trying, are still desirable.

The Twelfth house represents the region of the sky which planets enter shortly after rising on the eastern horizon. It is one of the houses which is susceptible to several layers of meaning. From the disposition of this house one may relate the incarnating soul to his eternal past with which he merges after mortal life is ended. It represents the journey's end, life after death, the pleasures of bed, imprisonment, and all kinds of outgoings and expenditure. The control of the individual over many of these aspects of life is completely absent. But the action and freedom aspect of this house, for which reason the presence of planets here is appreciated, pertains to moksha or liberation, "awakening from sleep" or disillusionment with material attachments, discharge of debt, the working out of past karma, "renouncing one's couch" or involving oneself in the struggle between darkness and light, and, finally, "going to another country." When planets are present in the Twelfth house, the forces generated thereby may energize and activate the individual towards his ultimate goal. The absence of planets in this house may encourage him to adopt the course of inertia, which will delay his final destiny.

To sum up, planets above the horizon will energize those aspects of life wherein one has much freedom to act; *action* is vital for changing the course of the individual's involvement with the world at large, turning him outward so as to expedite the attainment of his ultimate destiny.

Planets in the involutionary portion of the horoscope, represented by the houses below the horizon, will be able to provide pleasant conditions and a luxurious life, but they relate primarily to *one* life, the present one. Their influence will not generate fresh forces which affect the future lives of the individual. He has to bear them, whether they are pleasant or adverse. Planets in the evolutionary hemisphere, i.e., above the horizon, create forces which have far-reaching karmic consequences.

RULE 6
The Significance of a House is Deciphered by the Disposition of the Same House Relative to it.

This means that the significance of, for example, the Second house can be determined by taking into account the second house from the Second, which will be the Third. To give another example, the significance of the Third house should be decided in conjunction with the third from the Third, which will be the Fifth.

The above rule reveals certain deeper implications of the horoscope. It is an extension of the concept of the Mysterious Depth and the hexagon formed by the interlacing of the Spiritual and Material Triangles. The juxtaposition of the six-pointed figure on the Mysterious Depth produces the basic natal chart with its twelve house divisions. We can see that the Second, Sixth, Eighth and Twelfth houses fall in one category, while the Fourth and Tenth fall in another. The remaining six houses are represented by the various angles of the hexagon.

The Second, Sixth, Eighth and Twelfth houses, as we have mentioned earlier, constitute the Mysterious Depth. The primeval Sea of Immutability is not based on any other antecedent existence. It operates at its own level, undisturbed and unconcerned about any other force in existence. This is expressed by the fact that the houses representing this Sea of Immutability are not affected by the present rule. They only radiate their own basic impulses and do not reflect the features of any other house.

The Fourth and Tenth houses are also of the nature of the Mysterious Depth, but somewhat different. The Mysterious Depth represents completely universalized impulses, while these two houses differentiate that portion of the universal sea from which the course of the pilgrim's journey is carved out. The Fourth represents the place where all the forces generated by the incarnating soul are deposited, operated upon by the Divine Alchemy, and maintained till the end. The Tenth house represents the goal set out for the individual. Both these aspects of life represent tasks to be performed; these houses also radiate their own impulses without the influence of others.

Basic and Secondary Impulses of the Houses

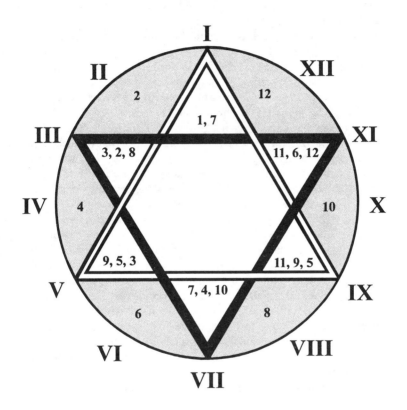

The Ascendant is very different from the other angles of the hexagon. It is not restricted or reflected by any other house division. Applying the rule, the Ascendant is the first house from itself, therefore no other house is involved in deciphering its results. However, the Ascendant is seventh from the Seventh house, so the significance of the Seventh must be examined in relation to the disposition of the First house. Thus the apex of the Spiritual Triangle (First house) influences the apex of the Triangle of Materiality (Seventh house). The depths in which the individual may immerse himself are directly linked to the heights toward which he may aspire. The potentiality contained in the Seventh house can fructify only with the approval of the First house. The Seventh represents partnership, whether in marriage or in business; it is also linked with death, dissipation of energy, and sexual pleasure. These are the basic impulses of the Seventh house, though according to the present rule it will also reflect the qualities of the Fourth house, as it is the fourth from the Fourth. The Seventh is also the tenth from the Tenth, hence it signifies the results of the Tenth house as well. In relation to the First house, it is difficult to say how much of the Seventh house will be reflected by the First, because the First house epitomizes the entire horoscope; nonetheless the basic fact remains that the First house does reflect some basic urges of the Seventh. Considering sexual relationships and sociability as the essential impulses flowing from the Seventh, the disposition of the First house must be potent enough to enable the fructification of these Seventh house impulses. For instance, if Venus is in Libra in the Seventh while Mars in Aries is in strength in the First, the individual will have lustful urges and a great desire for amiable social relationships, but Mars will make the First house so antagonistic to the social and sexual impulses of the Seventh house that these basic urges of the individual will be stifled. On the other hand, with Scorpio as the Seventh house and Venus in Taurus in the First, the individual may feel an inward repugnance toward sex and social relationships, yet he will be compelled by circumstances into just such situations. He would be psychologically averse to what he is doing physically. With Sagittarius as the Seventh house he will not be much interested in others, being self-centered and pursuing his own personal objectives of self-improvement even though the actualization of these basic impulses will be very restricted. Thus there is a kind of uneasy balance. In the case of Capricorn being the Seventh house, the social and sexual urges of the person will be very much inhibited, yet with Cancer as the First house the actualization of such basic desires will come to the surface eventually. Such individuals, even if they are basically moral, will find much stigma attached to them. This will not be the case with Aquarius as the Seventh. Denial of relationships, being the basic impulse, is only reinforced by the same type of influence from Leo, which will be the First house.

Examining the four angles of the hexagon, we find that the Third house is related to the Second and Eighth houses, as it is the second house counted from the Second, and the eighth from the Eighth. The Fifth house is linked with the Third house as it is placed third from the Third; the Fifth also happens to be ninth from the Ninth, so it is related to that house as well. Thus the Fifth house has two roles to perform: first, it has to reflect its own basic impulses, and second, it has to express some characteristics of the Third and Ninth houses.

The basic function of the Fifth house is to express creative urges and actions. But it also has the role of actualizing the urges of the Third and Ninth houses. The Third and Ninth are opposites which link up in the Fifth, thus uniting these three houses. The basic urges of the Third house are prowess, courage, and the will to action. These can be actualized only when favorable conditions are presented by the Fifth house. The Fifth house represents creative action, and unless opportunities for such action arise so that the individual may demonstrate his valor and courage, those forces will be still-born. But the opportunity for actualizing Fifth house creativity requires the support of the Ninth house. Thus, the influence of the Ninth house flows indirectly to the Third. Fifth and Ninth house relationships are considered auspicious because the opportunities for actualizing creativity are provided by the Ninth, while the Ninth house basic urge toward spiritual transformation can find its fruition only if the creative activity provided by the Fifth house is present.

The Third house represents lust for life. The Second house symbolizes death, as does the Eighth. As second from the Second and eighth from the Eighth, a strong Third house, imparting a powerful lust for life, will very much reduce ill health and stave off death. The Ninth house imparts the impulse to journey toward one's ultimate goal, thus greatly influencing the individual's basic attitude toward life. The earning of income and the process of socialization are some of the basic urges of the Eleventh house. Because the Ninth is the eleventh from the Eleventh, any effort towards achieving these objectives will greatly depend upon that general attitude toward life: otherwise one may remain a go-getter in mind only, without translating ideas into actuality.

The rule that the disposition of a house should be considered from the disposition of the house which occupies the same relative position vis-a-vis that house as does that house to the Ascendant is a basic indicator of the relationship of various impulses and their actualization. The first house in the series provides the clue to those urges, while the related house indicates the possibilities for their actualization.

RULE 7
The Nodes of the Moon, Rahu and Ketu, Represent Karmic Influences which are Difficult to Understand and which Cannot be Avoided.

Much care is needed in divining the results of the Moon's Nodes. They are called "the shadowy planets" as well as "the deceptive planets." The action of the Nodes eludes human imagination. For this reason, the diseases caused by Rahu and Ketu are hard to diagnose. The fateful quality of the results produced by these force centers is well-known. When the Nodes afflict a house, people dread the consequences and prepare to propitiate Rahu and Ketu — yet the inevitability of the results must be faced. These planets represent the karmic forces operating on the individual, which in many cases are a hold-over from earlier incarnations. They affect the individual's inner being in such a way that his psychological and psychic constitution is radically altered. Their importance, inevitability, inscrutability and depth of penetration are astounding, because the situations represented by the Nodes are prepared with specific objects in view from the standpoint of a soul's growth. As it is never easy to decipher the requirements of an evolving soul, the impact of Rahu and Ketu is deceptive and elusive.

The importance of Rahu and Ketu in esoteric astrology is considerable. A very exceptional yoga or planetary combination related to these planets is known as Kala Sarpa Yoga. Under this combination, all the planets in a horoscope are placed on one side of the Rahu-Ketu axis; the planets are said to be encircled by the Nodes. This planetary encirclement is said to make the individual poor and short-lived. This is, however, nullified or considerably reduced if there are kingly combinations (Raja Yogas) or several planets in exaltation. The adverse influence of this combination is also weakened if a few of the lords of the Second, Fourth, Ninth and Tenth houses are placed in angles or Trines without being in debilitation, afflicted by malefics, or flanked by malefics. But the adverse effects of Kala Sarpa Yoga are merely the outer symptoms of esoteric forces at work within. Past karmic forces (the Nodes) restrict the planets so that they become ineffective. This combination ordinarily occurs in the charts of people who have acquired considerable merit and maturity in past lives. The creative potential embodied in their planets is likely to be considerable, but certain past sins of omission and commission still hold them captive, rendering them frightened and helpless. The psychological frustration caused by this captivity is not intended to punish the person with illness or poverty but to impel him to seek the causes of that frustration and move toward a more spiritual existence. The *initial* impact of Kala Sarpa Yoga may make the individual frustrated, depressed, and regressive, but it can lead him to a life of philosophical reflection, of understanding and accepting his karma.

Mythologically, the Rahu-Ketu axis represents a unity. At the time of the churning of the ocean, the gods and demons were engaged in retrieving the nectar of immortality from the Sea of Immutability. The gods finally secured it but did not want to share it with the demons. One of the demons contrived to mingle with the gods and managed to consume a portion of the drink. When he was discovered he was cut in half by Vishnu, but since he had already drunk the nectar he could not be slain entirely. The two parts of the demon became two entities, the upper portion known as Rahu and the lower as Ketu; thus the Nodes are connected with the effort to obtain the nectar of immortality. Their general disposition is malefic, but in essence they work in collaboration with the benevolent forces of nature represented by the gods.

Astrologically, Rahu and Ketu maintain separate identities and have well-distinguished dispositions of their own. But together they represent an element of immortality, the wisdom that overcomes births and deaths. In obtaining this wisdom, Rahu and Ketu activate the churning of the ocean. This process is symbolic of the turbulence in our lives which leads to wisdom, which churns the forces of transformation within us. The wisdom obtained through the Rahu-Ketu axis carries the individual through the bondage of births and deaths and finally helps him overcome this chain of causation. This is the message imparted by the myth. In every horoscope, there are certain features which are essential to the understanding of the life-pattern of the individual. The Rahu-Ketu axis is one of these, showing the conflicts and trials that the individual will have to undergo in his life.

Rahu and Ketu are always opposite each other. If Rahu is in the Ascendant, Ketu will be in the Seventh house. Under such a situation, the individual's trials will be caused by his personal self and his partnerships. Rahu being the material circumstance and Ketu the wisdom arising from it, the individual is generally saddled with certain responsibilities, either real or assumed, which considerably distort his psychological make-up. Consequently, his married life is not smooth and his social relationships are self-centered. He will worry about the relationship aspects of his life to the exclusion of all else. Over the years he will see the cause of this imbalance by grasping the wisdom of his own self-nature. Thus he will be redeemed from his turmoil.

When Rahu is in the Second house, Ketu will fall in the Eighth, thus creating an unusual situation. Both houses are parts of the Deep Sea; both link the individual with his karmic past. Both houses are connected with death, which dissolves everything into nothingness. The Second house, however, is related to speech, wealth, and family relations, whereas the Eighth house represents secret affairs, spells, elusive diseases, and paranormal powers. The churning operation of the Nodes throws the individual into a vortex of physical and material problems. There may be speech defects, family troubles, scandals, loss of wealth, and psychic disturbance. Unless the individual develops complete detachment from materiality and begins to perceive the enduring nature of the spiritual path, the Rahu-Ketu axis will create problems with the inner workings of his emotions and relationships, expressing themselves externally in the form of congenital diseases, mental aberrations and sexual perversions.

In the Third house, Rahu will be at its best as regards success in achieving material objectives, but Ketu's placement in the Ninth house will make the individual thoroughly disenchanted with his gifts of success. The individual will suffer a perpetual conflict between material attractions and the futility of such attractions. There will be no peace of mind; nothing in life will satisfy. The individual will flit from one philosophy, religion, or political party to another, and from none of these will he obtain the satisfaction for which he yearns. Affluence becomes a beautiful carving on the front of an edifice which contains chaos within it.

Rahu in the Fourth and Ketu in the Tenth house make the individual thirst for love and affection, power and position. These factors can create unbearable pain for him. The Fourth and Tenth houses represent his past and future. When the Nodes afflict these houses, there is great agitation in the inner core of the individual; he always questions whether his activities are purposeful, whether his objects of love are perfect, and whether he is receiving his due in life. These strong feelings may not be perceived by others, but inside the individual there is great turmoil. In such situations he suffers much more within than any external symptoms of that psychological pain can ever reveal.

When Rahu is in the Fifth and Ketu in the Eleventh, the creativity of the individual is greatly restricted. The money he receives is tainted with cruelty, his friends and companions are disturbed. His thoughts are unclear and his children, if he has any, are of doubtful character. The Rahu-Ketu axis in this situation will force the individual to a life of poverty, chastity, and isolation; his society will be made up of social outcasts. His being discarded by society in spite of his positive attributes pains him acutely.

The Sixth and Twelfth houses are both parts of the Sea of Immutability. When the Nodes are placed here, something unusual happens. The rajasic or active proclivities of the incarnating soul are churned up to such a degree that there is radical transformation, bringing the individual to the verge of materialistic release. Material affluence, the overcoming of difficulties in life, and the externalization of latent capabilities raise the material confidence and status of the individual, but there is some disenchantment arising from his inability to enjoy his so-called prosperity. He begins to hear voices from the other side of existence. He sees new meanings and implications in every event. Difficulties arising in his life will be overcome, his diseases will be cured, his powers will reveal themselves, but they do not give him peace or tranquility. His sleep will be disturbed, his married life unhappy, his mind unsettled. He will then turn toward philosophies of the future. He will be so determined in his approach to the problems of life that adopting an unconventional mode of living, even at the risk of losing all that is socially coveted, will be of no serious consequence. His values will be different from those of other people.

In subsequent houses, the position of Rahu and Ketu will be reversed but the basic meanings will be the same; only the details will differ. What is important in the present context is to note that the Rahu-Ketu unity creates the fulcrum around which the entire life of the person will revolve. This axis is so important that the forces externalized by it will affect the very core of existence, and their origins will be rooted in karmic forces generated by the individual in past incarnations. There will be no escape from them. But these results are intended to transform the psyche of the person, as a result of which his entire course of life can change. The impact of the Nodes changes the whole direction of a life. In this process of transformation, materiality is squeezed out so that spirituality may emerge. This is inevitably an arduous process. Sometimes the process involves acquiring material affluence, sensual enjoyment, and high status — but only so that we may become disenchanted with these values when karmic forces raise their heads and force us into the alchemical crucible of transformation. On other occasions, there may be physical deprivation and poor health, so that even when opportunities arise one cannot enjoy them, which produces a feeling of helplessness and turns one's gaze toward the emptiness which is true reality. Often, the lessons of poverty, chastity, and self-control are learned after leading a life of indulgence, debauchery, and extravagance. It is a difficult task to decipher the course by which Rahu and Ketu will teach their lesson, but they will certainly fulfill their mission.

RULE 8

All Predictive Assessment should be done with Respect to the Ascendant, Moon and Sun before Pronouncing a Final Judgment with Regard to Any Aspect of Life.

The entire life of the individual is epitomized by the Ascendant. The importance of the First house, however, reflects the great significance attached to the physical level of our existence. Our psychological and spiritual lives are often neglected; even our astro-mental make-up (symbolized by the Moon) is not very well-recognized. The Moon is the channel through which the life-essence pours into the individual. It is important in the determination of one's life-span and general health conditions. The Moon is also connected with the Pitris, the guardians of humanity, the progenitors. Through the medium of the Moon, all the impulses which activate the human individual are energized. The fruit-gathering conditions of life as well as the action-oriented influences are, to a great extent, controlled by the lunar forces. Therefore, it has been suggested that the horoscope should also be read as if the Moon were the Ascendant — i.e. the house containing the Moon becomes the First house. If children are signified by the fifth house from the Ascendant, they may also be signified by the fifth house from the Moon. This principle is also applicable to the Sun. When examination of any aspect of life has been considered with reference to the Ascendant, Moon, and Sun, a final judgment can be made.

It is important to be clear about the basic differences between the results emerging from these three approaches. Occult literature has emphasized that the integrated personality takes into account the higher triad consisting of Atma-Buddhi-Manas, and the lower quaternary comprising thought, emotion, the aura and the physical body. The higher triad is comparable to the permanent part of the self which transcends physical birth and death and is the repository of all actions forming the aggregate of karmic forces; it is part of the eternal wisdom which regulates and guides the individual through the maze of incarnations until he attains his final liberation. The lower quaternary is that portion of the entity which lasts for only one life. The Sun represents the core of one's being or atman. That which it generates endures. If any aspect of one's life is examined in relation to the Sun, it will reveal the enduring meaning of that aspect of life. The fifth house from the Sun reveals our eternal creative potential rather than the birth of children. If the tenth house from the Ascendant is powerful while the tenth from the Sun is afflicted, the individual may attain status which is considered dignified by others, but he himself will feel chained and impeded by it. Only when a house is well-fortified when counted from the Sun, Moon, and Ascendant can an individual enjoy *complete* satisfaction in that aspect of life.

The Moon is the physical guardian of the incarnating soul. It provides the necessary impetus and power to sustain different kinds of activities. Unless support from the Moon is received, that impetus and power may be lacking. If the possibilities for achievement on the basis of the Ascendant are great, but the Moon offers no support, the achievements will either elude one at the last moment or will be short-lived. Moreover, the lunar influences are very powerful with regard to the physical and material conditions of the individual as well as the strength of his aura. For example, if matters relating to children, wealth, house and property are under consideration, or those relating to success, social relationships, reputation and the like, the lunar influence will be very determining. While predicting results based on the disposition of the Moon, the basic consideration is the direction of the life-force and the expansion of emotional and mental power. The results of lunar influence need not be enduring as in the case of the Sun, or much concerned with everyday events as in the case of the Ascendant. Supporting the physical achievement with energy and sustaining force and making the heart of the individual glow are the basic tasks of the Moon. Harmony between physical forces (Ascendant), life-sustaining impulses (Moon), and the enduring nature of the result from the soul's standpoint (Sun) is essential for any definitive prediction.

There are certain special combinations which are related to the Sun and Moon and which, if carefully understood, are an extension of the above principle. Two of these combinations are important in the present context.

First, Jupiter's aspect on the Sun or Moon is auspicious. In the former case, however, it bestows fame, glory, purity of motive and spirituality, while in the case of the Moon it dispels all impediments to one's physical well-being, enables the individual to overcome adversaries, and bestows wealth and status.

Second, the flanking of the luminaries by benefics on both sides is very auspicious. The absence of such a situation in the case of the Moon is considered a weakness in a horoscope. Various yogas, such as Adhi, Anapha, Sunapha, and Durdhara are based on benefics being either on one or the other side of the Moon. Adhi Yoga arises when benefics are placed in the sixth, seventh, and eighth houses from the Moon. This combination is not desirable in the case of the Sun. But in the case of the

Moon, which is helpful in supporting life-forms (whereas the Sun destroys material forms and encourages or sustains the enduring component of life), Adhi Yoga is important. Considered from the Ascendant, there are qualifying factors; except for Jupiter in the Seventh house, benefics in the Sixth through the Eighth houses are not favored. When the Sun is flanked on both sides by benefics, the various yogas are named Vasi, Vesi and Obhayachari, and are extremely auspicious. When the Ascendant is flanked by benefics, the individual receives unexpected and much needed support from others.

While considering each planet in a horoscope with respect to the Ascendant, Moon, and Sun, one must keep their basic differences in mind. Any influence which is not conducive to the enduring or eternal aspect of being will not be much supported by the Sun; that which is related to life-giving activities and supportive of birth and expansion on this earth as well as the development and expansion of consciousness will be strengthened by lunar influence; the Ascendant is related to every aspect of life in which the physical existence of the individual is concerned. Approached on this basis, it will be clear why it is laid down that the Moon in the first, fourth, seventh or tenth houses from the Sun will bestow scant wealth, in the second, fifth, eighth and eleventh houses will lead to an average level of prosperity, and in the third, sixth, ninth or twelfth from the Sun will promote abundance. In this connection, one may refer to the basic features of a horoscope as revealed by the Cardinal houses and the Spiritual and Material Triangles, along with the significance of the First-Seventh relationship. Other combinations are:

1. Jupiter in the Fifth house, Moon in the Third house and Sun in the Ninth house make the individual a very rich and affluent person. It may be noted here that Jupiter is in trine from the Sun, and the Moon in the seventh from it. From the Ascendant, Sun and Jupiter take their position at the base angles of the Spiritual Triangle, while the Moon will occupy a base angle of the Triangle of Materiality.

2. If the Sun in conjunction with the Moon in the Seventh house occupies its exaltation or a favorable sign, and benefics aspect it, a king or a king's equal is born, but his disposition will be fickle. The union of the Sun and Moon is a very mysterious combination with highly spiritual significance, but not very conducive to material affluence, especially as regards those aspects of life which are concerned with maturity of judgment. Under this combination, the cognitive process is subordinate to the solar influence. A benefic aspect on these planets is possible

only when Jupiter aspects the Seventh house from the Eleventh or Third house. The Eleventh and the Third houses happen to be the base angles of the Material Triangle. Often the above combination is said to yield powerful results when malefics aspect the Sun and Moon. Thus this combination emphasizes the activation of Sun, Moon and Ascendant by the malefics, that is, the materially inclined planets, besides the supporting influence received from Jupiter.

3. Another combination stipulates that if the birth is at midnight and the Sun in the Fourth house joins with Mercury, an aspect by Moon and Saturn in the Tenth house and Mars in the First house will produce a kingly person as far as affluence is concerned. Besides linking the Ascendant, Sun, and Moon, this combination stresses that the Sun must be dipped in materiality and its nature influenced by material planetary aspects.

The above combinations are described merely to emphasize that auspicious results require a combination of influences flowing through the Sun, Moon, and Ascendant. If these forces are affected by benefics, the harmonious currents are strengthened; otherwise, under materially inclined planets, the joint effect of these triple forces may lead the individual to more earthly pleasures. This astrological principle is a corollary of the basic rule that all considerations should be examined in relation to the Ascendant, Moon, and Sun in order to arrive at definite conclusions regarding any aspect, whether auspicious or inauspicious, spiritual or materialistic.

RULE 9
The Nature of a House is Regulated by the Lord of the Sign which is Occupied by the Lord of the House Under Consideration.

Every sign, as well as every asterism, is linked with its planetary deity by a magnetic affinity. When a planet occupies a particular house in a horoscope, it becomes subordinate to the planet ruling over the sign it occupies. The nature and disposition of the ruling planet will determine the kind of result expected in respect to that sign. Any planet in that sign will be influenced by this ruling planet, which is called the dispositor of the bhava. If the ruler endows that planet with benefic influences, its period in the life of the individual will be auspicious. If its influence is adverse, the individual will experience a trying time during its period of rulership.

For example, let us assume that Taurus is the Ascendant and its lord, Venus, is posited in the Third house in Cancer. The lord of Cancer is the Moon, which becomes the dispositor of the First house. If the Moon is placed in the Ascendant, which is its exaltation sign, the person will be very powerful. Using the same Ascendant, let us assume that Jupiter, the lord of the Eleventh house, is in the Fourth house in Leo, so that the Sun becomes the dispositor of the Eleventh. If the Sun is conjunct Jupiter in the Fourth, it will attain strength due to its ownership of the sign. The association of Jupiter will make it additionally auspicious. There will be much money in the life of the person and the period of Jupiter will prove very beneficial.

When examining a house, it is important to take into consideration the ruler of the sign constituting that house, the various aspects to it, and the influence of any planets which occupy it. In analyzing aspects, it is important to take into account their natural maleficence or beneficence. The temporary disposition of aspecting planets acquired due to house rulership or other factors should not be considered in this context. The timing of events connected with the house, the intensity of influence and the type of experiences to be expected will be dependent upon the dispositor of the bhava. This rule does not nullify other factors, but for specifying the *period* when specific results can be expected as well as the *kind* of results to expect, this rule is the decisive one. If the planetary ruler of a house is weak but its dispositor is strong and powerfully aspected by benefics, then that bhava will prosper.

If the principle is applied on the basis of the asterisms rather than the signs of the zodiac, it gives more accurate results. For example, if the Ascendant is Aries, whose lord Mars is at 26° 18′ Gemini in the asterism of Punarvasu, then the lord of Punarvasu, i.e., Jupiter, becomes its dispositor. If Jupiter is placed in the Seventh house in association with the Moon, it will aspect the Ascendant as well as the Ascendant lord; furthermore, Jupiter and the Moon conjunct in the Seventh house produces an auspicious combination of Cardinal house and Spiritual Triangle lords. The auspicious nature of this combination will be very much increased if Venus, the lord of the Seventh, is placed in the Fifth in association with the Sun, the lord of Leo occupying its own house. Such a combination may not be very beneficial for marital felicity, but the individual's fame will be universal, enduring and full of glory. If Jupiter is placed at 5° 54′ Libra, which lies in the asterism Chitra, ruled by Mars and symbolized by a pearl, and Venus is at 6° 20′ Leo in Magha asterism, ruled by Ketu and symbolized by a palanquin, the individual will accomplish courageous deeds on the battlefield and obtain easy victory over enemies, but there will be no cruelty in him. This illustrates the point that the rule applied on the basis of signs of the zodiac reveals the general indications of the house under consideration, but when applied on the basis of the asterisms the same rule will indicate more detailed characteristics.

Let us take another example. Assuming the Ascendant is Taurus, the Tenth house will be Aquarius, ruled by Saturn. Saturn is at 17° 36' Gemini in Ardra asterism ruled by Rahu. If Rahu is in Pisces along with Jupiter and the asterism in which Rahu is placed is Revati, ruled by Mercury, which in turns lies in Punarvasu, ruled by Jupiter and symbolized by a bow, the combination will make the individual be universally acknowledged as a great writer with tremendous command over written and spoken language. His writings will be on unconventional themes and he will carve out a niche for himself which may be difficult to fill for several centuries to come. Such detailed forecasting is not possible merely on the basis of zodiacal signs.

The importance of such indirect prognostication can be noted on the basis of several special yogas indicated in the astrological texts. Here we propose to indicate one known as Parijatha Yoga. It relates to the Ascendant lord. If the Ascendant lord is placed in a sign whose lord is placed in a Cardinal house, Trine, or its own or exaltation sign, the individual will be happy in the middle and last part of his life and will receive favor from highly placed people. He will enjoy a military career and possess expensive cars or other vehicles. He will conform to cultural traditions, customs, and established religion. He will be generous and famous. This result will also occur if the the lord of the Navamsha house which the Ascendant lord occupies is associated with a Cardinal house, trine, or its own or exaltation sign.

This rule is involved and requires careful application, but it predicts some of the inner forces working on the individual.

RULE 10
Patterns in Planetary Arrangement Reveal Important Problems in Life.

The reader has by now recognized the importance of the Cardinal houses, the Hexagons, and the Sea of Immutability. The planetary positions in relation to these broad classifications will suggest the type of life the individual may lead. Mention has already been made of the three primary attributes or gunas in relation to the zodiacal signs. Aries, Taurus, Gemini and Cancer are considered to be primarily under the influence of rajas or activity; Leo, Virgo, Libra, and Scorpio are tamasic i.e., they are primarily influenced by the tendency towards inertia; and Sagittarius,

Capricorn, Aquarius and Pisces are sattwic or harmony-producing signs. The distribution of planets among these three groups of signs will indicate the basic nature and disposition of the individual's behavior and relationships. A predominance of planets in the last four signs characterizes a highly evolved soul. It may have to undergo much suffering and face many ordeals in life, but these trials will influence the individual in such a way that his Divine nature unfolds and his spirituality is strengthened.

There are four primary motivational urges, namely artha (meaningfulness), dharma (righteousness), kama (passionate attachment to objects of sensual satisfaction), and moksha (liberation from the bondage of birth and death). These urges impel people toward different kinds of activity. The different asterisms have been classified according to these four categories as follows:

ARTHA	DHARMA	KAMA	MOKSHA
Bharani	Ashwini	Krittika	Rohini
Punarvasu	Pushya	Ardra	Mrigashira
Magha	Ashlesha	Purva Phalguni	Uttara Phalguni
Swati	Vishakha	Chitra	Hasta
Jyeshta	Anuradha	Mula	Purvashadha
Shravana	Dhanishta	Uttara Bhadra	Uttarashadha
Purva Bhadra	Shatabhishak		Revati

Depending upon the distribution of planets among these four categories of asterisms, it will be possible to understand the basic motivational urges activating different aspects of the individual's life. The quality of the inner man which directs the personality along different lines of activity can therefore be examined on the basis of these four categories of nakshatras.

In the early stages of evolution, the soul garners a multiplicity of experiences. The planets seldom assume any specific configuration. When sufficient knowledge of the different aspects of life has been gathered, the soul begins its specialized mission. At this stage, swift cancellation of karmic debts has to be made, fresh lessons have to be learned without losing much time, and the course of evolution becomes specialized. In this phase, the planets begin to take on very meaningful configurations.

Often one will find that the lords of auspicious houses are placed in *their* inauspicious houses. That is, the lord of the Tenth house will be placed in the twelfth, sixth or eighth houses from the Tenth, which will reveal fruitless efforts. The lords of the Second and Fourth in similar position imply the squandering of wealth and many inconveniences in life. The lord of the Fifth house in a similar position will indicate frustration from progeny. The Ascendant lord in the Twelfth house may portend grand failure of the life in general. Such conditions with regard to a large number of houses will indicate that the individual had been very cruel, acquisitive and demanding in his past lives, without any consideration for the feelings and rights of others. Such individuals will suffer as a result of their past sins of omission and commission so that they may become sensitive to the legitimate rights of others and be oriented toward helping people.

Similarly, one may find that the lords of most of the houses are in their inimical signs. Again, when the auspicious effect of a benefic is spoiled by conjunction with a malefic, some karmic force is at work. This rule is applicable only when these conditions are present in a spectacular manner, not just in one or two instances.

When correct behavior in an individual becomes prominent, that individual receives helpful conditions. These conditions are noticeable by the presence of planets in trine to each other (five houses apart). If such situations arise, it can be surmised that the life of the individual will be very creative. He will have a special set of opportunities with which he can make an impact. He will be a pioneer in several lines of activity.

Often it is found that many planets are clustered in one or two houses of a horoscope. Such configurations show that the individual's life has begun to crystallize. The individual has entered incarnation in order to fulfill certain special tasks. All the prognostications in such cases should be made with special regard to those house divisions. Such an individual is provided with special opportunities and ordeals, each of them intended to develop certain qualities urgently needed for his mission and to strengthen those qualities which enable him to achieve it.

2
SPECIAL PLANETARY
COMBINATIONS

AVATAR OR AMSAVATAR YOGA

Evolved souls incarnate into this world with special missions to fulfill, and astrological configurations sometimes reveal this quality in a soul, as well as its mission. Such highly evolved persons are rare. During the course of our lives, we may encounter only one or two people whose inner development and union with the life-force are so highly realized, whose consciousness transcends birth and death. This sensitivity of consciousness is a quality which has developed over several lives. The individual concerned need not be aware of those past lives, but an intuitive knowledge of human psychology, a profound grasp of ancient wisdom, and an impersonal approach to life reflected in detachment from the fruits of effort will reveal that maturity of soul. Some intimation of spiritual purpose may be gleaned from such an individual's natal chart.

There are three conditions for the yoga or planetary combination which describes such an individual. First, the Ascendant must be in a Cardinal sign. The yoga is effective whether the Ascendant is Aries, Cancer, Libra or Capricorn, but in actual practice the ascending sign will reveal a great deal about the specific mission of the incarnating soul. With Aries as the Ascendant, the soul is struggling to begin something new in the world, which can imply changing the course of human thinking and lifestyle. Such persons will be heralds of new ideas, new utopias and philosophies. When Cancer is the Ascendant, the individual will function like a mighty ocean; diverse kinds of people will come to him with their woes and sorrows, problems and confusion, and the person will enlighten them and assuage their sorrows. Libra ushers in a soul which is externally very quiet and balanced, but which inwardly shoulders the problems and pressures of the world. Such persons will suffer for others, but will provide some kind of peace and harmony to the world and society in which they live. Individuals born under Capricorn have the potential to reach great heights; such a person may be born to relinquish completely his personal life in order to realize universal feelings and emotions. When an individual is ready for self-regeneration at a higher level of existence, he is born under Capricorn Ascendant. For Avatar or Amsavatar Yoga, the first condition is that the individual must be born with a Cardinal sign rising.

Second, Jupiter and Venus must be in a quadrant, i.e., in one of the Cardinal houses. This condition, as will be clearly seen, is a reflection of spirituality of the soul. When Jupiter is angular, it will powerfully influence the individual as well as his involvement in the external world. A kind of altruism, philanthropy and deep insight into ancient wisdom will be ingrained in him. Such an attitude results from maturity acquired in previous lives. With Venus in one of these houses, one does not incline towards indulging in the base or material aspects of life; rather, one possesses a highly sensitive consciousness which is electrical in its operation and swift in understanding the feelings and emotions of others. Jupiter and Venus in the quadrants by themselves are sufficient to raise the evolutionary level of a person.

Third, Saturn must be exalted (i.e., in Libra). The exaltation of Saturn is fairly uncommon and occurs only for a period of two years during the twenty-nine year orbit of the planet around the zodiac. An exalted Saturn produces a seer whose sight transcends the known and the living. It encourages tremendous spiritual powers. In personal life it may create hardship and deprivation, but detachment, magic powers, control over the invisible forces of Nature, and the strength to face the annihilation of the ego are some of the features of an exalted Saturn in the Cardinal houses.

The individual whose horoscope contains all these elements will have profound wisdom and be learned in ancient traditions. His personal life will be spotless and people will gather around him, providing the temptation for his ego to become infatuated. He will wander far and wide, meet many learned persons and establish religious movements which give solace to many people. He will have a large following, and much power at his command. He will be able to shape the destiny of the society in which he lives and the people who surround him. Such a destiny may seem very attractive, but individuals with this yoga are not necessarily happy in their personal lives; often they have to undergo many hardships. Their longevity may not be exceptional. This yoga indicates an extremely special person, but the price one has to pay for his gifts may be very high.

PANCHA MAHAPURUSHA YOGA
Five Combinations of Exalted Beings

The exaltation of the individual spirit, according to the astrological approach, does not depend upon material affluence, status or erudition; it is founded upon the maturity of the soul. The life of a human being is a continuity extending over various incarnations and several aeons during which different life-currents are vivified. For a better understanding of this concept, one may consult Shankaracharya's *Viveka Cudamani*,[1] wherein he describes the essential nature of man and the various sheaths which constitute that essence.

Astrologically, different planets have affinity with different principles whose unfoldment and maturity determine the real stature of man. The highest principle in man is energized by the Sun. The passive or receptive principle has affinity with the Moon, which is also linked with Mahat or cosmic ideation. On the objective realm of existence, Mercury and Venus together hold sway over the Anandamaya Kosha, Vijnanamaya Kosha, and Manomaya Kosha, which reflect the association of atman with tamas (egotism) and avidya (creative illusion).[2] Mars is connected with the Pranamaya Kosha, which directs the vivifying life-current to the human personality and circulates blood through the veins. Jupiter channels the akashic element and sustains the etheric double of the person, which enables him to maintain the integration of his consciousness with the body and all its passions. Saturn is associated with Annamaya Kosha, reflecting the five organs of activity and protecting the dissipation of the gross physical body into the five elements constituting the physical personality of the person.

The exaltation of the human being from the point of view of the enduring soul depends upon the maturity and perfection of the different energy-impulses which ensoul the five objective levels of existence. The luminaries, being concerned with the formless component of being, are always subjective and as such they do not contribute to this astrological combination for exaltation of the individual. In fact, their association or aspect on the planets will nullify the effect. The Nodes of the Moon, being the dispositors of karmic restrictions on the individual's activities, spoil the exaltation of the individual by their association or aspect. The astrological combination indicating the exalted nature of the inner man depends upon the five planets — namely Mercury, Venus, Mars, Jupiter and Saturn — being in exaltation, mulatrikona, or in their own signs and

---

1   This work is usually rendered in English as *The Crest Jewel of Discrimination.*

2   The koshas are subtle "sheaths" surrounding the physical body. A fuller discussion can be found in Volume III of the present series (forthcoming), in Shankaras's classic (cited above), or in *From the River of Heaven*, by David Frawley, Salt Lake City, Passage Press 1990. pp. 100-101.

posited in quadrants. Whichever planet is thus posited will reflect a corresponding maturity of the principle signified by that planet in the consciousness of the individual. This combination does not require all five planets to be so placed simultaneously: that is, in fact, an impossibility.

There are four conditions for the applicability of this combination. First, one or more of the five planets must be exalted, in mulatrikona, or its own sign. Second, the planet involved in the combination must be in a quadrant; that is, in the First, Fourth, Seventh or Tenth house. Third, the aspect or association of the lords of the Third, Sixth, Eighth and Twelfth houses will spoil the yoga. Fourth, the association of the luminaries with the planet bestowing this yoga will dim its influence, though the nature of the planetary combination will remain auspicious to a great extent.

When MERCURY causes this yoga, its effect is primarily on the Mahat Principle, implying that it activates the mind's potential. The possibility of discovering the truths of Nature is greatly increased, and, on discovering the same, the knowledge is disseminated to the world for its general use. Piercing intelligence, an attention turned towards earthly advantage, and success in all endeavors are the chief influences of this combination. Mercury links abstract subjective principles with objective existence. That is why Hermes has winged heels and Narada frequents both Heaven and Earth at his ease. The Mind Principle is the root of mental phenomena at all levels. It is expressed as cosmic ideation of the unmanifest cosmic Logos at the highest level and is then reflected in mental phenomena of all degrees of subtlety in different realms of manifestation. The perfection of this principle will bestow immense confidence, the power to raise one's consciousness to the highest level of abstraction, profound learning, and eagerness to share one's wisdom with others. Under such an influence, the individual may also be opinionated, willing to teach others but reluctant to receive suggestions from them; he will be unforgiving to his own relations. He will be spiritual in nature, but his libido will also be very strong. In its full expression BHADRA YOGA, as this combination is called, will make the individual look upon others as his responsibilities. He will be rich, affluent, surrounded by a loving wife and children, but his heart will pine for something he has not yet achieved. Bhadra Yoga is a mysterious combination of spirituality and gross earthiness.

MALAVYA YOGA is present when VENUS is involved. Knowledge, egotism, and a veil over the spiritual world produce the creative impulse which leads the soul towards deeper layers of materiality. Such a creative impulse provides the individual with a unique luster; his ethics may be less remarkable than his sociability. He enjoys all the conveniences of life. His knowledge of spiritual literature is extensive — and he may use that knowledge to convince others of his point of view and to justify his activities. He has competence, energy and initiative; he has the required skill to utilize the secret laws of Nature for his own advantage and to attain his desires. Venus represents the Divine impulse moving towards intensifying the manifestative process. As such, Malavya Yoga leads to the acquisition of material comforts and sensual enjoyment (often including deviant sexual acts), but the person with Malavya Yoga nevertheless provides sustenance to a large number of persons.

With MARS in exaltation, mulatrikona, or his own sign posited in a quadrant, RUCHAKA YOGA activates the life principle and vivifies the Pranamaya Kosha. Inaction, introversion, or a smooth course of life will destroy the vital spirit of such a person. He wants to kill his prey with his own strength and earn his food with the sweat of his brow. He knows how to achieve his mission. He has the necessary energy and skill to gain his purpose. Ruchaka Yoga provides all that a man of the world desires: tremendous power, victory over enemies, accomplishment in spells, the power to kill as well as to attract, devotion to learned men and respect for saints and sages. The keynote of Ruchaka Yoga is energy in action which can brook no resistance, but once the adversary is subjugated the victor will be generous. People born with Ruchaka Yoga love conflict, express themselves in perfection only when there are difficulties, show quick judgment, are sensitive to the finer feelings of others, and can be very affectionate. They are highly spiritual, but cruel at times; they seek order and discipline, but they love struggle and strife. When confronted with serious difficulties, their balance of mind, discriminatory intelligence, and inner understanding of the laws of Nature blossom forth. They always work from the center to the circumference, which introduces the element of polarity or contradiction in their day-to-day living.

HAMSA YOGA is produced by JUPITER, the adviser of the gods, learned in scriptures. The Jovian influence protects and sustains manifestation. When this planet produces the exaltation of the individual, he has a quality of benediction wherever he goes; he radiates Divine spirituality. Operating on the material planes of existence, he is highly productive, creative, and protective. He regulates his own personal conduct and is capable of advising others on their spiritual path. He is graceful, attractive, and commanding. He is known for learning, well-versed in exoteric knowledge, and engaged in producing learned treatises, but his greatest weakness is his libidinous disposition. He may be married to a very desirable woman, but he is never satisfied with any one woman. Hamsa Yoga produces an insatiable urge for sexual relationship, and anyone coming in contact with such a person will be regarded as a sexual object.

But the possessor of Hamsa Yoga will command respect despite his insatiable sexuality.

SHASHA YOGA is produced by the exaltation of SATURN. This yoga also produces a great urge for sexual relationship, but of a different kind. The individual has the disposition of a leader, and though physically he is not beautiful, he likes sex in its various expressions. He does not treat sex merely as an act for satisfying carnal passions, but rather as a means of establishing rapport with the inner core of the other person. Any expression of pure lust repels him, but the expression of erotic feelings as indicators of a love relationship between two persons soothes him immensely. As a result of his relationship with different types of persons, he acquires much insight into their problems and modes of expression. This gives him insight into human character. He can see the faults and weaknesses of others very easily. He is often learned. His knowledge consists of esoteric wisdom; his wanderings among forests and inaccessible places are induced by his thirst for spiritual experiences. Shasha Yoga makes the individual outwardly an ordinary person with ordinary conveniences in life, but his leadership ability is phenomenal. He leaves an imprint on the society in which he lives. He may establish a school of philosophy which contains much wisdom. He leads large numbers of people by his good advice and spiritual knowledge. Shasha Yoga does not so much operate on the external plane as on inner and subjective levels. The individual's fondness for lonely places, mountains, rivers and fortresses are expressions of his essential subjectivity, which is less favorably expressed as impatience, cruelty and an unconventional lifestyle. Shasha Yoga produces inner greatness through a vision of eternity and complete detachment from worldly life.

NEECHABHANGA RAJAYOGA
Cancellation of Debilitation

Neechabhanga Rajayoga is the cancellation of the debilitation of a planet. Debilitation radically changes the nature of a planet. Even a benefic planet, when in debilitation, loses its power to generate auspicious results. The destructive nature of a malefic planet is greatly enhanced under this situation. But there are certain configurations under which the adverse nature of a fallen planet is transformed into one producing unusual prosperity. Basic astrological principles indicated earlier might indicate the rationale for such a transmutation, but the emphasis here is not merely on the nullification of adverse effects, but on turning the adverse into the beneficial. Under this combination, the planet concerned bestows exceptional results in improving the status of the individual.

There are several variations of this combination. Basically, it involves the planet which rules the debilitation sign of the planet involved or the planet which rules the sign in which the fallen planet would be exalted. The most important variation involves three conditions. First, the planet in question must be in its debilitation or fall. Second, the ruler of the sign in which the concerned planet is fallen or the ruler of its exaltation sign must be in a certain relationship to the Ascendant or Moon sign. Third, the specific relationship must be that the planet ruling the exaltation or debilitation sign must lie in a kendra (angle) from the Moon or Ascendant. This is the most important Neechabhanga configuration.

Another version of this combination stipulates that the lord of the debilitation sign of the planet and the lord of its exaltation sign should be in angular relationship to each other. This condition does not necessarily require them to be in any special relationship with the Ascendant or Moon sign.

The third variation of this combination stipulates that the lord of the debilitation sign of the planet must aspect the debilitated planet. This combination only acquires great strength if the debilitation does not occur in the Sixth, Eighth or Twelfth houses.

The fourth type of combination occurs when the Navamsha lord of the debilitated planet is in a Cardinal house or trine with respect to the Ascendant and the Ascendant is in a Cardinal sign.

The effect of these configurations will differ according to the nature of the planets concerned and the special combinations which obtain in any natal chart, but all of them indicate a life of affluence, status, respect from the authorities, and honor from the state.

It may be interesting to examine some specific examples of these combinations. Let us suppose that the Sun is debilitated in the Fifth house, indicating that the Ascendant is Gemini. We shall assume that the Moon is in Aquarius. The planets which must generate Neechabhanga will be either Venus, lord of the sign of the Sun's debilitation, or Mars, the lord of the Sun's exaltation sign. These planets must establish a certain relationship to the Gemini Ascendant or with respect to the Moon sign, Aquarius.

If Venus has to generate Neechabhanga, it must be either in Virgo or in Sagittarius (quadrant from the Ascendant) or in Leo or Scorpio (quadrant from the Moon). Wherever Venus is placed in order to produce the beneficial effect of this combination, it will greatly strengthen the inherently benefic nature of the Sun or Moon. The placement of Mars, lord of the Sun's exaltation sign, will have to be either in the quadrants, where its power to bestow material riches and status is greatly enhanced, or in the Third or Sixth, where Mars acquires exceptional disposition.

We may examine other planets and variations of this combination, but we shall find that all the emerging situations lead to exceptional permutations and combinations of benefic effects. We need not go into details regarding every possible combination. We may, however, note that the debilitation of the Sun, unless nullified by this combination, would have made the individual bigoted, self-centered, dictatorial, and extremely selfish. As we have indicated earlier, any factor may be interpreted from the viewpoint of the Sun and Moon as well as the Ascendant. Thus we find in the present example that the lord of the eleventh house from the Sun (the Sun itself) is fallen, which will be detrimental for material gains. Putting the lord of the eleventh house from the Ascendant (Mars) in a favorable position greatly enhances the financial prosperity of the individual. Alternatively, the lord of the Fifth house (Venus) in a favorable position will counteract the depressive psychological traits of the Sun's fall and bestow benefic effects. If we could examine all possible situations involving Neechabhanga, we would find that there is always a sound reason for the affluence promised by this yoga. In fact, Neechabhanga Rajayoga may be considered as the summation of a number of basic principles and is intended to help the astrologer in pin-pointing the possibility of immense prosperity despite the seemingly adverse disposition of a given planet.

RAJA YOGAS
Kingly Combinations

The attainment of royal status or its modern equivalent in wealth and power is desired by almost everyone. Such a destiny is achieved by a combination of effort and good luck. Material affluence, riches, property and a legacy can be had by sheer fortuitous circumstances, but to command respect from others one has to develop many virtues. In astrological prediction, one distinguishes three features in this context. First, legacy or inherited wealth, wealth given by others or wealth acquired by surreptitious means belong to one category of affluence. Second, income earned through one's profession through the discharge of social obligations and through that which may be termed one's vocation or calling is classified in another category. Third, there are situations when the wealth possessed by an individual has little relationship with the status he enjoys. Such a situation can arise in the case of a learned person or a venerable philanthropist who is engaged in serving others; it can happen also in the case of a person whose demeanor is so powerful that everyone coming in contact with him experiences a sense of awe, a feeling of reverence, and a realization of his greatness which is unconnected with anything external to him. Astrologically, all three are distinguished according to planetary combinations. Raja Yogas are popularly understood as configurations which bestow wealth and power, but this is a misunderstanding. The confusion has arisen from the fact that ancient sovereigns enjoyed both power and wealth; such a position was related to planetary Raja Yogas. Since we live in a society which is no longer based on the power of monarchs, many people have come to believe that Raja Yogas "don't work." For this reason, it is necessary to clarify that the "kingly status" implied by Raja Yogas is not *necessarily* linked with monetary or financial possessions — though wealth is certainly possible with these combinations.

The kingly combinations or Raja Yogas occur primarily as a result of close relationships between the lords of Cardinal houses and trines, though there are numerous variations of this basic relationship. We have already dealt with the importance of Cardinal houses and the Spiritual Triangle and have stated that the Fourth and Tenth houses, as well as the Fifth and Ninth, have special importance in revealing karmic influences on the individual. Any relationship between the lords of these houses will indicate that past forces are contributing to the present activities of the native. Such factors generate conditions which are much more powerful than those which relate only to the present incarnation. Depending on the planets and houses concerned, the relationship between the lords of the Cardinal houses and the Spiritual Triangle produces the kingly combinations, elevating the status of the person to great heights.

The relationships stipulated under this combination are of four different kinds: first, an exchange in which the lord of a particular sign is in a sign whose lord is placed in the sign of the first planet. For example, Aries belongs to Mars and Leo to the Sun, so if the Sun is in Aries and Mars in Leo there is an interchange of sign lords.[3] Second, mutual aspects: for example, if Mars is placed in Cancer while Saturn is in Libra, Mars aspects Saturn with its fourth house aspect while Saturn aspects Mars with its tenth house aspect. This is an example of mutual aspects. Third, relationships established by only one aspect: for example, if Mars is in Leo and the Sun is in Pisces the Sun does not aspect Mars but Mars aspects the Sun — thus a relationship exists between the two. Fourth, the placement of planets in the same sign. If the lords of Cardinal houses and trines form

---

3   In Western astrology, this phenomenon is called mutual reception.

any of these relationships, Raja Yoga is created. The relationship established between only one of the quadrants and one of the trines is sufficient
for the production of this combination; if more of these houses are related,
the combination is greatly strengthened. While examining the generation
of Raja Yoga, it is important to see that the planets are not afflicted in any
way, either by association with the Third, Sixth or Eighth houses or with
their lords. This affliction nullifies Raja Yoga. Any other affliction, though
it may reduce the power of the yoga, does not nullify it completely.

Some of the variations of Raja Yoga are as follows:

1. The lord of the Ninth house is placed in the Tenth and the
lord of the Tenth is placed in the Ninth.
2. The lords of the Ninth and Tenth houses are both together in
the Ninth house.
3. The lords of the Ninth and Tenth houses are both in the Tenth
house.
4. The lord of any Cardinal house is linked with the lord of any
trine and with the lord of the Tenth.
5. (a) The lord of the Ascendant is in the Fifth House;
    (b) The lord of the Fifth is in the Ascendant;
    (c) The atmakaraka or planet which has attained the highest
longitude in any sign and the Putrakaraka, i.e., Jupiter, should
be in the Ascendant, Fifth house, their own Navamsha or their
exaltation signs, and aspected by a benefic. This combination
generates a combination for the attainment of supreme status
known as Maharaja Yoga.
6. The lord of the Ninth house and the atmakaraka are in the
Ascendant, Fifth house or Seventh house and aspected by
benefic planets.

In the present context, one may mention other combinations related
to the basic principle of relationship between the Cardinal houses and the
Spiritual Triangle. In order to appreciate the following kingly combination, it may be useful to note that there are several conditions under which
a planet assumes the role of a karaka planet or dispositor for the horoscope.
When planets are in their own, exaltation or friendly signs and in mutual
angles, they become karakas and produce auspicious results. If a planet
in either its own sign or in exaltation is in Cardinal houses, it becomes
yogakaraka, but its placement in the Tenth house strengthens its benefic
power even more. If the Second, Fourth and Fifth houses from the karaka
planet or from the lord of the Ascendant are associated with benefic
planets, the configuration not only raises the status of the native, it also
bestows much wealth.

Some other combinations which may be mentioned in the present context are related to the exaltation and debilitation of planets. When a planet attains exaltation, it acquires special benefic strength and is capable of bestowing many favorable results. Similarly, when a planet is posited in one of the houses which comprise the Sea of Immutability it generates mysterious influences which under certain situations could prove very favorable for the native. When one of the lords of the signs constituting the Sea of Immutability or a planet in exaltation is placed in houses which are related to wealth, honor and status, a large number of forces come into operation. Each of these combinations will have its own unique influence on the native, but their auspicious potential will certainly come into fruition. Some of these combinations can be described as given below:

1. The Ascendant, Second and Fourth houses are occupied by benefics, and the Third house afflicted by a malefic.

2. The Second house is occupied by the Moon, Jupiter, Venus or Mercury in exaltation.

3. The Third, Sixth or Eighth house is occupied by a planet in debilitation, while the Ascendant is aspected by its lord from its own or exaltation sign.

4. The lord of the Tenth is posited in its own or exaltation sign and aspects the Ascendant, and all the benefics are placed in Cardinal houses.

5. The lords of the Sixth, Eighth, and Twelfth aspect the Ascendant while in their debilitation.

6. The lords of the Fourth, Tenth, Second and Ascendant aspect the Ascendant, and at the pada there is the association of a benefic planet, and the Eleventh house from the pada is aspected by Venus: under this combination the native becomes a ruler or like a ruler. (Pada is decided on the basis of the placement of the lord of the Ascendant. If the Ascendant lord is in the fifth house from the Ascendant, then the fifth house from the Fifth house will be the pada of the Ascendant. If the lord of the Ascendant is in the sixth house from Ascendant, the sixth from the Sixth house is the pada).

There is a general rule that any relationship between the lords of the Ninth, Tenth, Eleventh, First and Second makes these houses very auspicious for the native and provides much wealth and income for him. In this context, it is not necessary that *all* the related planets must be placed in the stipulated houses; if even one of them is so placed, the auspicious behavior of the planet is assured. In fact, the kingly combinations are many and their results have to be carefully assessed. Even malefics and badly placed planets (e.g., in debilitation signs) sometimes, as we have seen above, produce very auspicious combinations. Even if a planet is malefic by its rulership of the Third, Sixth, or Eleventh house, it produces auspicious results during its sub-period under the main period[4] of the dispositor of the Raja Yoga. Even Rahu and Ketu, which are ordinarily considered as malefics generating karmic retribution, produce Raja Yoga if they are posited in a quadrant and establish relationship with the lord of a trine, or if they are posited in a trine establishing relationship with the quadrant lord. In this case, it is to be noted that only one of the Nodes will be so placed in this situation: in a trine, both the Nodes will not be so placed.

There is one condition for the nullification of Raja Yoga. If the combination is formed by the association of the lords of the Ninth and Tenth houses, and one of these is also the lord of the Eighth or of the Eleventh house, their association does not constitute a kingly combination, though the planet generating the combination may bestow mildly auspicious results.

Raja Yoga combinations are nullified under certain conditions which generate contrary forces. The most important nullifying combinations are REKHA, which produces poverty, PRESHYA, which leads to dependence and servitude, and KEMADRUMA, under which the person becomes sorrowful, dependent, and involved in wrong-doing. If all the malefic planets, namely the Sun, Mars, Saturn and a weak or waning Moon are in Cardinal houses which correspond to their debilitation[5] or inimical signs, and if, at the same time, they are aspected by benefic planets occupying the Twelfth, Eighth and Sixth houses, the combination will destroy Raja Yoga. The number of combinations which exemplify this rule is in fact rather limited; the degree of restriction should be judged according to how many planets are actually involved.

REKHA YOGA is constituted by eight types of combinations:

1. The Ascendant lord is weak and is aspected by the lord of the Eighth house while Jupiter is combust.
2. The Navamsha lord of the Fourth house lord is combust and is aspected by the lord of the Twelfth house.

---

4   For planetary periods and sub-periods, see Volume III of the present work (forthcoming).
5   For instance: the Sun is debilitated in Libra, the seventh sign. This corresponds to the Seventh house, which is a cardinal house.

3. The lord of the Fourth house is aspected by the lord of the Sixth house, the lord of the Ninth and the lord of the Eighth house are in the Fifth, and the lord of the First house is in its debilitation sign.

4. Benefics are posited in the Sixth, Eighth and Twelfth house, the quadrants and trines hold malefics, and the lord of the Eleventh house is weak.

5. The Ascendant lord is associated with malefics, Venus and Jupiter are combust, and the lord of the Fourth house is both associated with a malefic and combust.

6. The lord of the Ninth house is combust while the Ascendant lord and the lord of the Second house are in their debilitation signs.

7. Three planets are either debilitated or combust while the Ascendant lord is either weak or placed in the Sixth, Eighth, or Twelfth house.

8. There are malefics in the First, Second, Third, Fourth, Fifth, Seventh, Ninth, Tenth, or Eleventh houses aspected by debilitated, inimical or malefic planets.

In any of these combinations, the individual will suffer from poverty, sorrow, disease, and misfortunes of various kinds. Raja Yoga will lose much of its strength in the presence of any of these combinations.

PRESHYA YOGA is of several kinds. Some of the more important combinations are as follows:

1. When the Sun is in the Tenth house, the Moon in the Seventh, Saturn in the Fourth, Mars in the Third and the Ascendant is Cardinal while Jupiter is in the Second house, the native works "the graveyard shift," for others rather than for himself.

2. In the case of a person born with a fixed Ascendant, if Venus is in the Ninth, the Moon is in the Seventh, Jupiter is lord of the Ascendant or the Second house, and Mars is in the Eighth, Raja Yoga is nullified and the person becomes the "unappreciated employee of another."

3. If the birth is at night-time, the Ascendant in a Cardinal sign, the Ascendant lord at the bhava sandhi (i.e., at the border of two house divisions), and a malefic occupies a quadrant, the individual labors for an unsympathetic employer. The same is true if the birth is during day-time and Saturn, the Moon, Jupiter, or Venus occupying a quadrant or a trine are at the border of two house divisions while the Ascendant is in a fixed sign.

4. Preshya Yoga will operate when Mars is at the border of the

Sixth house, Jupiter at the border of the Fourth, and the Sun at that of the Tenth. This configuration completely strips the three most important planets of their power.

5. One is likely to overlook the effect of a malefic Navamsha which radically changes the disposition of an auspicious configuration of planets. If the Moon is in the Navamsha of a malefic planet, then — even if it is in a benefic sign while Jupiter is in conjunction with the Ascendant lord — misfortune will follow the native.

6. An inauspicious Jupiter in debilitation occupying the Eighth, Twelfth, or the Sixth house while the Moon is in the Fourth will greatly limit the status of the individual, making him occupy a very humble place in society.

7. Saturn spoils Raja Yoga if it is lord of the Ninth and is in the Second or the Fifth house aspected by a malefic, or if it occupies the Sixth house along with a malefic. A similar result occurs when Saturn is in the tenth house from the Moon, or in the Second, Fifth or Ninth house (from the Ascendant) while the Eighth house is occupied by a malefic.

We have seen above the nullifying effects of an adverse Saturn or a weak Moon, or of combustion and powerlessness of the benefic planets. KEMADRUMA YOGA results in the absence of any planet being on either side of the Moon. (The Sun is not taken into account in this configuration). In the presence of Kemadruma, all Raja Yogas become powerless. But there are many factors which nullify Kemadruma itself. One of the most important of these factors is when the Moon is in a quadrant or associated by conjunction with any planet. If the Moon occupies the Navamsha of a sign occupying a quadrant, the effect of Kemadruma Yoga is eliminated. If *all* other planets aspect the Moon, even when it is Kemadruma, the power of the luminary is greatly enhanced, and if Raja Yoga is present in the horoscope it is very much strengthened by this configuration. Auspicious results blossom forth when the Moon under Kemadruma is full and in the sign of a benefic.

The presence of Raja Yoga in a horoscope raises the status of the individual, and, under certain favorable conditions, it also generates much wealth for the native, but there are many nullifying conditions, mainly arising from the inauspicious placement of the benefics. An adverse Saturn, a weak Mars or Sun, an afflicted or unsupported Moon greatly reduce the impact of Raja Yogas but even when the kingly combinations are nullified by other configurations in a natal chart, they are not *com-*

pletely wiped out and they do make an impact on the life of the person concerned.

MOON-JUPITER COMBINATIONS

The Moon and Jupiter are the two most important planets for sustaining and protecting humankind. Combinations between them generate helpful influences. Some of them have already been referred to, but there are two very significant yogas connected with these planets which may be highlighted here. They are known as GAJAKESHARI YOGA and SAKATA YOGA. Under the influence of the former, the individual is said to destroy all his enemies like a lion. He will speak gracefully in assembly; he will be passionate in his behavior. He will be long-lived, highly renowned and exceedingly intelligent. Sakata Yoga, however, is an inauspicious combination which often makes the individual lose his wealth and status, though he will regain the same again and again. The individual with this combination will be a very ordinary and insignificant person in the world: he will suffer from mental anguish and encounter several heart-rending calamities. Mention has already been made of ADHI YOGA, which stated that benefic planets occupying the Sixth, Seventh, and Eighth houses from the Moon raise individuals to the heights of prosperity and pleasure and help them overcome their foes and live long lives free of diseases and dangers.

Gajakeshari Yoga

Gajakeshari Yoga stipulates that Jupiter must be in an angle from the Moon, or that benefics such as Venus, Jupiter and Mercury, without being debilitated or combust the Sun, should aspect the Moon. In the latter version of the combination Mercury and Venus must occupy the seventh house from the Moon, otherwise they cannot cast an aspect upon it, while Jupiter may be in the fifth or the ninth house from the Moon. The classical astrological texts have indicated several other variations for the occurrence of Gajakeshari. Parashara[6] stated that Jupiter in a quadrant from the Ascendant or Moon in association with or aspected by benefics which are neither debilitated, combust, or in the Sixth house produces Gajakeshari Yoga. All these combinations are considered auspicious: they make the native graceful, powerful, indomitable, wealthy, intelligent, learned, skillful and favored by the state.

---

6   Parashara was one of the astrological sages or rishis, author of the important astrological scripture entitled *Brihat Parashara Hora Shastra.*

Essentially, Gajakeshari Yoga refers to the capabilities of the Moon. The basic influence of this luminary is to develop the inner Divinity which reflects the universal Sun. When the Moon is weak or afflicted, its capabilities cannot blossom, but under the favorable impact of Jupiter — who develops latent faculties, protects the individual from any harm, and sustains evolving entities — the Moon is empowered to bestow all its potential blessings. This can happen when Jupiter is in the seventh house from the Moon, but it is better still when in the fifth or ninth from that luminary. Planets in affliction, fall, or adverse houses lose their benefic nature, thus such aspects are detrimental for the unfolding of lunar impulses. If the Moon enjoys Gajakeshari in any of its variations, it should enable the individual to overcome any difficulty he may have to confront; it will certainly provide him with adequate opportunities whereby he may succeed in developing his latent faculties and attain a higher status in life.

Sakata Yoga

The placement of Jupiter in the sixth or eighth house from the Moon also implies the Moon in the eighth or sixth from Jupiter. The two planets involved in this yoga are the greatest benefics of the planetary system, while the two houses concerned are the most inauspicious houses. The relationship between the two, though dreaded, does not necessarily produce devastating results. The combination exists in the natal charts of many persons who have attained very high status in life. The occurrence of this relationship between the two planets is common. The texts qualify this yoga by stating that it is nullified when the Moon is angular, though in fact either the Moon *or* Jupiter in a quadrant will counterbalance the malefic influences of Sakata Yoga, and the alleged malefic influence of this combination itself must be understood clearly.

The Sixth and Eighth houses are part of the Sea of Immutability and, as such, they help to churn up the eternal component of each individual and bring it to the surface. But before the life-giving nectar is received, the poison which emerges has to be assimilated into the system. In the sixth or eighth house relationship between the Moon and Jupiter, this process of churning the Sea of Immutability is intensified on the Buddhic plane represented by the Moon. The churning is done by Jupiter, and the basic objective is to spiritualize and transmute the animal nature into the Divine. When these two planets are unconnected with angular houses or trines, the churning does not reach the enduring part of one's eternal existence. Under such a situation, the mind is agitated by deprivation or denial of certain physical aspects of life without any satisfying outcome. The individual feels sorrowful. One often observes that the precise effects of Sakata Yoga are almost impossible to predict; only loss, deprivation, sorrow, mental anguish and other such reactions can be anticipated. These reactions are expressions of lunar agitation. Jupiter in the sixth or eighth from the Moon agitates the eternal substratum of the Buddhic consciousness. If the Moon is in a sixth or eighth house relationship with Jupiter, or Jupiter in such a relationship with the Moon, the Jovian influence of protecting, sustaining, and developing or unfolding the spirituality is struck by the cold-wave of the Moon: Jupiter is fruitful when the individual is active (i.e., with a Cardinal house emphasis) because only in such a situation can there be transformation, which is the prime objective of Jupiter's influence. The sixth-eighth relationship between the Moon and Jupiter affects the flow of consciousness. Activated by the external conditions of life, these influences guide the individual to realize the enduring aspect of the Self, which is expressed as transformation. Transformation is possible only when the past forces represented by the trines or vital activities represented by the quadrants are activated. Otherwise, Sakata Yoga may produce only mental anguish without any redress. And because the Moon is involved in it, and because Sakata Yoga is a combination which operates throughout one's life and aims at changing one's outlook toward the various events of existence, the periodicity or cyclical nature of the Moon will always be present.

KALA SARPA YOGA

Kala Sarpa Yoga is neither a combination of penury nor of affluence, but a mysterious configuration revealing that the Lords of Karma have made certain important decisions regarding karmic retribution in the life of the person concerned. The very word Kala, which ordinarily means "Time" or a portion of Time, also refers to the Supreme Spirit as the destroyer of the universe, personified as Yama, the god of death. Sarpa is a serpent, but the word also refers to a serpentine or winding motion, something undulating. As a compound, Kala Sarpa means the undulation of time, the inner hidden forces creeping stealthily through life. The planetary combination denoted under this name produces its unhappy results *mysteriously*, without any other astrological indications. In this sense, Kala Sarpa Yoga is a dreaded combination. It foils all human efforts to transcend it; its hold is firm and escape from it is impossible.

Kala Sarpa Yoga is produced when all the planets are encircled within the two Nodes of the Moon. If, for instance, Rahu is at 15° Gemini and Ketu at 15° Sagittarius and all seven planets lie within this distance (either between Gemini and Sagittarius or Sagittarius and Gemini) Kala Sarpa Yoga is created, though some astrologers believe that its effect will be different depending on which side of the axis the planets lie. For instance, if they are situated in the houses between Gemini and Sagittarius, the combination will deny the fruits of past karma, i.e., destiny and "good luck," while the native's personal initiative, career potential, social and intellectual activities and religious pursuits will not be impeded. This is because the signs which lie between Gemini and Sagittarius (i.e., Cancer, Leo, Virgo, etc.) are concerned with aspects of life which come to us from our karmic past, whereas the opporite half of the zodiac (Capricorn, Aquarius, Pisces, etc.) is more concerned with actions accomplished in *this* incarnation. One must, of course, give further consideration to the bhavas or houses in which the signs fall — i.e., the first seven houses are concerned with the fruits of the karmic past while the latter seven (assuming that only half of the Ascendant and the Seventh house lie on either side of the horizon, as noted in Rule 5 under 'Rules of Interpretation') represent the native's initiative and worldly activity. The meaning of Kala Sarpa Yoga in any given chart, therefore, is assessed by synthesizing the meanings of the relevant houses and signs.

According to a second view, however, this combination weakens the entire horoscope. The native feels helpless and is unable to achieve much in life; he fails to achieve even his legitimate rewards in any field of endeavor.

There is yet a third view, which holds that if all the planets lie in the sector between Rahu and Ketu, the native will suffer deprivation in terms of physical comforts and the material world, while if the planets lie between Ketu and Rahu, he will suffer karmic or psychological frustration in the form of complexes and general morbidity. Nothing in life will give such a person any sense of satisfaction.

Certain exceptions have been indicated for this combination. The effect of Kala Sarpa Yoga is considerably reduced with the presence of two or three exalted planets in the chart, along with a few Raja Yogas. If a few of the lords of the Second, Fourth, Ninth, and Tenth houses occupy quadrant positions or are in trine houses without being debilitated, aspected or flanked by malefics, and if instead they are exalted or in their own signs, the impact of this unfortunate combination is greatly alleviated and only minimal effects of the same are experienced. Many renowned persons who have made their mark on the society in which they lived, or persons who possessed much wealth, had Kala Sarpa Yoga in their natal charts. In view of such observations, the commonly held view is seriously questioned.

The importance of this combination is revealed by its association with a serpent, the Rahu-Ketu unity. In this form, Rahu-Ketu was certainly demonic, but had cooperated with the gods in order to retrieve the nectar from the Sea of Immutability, the Kshirasagar. Having partaken of the nectar, it has become immortal and assists the gods (the Divine Plan) in externalizing the contents of the Sea of Pure Essence, the latent powers in man and the powers hidden in Nature. The way this result is achieved is difficult to anticipate, but the Nodes act as agents of nemesis. They produce retributive justice; in all their operations they bring forth certain unique qualities of being, they externalize certain capabilities which otherwise might have remained latent for a long time.

Kala Sarpa Yoga is an uncommon combination: it occurs rarely. It is found in powerful personalities. What happens is that these individuals, during the course of their past lives and as a result of their reactions to certain conditions of life, have generated adverse forces harmful to their own growth. Being powerful personalities they have acquired strength and maturity in many ways. These qualities, once acquired, become an eternal part of the soul. When these adverse forces have to be counter-acted, the opportunities and initiatives of the individual have to be curbed and impeded. Such an impenetrable wall against individual effort creates frustration. Effort, though very powerful, proves ineffective against the invincible past. The serpent is a symbol of the eternity which preserves the memory of all our actions and produces appropriate counterbalancing forces in due time. When such handicaps are produced, an individual chafes, feels frustrated, and senses his own smallness in the face of a greater power. Realization of the difference between the individual and the universal produces the unhappiness that goes with this astrological combination.

Kala Sarpa Yoga expresses karmic nemesis. It enables the individual to realize that he has to function in a framework which is greater than himself. Any frustration or helplessness, whether arising due to limita-tions of wealth, bad health, family discord, social obloquy, or denial of opportunities, should be considered as the expression of a karmic coun-terbalancing force which may enable the individual to transcend the very sorrow and helplessness experienced as a result of this planetary config-uration. The presence of strong and benefic planets shows that the individual has already acquired maturity in many ways, and that it may be possible for him to absorb and assimilate the fruits of this combination easily and sensibly.

PARIVRAJYA YOGA
Combinations for Asceticism

Ascetism may be defined as the complete withdrawal from material-istic involvements and the alignment of oneself with the spiritual forces of nature. Such enlightenment comes after much preparation. Before the final stage of liberation or Nirvana is reached, the individual must develop altruism, philanthropy, charity, and spiritual perception. Passing through the preparatory stages, one must conform to certain mystical precepts whereby individual consciousness is disentangled from the non-essen-tials. The experience of these preparatory stages showing religious pro-pensities, a righteous attitude, the observance of rituals, psychic attainments, the initiation process, and the renunciation of material attach-ments can be predicted from various planetary combinations. Such an assessment, however, cannot be made merely on the basis of exoteric astrological rules; it requires an understanding of the spiritual occult laws guiding and regulating the individual and the society in which he lives, and the esoteric disposition of the planets. A planet in a particular house may produce excellent results, but the discerning astrologer, using his deeper understanding, may recognize the imperceptible uniqueness which, under seemingly similar planetary configurations, raises the indi-vidual to spiritual heights. In determining the efficacy of Parivrajya Yoga, one has to be very careful lest the thin line dividing it from combinations for penury is overlooked.

For asceticism, three planets, namely Saturn, the Moon and the Sun are very important. Esoteric astrology has assigned great significance to these planets. By considering the Sun as the soul of the universe, it not only states the physical importance of this fountainhead of life-giving energy, but also points to its sacred role as the highest hierophant on this Earth. It is only with the permission and active participation of the solar deity that aspirants to the secret knowledge of nature may pass through the portals of the mystery temple. The Moon represents the channel which must be purified in order to receive the secret — prior to which occult principles and practices will seem like meaningless abracadabra. Support from the Moon is essential for every kind of enlightenment. Saturn ignites the fire, burns the dross, destroys the material base of perception and understanding, makes the personal life of the individual desolate, and confronts him with the hard realities of life. It is only when the material dross has been burned away by Saturn and pure gold has been produced that the individual is united with his highest principles (represented by the Sun and Moon) and attains final liberation and renunciation of the material life. When life appears to the person in all its pristine glory without any veil of shadow, the individual is enlightened; he becomes one with life and light. Saturn, which is the planet of materialization, is also the planet without whose active instrumentation none can expect redemption from its thraldom.

In determining the combinations for enlightened asceticism, the association of Saturn with the Triangle of Spirituality is important. The Fifth house, an important angle of the triangle, represents intelligence, which, penetrating the veil of shadow and piercing the avarana shakti (the distortions caused by illusion), leads to understanding the laws of nature and love of God. The Fifth house impulse intensifies devotion to God. Under the impact of the Ninth house, the urge to involve oneself in spiritual pursuits, thus integrating everyday life with spiritual understanding, is intensified. With the appropriate influence from Saturn, the individual is denied the fruits of his efforts, and consequently he withdraws to dwell upon his religious practices and spiritual pursuits. That, in essence, is the beginning of asceticism. For the effective production of ascetic yogas, the integration of the Spiritual Triangle with Saturn in one way or another is essential.

If there are four or more planets in any one house of the birth chart, the natural astrological rules do not operate. Apart from combustion, which is merely one of the possibilities here, the interaction of divergent planetary impulses almost paralyzes the individual. Life becomes a serious problem for him; he finds the Gordian knot difficult to unravel. But, if one planet in the house is especially strong, it will induce the others to follow its lead and enable the individual to renounce the world. The nature of the strongest planet will determine the nature of the specific religious path that he will follow.

If the strongest planet is the Sun, the individual will adopt Vanyasana or Vanaprastha, under which he will lead the life of a recluse while still living in the world, unconcerned with affairs of the society in which he resides. Often, such persons "retire to the forests," but do not necessarily cut their links with society. The characteristics of such persons are simple living and exalted thinking, denoting a high intellectual and spiritual development. The powerful pull from the Sun will draw all the proclivities of a man or woman and absorb them in its inner essence: under such an impulse the psychic and psychological orientation of the person will be turned inward and he will transcend the chains of astro-mental compulsion.

Under the influence of the Moon, the individual will become a Vridha, meaning a venerable old man, or a guru, meaning a wise teacher. The removal of every impurity from the individual's consciousness also removes the distortions which lead to unreal relations — hence the ascetic with a powerful Moon can establish contact with the highest subjective core of his being. With an unimpeded flow of consciousness from the highest level of enlightenment, he will understand the universe and the Supreme Creator. A strange sense of humility captures the native, and he is swayed by the urge to "move from place to place with a skull-like begging-bowl in his hand."

When Mercury becomes the strongest planet in the group, the individual adopts the attitude of a Jivika or Dandin, who wanders around with mysterious understanding of the laws of life and the conditions surrounding everything, but is unattached to the external environment. All his experiences strengthen his understanding of reality, which in turn intensifies his dispassion. Venus produces an ascetic of the Charaka type who moves in regal splendor, externally enjoying all comforts, but inwardly poised in a sanctum sanctorum linked to the primordial cause. If Mars holds the power among the cluster of planets, the individual becomes a Shakya, a mendicant who worships Shakti or the female form of power, who believes in action and in transforming the world with the *power* of intelligence, like some types of Buddhist monks. When Jupiter becomes the predominant planet, the individual becomes a learned mendicant, a Bhiksu who wanders around begging for his living and disseminating knowledge and Divine wisdom, i.e., especially the Sankhya philosophy of manifestation.

Saturn as the most powerful among the planets producing the combination for asceticism impels the individual to abdicate everything, often even his clothes; all wisdom, all possessions. The asceticism of Saturn is extremely arduous, without any material support. Such individuals will have ethics of their own, dwelling on emptiness and communicating with God in the wilderness.

The asceticism produced by the planets, however, will take different forms depending upon the time and kind of society in which the individual lives. It is said that a man in the Vanaprastha order inspired by the Sun is "engaged in the practice of rigorous and devout penances." One under Saturn is "a naked ascetic dwelling in hills and forests." A Bhiksu under Jupiter is "an illustrious ascetic with a single staff, engaged ever and anon in contemplation of the truths of the sacred scriptures." One under Venus "wanders in many countries, undergoing different experiences." A Shakya under the impact of Mars is "impetuous, difficult to tame, often behaving in a disorderly manner." The Moon makes one "a celebrated teacher endowed with royal splendor," while the ascetic under Mercury is often "garrulous and gluttonous."

Obviously, the precise delineation of the nature of asceticism will depend upon the sign as well as the house in which the combination occurs, but essentially the clustering of four or more planets in a house without aspects from any other planet, and with at least one planet showing exceptional power, will produce an ascetic. If any kingly combination or Raja Yoga is present, the ascetic yoga will definitely manifest.

The influence of Saturn in producing asceticism can be observed in the following combinations as well:

1. The unaspected lord of the Ascendant aspecting Saturn produces asceticism.

2. An unaspected Saturn aspecting the Ascendant lord produces the same results. It is noteworthy that a mutual aspect between Saturn and the lord of the Ascendant does not produce asceticism. However, if there is such a mutual aspect, Divine discontent may be acute. One's own individualism will often clash with the annihilating influence of Saturn, but the essential dominance of the Supreme which must be present in order to manifest an ascetic yoga will be absent. For asceticism it is necessary that either the lord of the Ascendant should aspect Saturn or that the latter should aspect the former, but there should be no *mutual* aspect, no other planet should aspect either of them, and the strength of the two planets should not be equal.

3. The lord of the sign in which the Moon is placed is unaspected by any planet, but it aspects Saturn; if so, there will be asceticism.

4. If the Moon is in a Drekkana of Mars or Saturn and is unaspected by any planet *except* Saturn, asceticism arises. If, under this situation, the Moon is also in the Navamsha of Saturn, the ascetic yoga becomes very powerful.

From the above, it can be observed that Saturn's aspect on the lord of the Ascendant as well as on the lord of the Moon sign (unless it is nullified by any other aspect) produces a strong revulsion to the material world. Under such an influence, the individual does not enjoy his material attainments, but wishes to merge his individual life-spark in the universe. The annihilation of one's separate existence, of all consciousness of separateness, is the essential outcome of these ascetic combinations.

One of the ascetic combinations which creates much turmoil in the life of the individual and under which he becomes helpless and follows the path of renunciation arises from a combination of Saturn, Jupiter, the Moon and the Ascendant. We have already emphasized the importance of these planets in producing spiritual tendencies, and that the association of the Spiritual Triangle shows the involvement of karmic forces. The asceticism of this yoga does not arise due to any frustration with the material world, for the presence of a Raja Yoga is an essential feature of it. This yoga requires that Jupiter, the Moon, and the Ascendant be aspected by Saturn while Jupiter occupies the Ninth house. Such a person, born with a Raja Yoga, becomes a holy and illustrious founder of a system of philosophy and remains unattached to the world.

APPENDICES

CASTING THE
HOROSCOPE

STEP ONE

Casting a horoscope nrequires a sidereal ephemeris (Lahiri in this case) for the year concerned, and a table of Ascendants.

An Ephemeris gives the sidereal time as well as the longitudes of different planets. The first step in the preparation of a horoscope is to convert the time recorded at birth into Local Mean Time. Indian Standard Time is 5 hours 30 minutes in advance of Greenwich Mean Time: at 12 noon GMT, the IST will be 5:30 PM. We will assume that the birth took place at 25° 47' North and 84° 43' East, which implies that the time has to be advanced. For each degree of longitude, a time differential of 4 minutes is to be reckoned. If the longitude is east of Greenwich, the differential is to be *added* to the GMT, but if it is west of Greenwich, it has to be be *subtracted*. In the present case, the birth place is east of Greenwich, so the time differential is added. The time differential is obtained as follows:

84° 43' (or 84.7166667) degrees
    × 4 minutes
338. 8667 minutes = 5 hours 38 minutes 52 seconds

As IST is 5 hours 30 minutes in advance of GMT, the Local Time at the birthplace will be 8 minutes 52 seconds ahead of IST.

Assuming that birth took place at 11 hours 15 minutes in the morning (i.e., 11:15 AM) the Local Time will therefore be (11 hours 15 minutes) + (8 minutes 52 seconds) = 11 hours 23 minutes 52 seconds. (Often there is a slight correction to be made, which is also generally given in the ephemeris. For practical purposes we may ignore it, because very few births are recorded accurately to the second.)

STEP TWO

In order to find the longitudes of the different planets, we consult the ephemeris. We will assume the date of birth is 8th Februrary 1925 at 11:15 AM. Having converted the IST into Local Mean Time, we now consider the time of birth as 11 hours 23 minutes 52 seconds on 8th February 1925. First we shall consider the Moon's longitude.

From the ephemeris, we find that the daily motion of the Moon on that day was 12° 5', which is obtained by subtracting the Moon's longitude on 8th February 1925 as 21° 51' Cancer and 9° 46' Cancer on the previous day. This position is for 5:30 PM.

To obtain the longitude of the Moon at 11 hours 23 minutes 52 seconds, we have first to find —

Motion Log for 12° 5 minutes = .2980

As the time of epoch is 17 hours 54 minutes after 5:30 PM on 7th February, we have to get —

Time Log for 17 hours 54 minutes = .1274
Total of the two = .4254

The sum of the two is Log of 9 degress 15 seconds. Therefore the Moon's degree would be —

9° 46'Cancer + 9° 15" = 18° 46' 15" Cancer.

(NOTE: The above calculation has been done with the help of a logarithm table appended to the ephemeris, but the same can be worked out by simple arithmetical procedure on the basis of the time difference between the two intervals for which the longitudes of the planets are given; therefore the daily motion of the planets is available for calculation.)

STEP THREE
The determination of planetary longitudes is done similarly, on the basis of their postions in the ephemeris. If the daily motion of the planets is given, one could easily, as in the case of the Moon, work out the exact longitude of the planets. If the longitudes are given for longer intervals, the method is the same, though the process may be a little more complicated. But given the position for two different points of time, and having the time differential of the epoch from the beginning of the time interval, the simple arithmetical calculations or those based on the logarithmic tables, the required planetary positions can be ascertained.

For the above mentioned time, 11 hours 23 minutes 52 seconds on 8th February 1925, the planetary positions would be as follows:

1. Sun   26° 10' Capricorn
2. Moon 18° 46' Cancer (as already worked out under Step Two)

3. Mercury 8° 54' Capricorn
4. Venus 7° 32' Capricorn
5. Mars 9° 00' Aries
6. Jupiter 18° 45' Sagittarius
7. Saturn 21° 20' Leo
8. Rahu 20° 49' Cancer
9. Ketu 20° 49' Capricorn

STEP FOUR

Having fixed the position of different planets, the Ascendant is to be determined. This has to be done carefully. Generally speaking, adjustments have to be made in relation to the date, month, year and the place; therefore one has to examine the ephemeris as to whether and how many of these adjustments are needed for the sidereal time given there. In the present case, on the basis of sidereal times given for different dates of the year, it is found to be 21 hours 8 minutes 51 seconds for February 8, for which the correction for January–February 1925 was (+ 2 minutes 28 seconds), so the sidereal time for 8 February 1925 is found to be 21 hours 11 minutes 19 seconds.

The birth time is 36 minutes 8 seconds before the sidereal time, so the sidereal birth time is estimated at 20 hours 35 minutes 11 seconds.

STEP FIVE

On the basis of the table of Ascendants, one must now find the Ascendant for the given epoch. For the given latitude of the birthplace, the nearest available Ascendant is for 25° N 23', which is good enough for 25° N 47'. The Ascendant for 20 hours 36 minutes is given as 27° 13' Aries. The differential for 4 minutes is given as 1° 9', on the basis of which the differential for 50 seconds of sidereal time would be about 15 minutes less than the Ascendant given for 20 hours 36 minutes of sidereal time. The Ascendant for 20 hours 36 minutes is given as 27° 13' Aries, so 15 minutes can be subtracted from it to give 26° 58' Aries as the Ascendant.

On the basis of the data worked out above, the detailed Rashi chart can now be constructed.

GLOSSARY

Abhijit	A lunar mansion between Uttarashadha (21) and Shravana (22) formed by three stars including Vega. Being away from the path of the ecliptic, it is (generally) excluded from the twenty-seven nakshatras
Adi	Commencement, the First, Primordial
Aditi	The mother of Adityas; the Earth, Eternal Space or Boundless Whole; Cosmic Mother or the Primordial Substance (Mula-Prakriti)
Adityas	The sons of Aditi taken collectively; eight or twelve suns all of which shine together only at final dissolution; Divinity in general
Agni	Fire, the deity representing the life-giving energy in men and the entire manifestation. Agni (fire), Vayu (air), and Surya (sun) together constituted the Vedic trinity
Ahir Budhnya	The Dragon of the depth of the cosmic sea or wisdom
Ahi-Vritta	Literally the circular or round demon, serpent-demon; metaphysically, the indestructible force which impels the ego in the chain of life and death. Also refers to Rahu, a Node of the Moon
Aja	Unborn, eternally Brahma, an epithet of the Almighty. A ram, the sign Aries, a name of the Moon and of Kamadeva, the Indian Cupid
Aja Ekapad	The One-footed Goat. The Vedic deity without any objective existence while it sustains the entire universe: he makes the heaven and earth firm with his strength
Akasha	Sky, space, ether of the five elements. The primordial substance or spiritual essence which pervades all space
Alaya	A receptacle, the Universal Soul, identical with Akasha in its mystic sense
Anima Mundi	Life principle or world soul that pervades all

Artha	Object, purpose, aim, significance, import; attainment of worldly riches, prosperity, one of the four ends of human life
Ark	Essence, a flash of light, the sun, number 12
Aruna	Dawn personified as the charioteer of the Sun
Astral Light	A subtle principle surrounding our globe containing within it all its moral, psychic and physical emanations and radiating them back to the earth and establishing a link between the past, present and the future of human and terrestrial evolution
Atma	Essence, soul; the highest principle in man ever watching, and guiding the incarnating ego towards its Ultimate Destiny, contains within it no impurities or illusions concerning earthly birth and deaths
Atman	The Supreme Soul, the personified universal spirit, the highest principle in man and the universe
Aum or Om	The sacred word uttered as holy exclamation, represents Vedic trinity
Avidya	Ignorance, opposite of knowingness; illusion as well as illusion personified as Maya, the cause of incessant chain of births and deaths as well as the power enabling one to perceive the world around oneself; one of the twelve Nidanas of the Sankhya philosophy which are the twelve causes of sentient existence
Bhanu	The Sun
Bhumiputra	Son of mother Earth, the planet Mars
Bija	Seed
Bindu	Point
Brahma	The creator, one of the Hindu Trinity; others being Vishnu and Shiva
Buddhi	Intelligence, the second of twenty-five elements of Sankhya; an aspect of the higher triad of human individuals, others being Atma and Manas
Chakras	Circular disc, the force-centers located in human body
Chitra	The name of the fourteenth lunar mansion
Citta	Consciousness, one of the triple-aspect of divine consciousness; others being Sat (truth) and Ananda (happiness, bliss)

Conch   Shell-fish used in religious rites for invoking
                     Divine presence

Daitya   A demon

Daksha   Skillful; one of the ten sons of Brahma; father of
                     twenty-seven lunar mansions

Damaru   A small drum-like musical instrument resembling
                     an hour-glass and generally used in the worship of
                     Shiva and by Kapalikas

Deham   Body, the physical basis of any manifestation

Devas   Gods

Dharma   Customary observances, righteousness, that which
                     holds a being or any organization, essential
                     property or characteristics, one of the four ends of
                     human existence; others being artha (material
                     existence), kama (desire), and moksha (liberation)

Dwaja   A flag, standard ensign, the organ of generation

Dyuta   Gambling

Fohat   The essence of cosmic electricity, the active or
                     male potency, the Sakti or the female reproductive
                     power in nature

Guna   A quality, basic nature, characteristic property; one
                     of the seven categories or padarthas of the
                     Vaiseshikas; anyone of the three properties
                     belonging to all created things, these properties
                     being Sattwa (harmony), Rajas (activity), and
                     Tamas (inertia)

Hasta   The hand, trunk of an elephant, thirteenth lunar
                     mansion symbolized as a palm

Hiranyagarbha   Shinning, resplendent, the Golden Egg, the nuclear
                     matrix from which Brahma was born; Mother
                     Nature in essence

Ida/Ila   Androgynous daughter of Manu; wife of Budha
                     (Mercury. A channel of Prana on the left side of the
                     spine through which the feminine force flows up.
                     One of the three vital airs, the other two being
                     Sushumna and Pingal

Jagrata   Wakefulness, one of the four states of
                     consciousness, the other three being: Swapna
                     (dream), Sushupti (profound sleep), and Turiya (the
                     fourth state in which the soul becomes one with the
                     Supreme Spirit)

Jiva	Living or existing being; individual soul enshrined in the human body called Jivtma as opposed to Paramatma, the Supreme Soul Life, as the Absolute; also Atma-Buddhi
Jyestha	An eldest sister; name of the eighteenth lunar mansion; the middle finger, an epithet of the Ganges
Kaivalya	Detachment of the soul from matter, identification with the Supreme spirit; final emancipation; related to the Twelfth house in the horoscope
Kala	The black or dark-blue color, time, proper occasion for undertaking any work; time considered as one of the nine dravyas (elements) of the Vaiseshikas; Shiva or the Supreme spirit regarded as the destroyer of the universe; Yama, the God of death; the planet Saturn
Kala Purusha	The cosmic creative principle operative in time; the all pervading subtle principle; the manifested deity; astrologically macrocosmic being whose pulsating impulses throb in every form of manifestation including every human individual
Kalatrasthanam	The place of the wife, the location of the royal citadel; the Seventh house in the horoscope
Kama	Sexual urge, the God of love (Kamadeva), the principle of desire either cosmic or individual; the clinging of existence, usually the powerful weapon of Mara, the tempter; Desire as one of the four ends of existence
Kama-Manas	the desire-mind principle in man
Kama Rupa	The subjective form created through the mental and physical desires and thoughts in connection with things of matter, by all sentient beings, a form which survives the death of their bodies
Kanya	A maiden; name of Durga; Virgo, the sixth sign of the zodiac.
Karkatam	A crab; Cancer, the fourth sign of the zodiac
Karma	Action, duty, fate, consequences of acts done in former lives or during an earlier period; the law of cause and effect or ethical causation; its three types being Sanchita (accumulated), Prarabdha (starting or allocated during a specified period), and Agami or Kriyamana (future)
Kartikeya	Name of Skanda, the Indian God of War, son of Shiva, the personification of Logos; the planet Mars

Kendra	The center; the four Cardinal houses in the horoscope namely, the First (Ascendant), Fourth, Seventh, and the Tenth house
Klesha	Pain, anguish; pain and misery especially those arising from love for life; mainly connected with the Sixth house in the horoscope
Krittika	The third of the lunar mansions; foster mother of Kartikeya
Kshetra	The abode, repository, a place of pilgrimage, the sphere of action; the Great Deep, Prakriti, Space; Yoni, the female generative organ
Kshetrajna	The knower of the field, the Conscious Ego in its highest manifestation, the Soul; the reincarnating Principle
Kumbha	A pitcher; closing of the nostrils and mouth so as to suspend breathing; Aquarius, the eleventh sign of the zodiac
Kundalini	Decorated with earrings; circular, spiral, winding, coiling as a serpent; the Serpent Fire, one of the three types of Primordial Energy surrounding the Earth and inhering in man, the other two being Prana (life-breath) and Fohat (the essential cosmic electricity)
Lagna	Ascendant; the First house in the horoscope
Lokas	Planes, world or realms of beings
Mada	Pride, egotism
Mahabharata	An Indian epic depicting the war between Pandavas (the five) and the Kauravas (the hundred) who were brothers, Lord Krishna in this war was the charioteer of Arjuna from the side of the former while Brishman Pitamah who was their grand sire commanded the Kauraves till he was wounded on account of his own machination
Mahamaya	The great illusion; the mystic power of manifesting oneself in different objects of sense perception possessed by the World Mother (the cosmic generative principle); the Buddha's immaculate Mother-Mayadevi
Mahat	The great one; the first principle of cosmic mind and intelligence, the producer of mind and egotism; the second of twenty-four elements or tattwas

Makaram	A crocodile, an emblem of Cupid, an earring in the form of a crocodile; one of the treasures of Kubera; the tenth sign of the zodiac; esoterically, a mystic class of devas; the vehicle of Varuna, the water-god; a pentagon, the ten faces of the universe
Makka/Magha	The tenth lunar mansion
Manas	Mind, intelligence, the thinking principle or synthesizing sense which organizes and relates the sense organs with the sense objects. When unqualified it means the Higher Self or spiritual soul in contradistinction to its human reflection — Kama-Manas
Manomaya Kosha	The sheath of mental activities which receives all sense impressions and forms its own ideas thus giving rise to the idea of "I" and "Mine" and creates avidya or illusion
Mantra	A combination of sounds whose repetition can bring about certain definite results; Vedic hymn or sacred prayer addressed to any deity; a charm, spell or incantation; a secret
Manu	Vedic original man or father of the human race, a cosmic progenitor
Marg	A path, way; the path or course of a planet; the fifth constellation called Mrigashirsha
Maya	Illusion, enchantment, unreality; philosophically, matter, wealth and worldly attainments; another name for Prakriti, matter
Meenam	A fish, the twelfth sign of the zodiac; the first incarnation of Vishnu
Mithunam	A couple, twins, sexual union, the third sign of the zodiac, Gemini, the first androgyne, the Ardhanareeswara — the deity representing half male and half female
Mitra	An ally; the Sun, name of Aditya and usually associated with Varuna, a Vedic deity
Moksha	Liberation, final emancipation of the soul from cycle of birth and death, Nirvana; after-death state of rest and bliss. Liberation as the last of the goals of human life
Mula	A root, lowest edge or extremity of anything, beginning, foundation; the nineteenth lunar mansion
Mridangam	A kind of drum

Mrigashirsha	An antelope, an enquiring mind; the fifth lunar mansion
Mumukshattwa	The urge or striving after Final emancipation
Nada	Sound, vibration; the primary, all embracing vibration of which all other vibrations in the manifested universe are constituted; the power hidden in Sound
Nirvana	Liberation from existence; reunification with the Supreme Spirit. In Buddhism, absolute extinction of individual or worldly existence; merging of individual separate consciousness with the universal life-force; in Vedantic terminology, it corresponds to Kaivalyam
Nirayana	Fixed or Sidereal zodiac; position of the planets without taking into account precession
Nvritti Marg	The path of return or cessation from worldly involvements
Nritti	A goddess of destruction or negation, the presiding deity of the asterism Mula
Pada	A foot, a ray of light, a quarter, one-fourth of the whole
Padma	A lotus, a mode of coitus, a symbol of creativity
Pitta	Bile, one of the humors of the body; others being Kapha (phlegm) and Vata (air, wind)
Purva Punya	Auspicious deeds done on earlier occasions, generally during past lives; astrologically related to the Ninth house in the horoscope
Prakriti	Principle of materiality or objective existence, the passive or feminine creative principle, Mother Nature
Pranava	The sacred word Aum; an epithet of Vishnu or the Supreme Being
Pranayana	Cessation of inspiration and expiration, regulation of breathing; in Yogic literature it refers to control and regulated distribution of Prana or the Vital Force energizing the human body

Precession	refers to the earlier occurrences of the equinoxes in each successive sidereal year because of a slow retrograde motion of the equinoctial points along the ecliptic caused by the gravitational force of the Sun and the Moon upon the earth. This shift is not taken into account in the Indian astrological system where the longitude of celestial objects are measured from a point occupying a permanent position on the ecliptic fixed among the stars. The distance or longitude of this fixed initial point from the initial Vernal Equinoctial point is called Ayanamsa or the precession. The longitude measured from this initial (fixed) point is called Nirayana or Sidereal longitude. In modern or the European system of astronomy, the celestial longitude of planets and stars are measured along the ecliptic starting from the first point of Aries or the Vernal equinoctial point and this initial point does not occupy any fixed position among the stars
Prithvi	The earth, the earth as one of the five elements; Mother Earth
Purusha	A male or man, the positive generative force; the Spirit or the Supreme Being, Atman. In Sankhya, Purusha is the inactive witness of Prakriti
Pushya	A flower, the eighth lunar mansion
Rajas	Activity, energy, agitation, the second of the three constitute qualities of material substances predominant in man, gives motivation and ambition
Revati	The twenty-seventh lunar mansion; the wife of Brahma
Rohini	A red cow, a young girl in whom menstruation has just begun; lightning; wife of Vasudeva and mother of Balarama; fourth lunar mansion in which the Moon acquires special strength
Rudra	Name of Shiva; the roarer or howler, the storm of God; the destructive and regenerative force of Shiva
Rupam	Form, appearance, any visible object or form, natural state or condition; the number one; form or the quality of color as one of the twenty-four gunas or attributes of the Vaiseshikas
Sahasrara	The thousand petalled chakra — force center — at the top of the head which fully blooms when the Kundalini Shakti is fully at use

Sakat	A cart, carriage; name of a demon slain by Krishna when quite a boy; in astrology, refers to planetary combination when the Moon and Jupiter are placed in the sixth or eights house from each other
Samadhi	Highest state of deep meditation
Sattwa	Quality of purity, goodness, harmony and balance; one of the trigunas or three divisions of nature
Saumya	Graceful, auspicious; one of the nine divisions of the earth; a particular class of Pitris, the ancestors or creators of mankind; the planet Mercury
Sayana	The moving zodiac; position of planets and celestial bodies by taking into account precession. In modern system of astronomy on which the Western astrology bases the position of planets is determined according to Sayana or the Tropical system
Shravana	The ear, the act of hearing, that which is heard or revealed; the Vedas; the twenty-second lunar mansion
Shikhin	Pointed, proud, a peacock, a lamp, a religious mendicant; the planet Ketu, the descending Node of the Moon; the number three
Sushupti	Deep or profound sleep; the third state of consciousness prior to its assimilation in the Nirvanic state
Tamas	Darkness, dullness, inertia. An epithet of Rahu, the ascending Node of the Moon; one of the three gunas, attributes of nature
Tantra	Medieval Hindu teachings; provides the measure for calculating the duration of Kaliyuga. A peculiarity of Tantra is the worship of Devi or the female powers personified as Shakti. Some Tantras are connected with sexual rites and the practice of black magic
Tauli	That which weighs, the seventh zodiacal sign
Turiya	Fourth, four. The state in which consciousness is raised to the highest or the Nirvanic state of Samadhi, beyond the three lower states of waking (Jagrat), dream (Swapna), and deep sleep (Sushupti)
Udyama	Strenuous or assiduous effort, exertion, preservation; raising, elevation; firm resolve, preparedness
Vanika	Trader, seller, purveyor

Vibhuti Pada	the chapter on accomplishments; refers to third chapter of Patanjali's *Yoga Sutras* wherein he mentions the various possibilities of acquiring special yogic faculties including the knowledge of planets and their astrological impact. It also refers to the significance of omens and the language of birds and animals
Vishnu	The second deity of the Puranic Triad (others being Brahma, the creator, and Shiva, the destroyer) entrusted with the preservation of the world which duty he is represented to have duly performed by his various incarnations; the Lord Rama and Krishna were his reincarnations, avataras, undertaken for special preservation missions. Literally means that which has expanded
Vishwa	The whole, the manifested universe, the Earth
Vrischikam	A scorpion, the eighth sign of the zodiac; esoterically, stands for Vishnu, and as Vishwam, the manifested universe, itself is Vishnu, Vrischikam signifies the Universe in thought or the universe in the divine conception
Vrishabha	A Bull, the bull of Shiva, a strong or athletic man, a lustful man; the second sign of the zodiac, Taurus; the word is used in several places in the Upanishads and the Vedas to mean Pranava, the Sacred Word Aum
Yasha	Fame, reputation, glory, renown, approbation
Yoga	Combination, connection; deep and abstract meditation, concentration of mind and contemplation of the Supreme Being taken together as a result of which unification with the Universal Spirit is established, the second division of the Sankhya philosophy generally associated with the name of Patanjali. One of the six Darshans or schools of philosophy of India. Astrologically, it refers to planetary combinations and special relationships which produce important results. Name of a particular astronomical division of time, twenty-seven such Yogas are usually enumerated

Yoga Sutras	Aphorisms of Yoga; the treatise associated with the name of Patanjali which contains four sections dealing with Samadhi (meditation), Sadhana (practice), Vibhuti (accomplishments), and Kaivalya (Liberation). The yogic discipline continued from a very early period, even prior to Patanjali; it is said that the doctrine that helped the Lord Buddha came from Yajnawalkya, the writer of the *Shatapatha Brahma of Yajur Veda*, the *Brihad Aranyaka*, and other famous works
Yuka	A parasite, a louse, one who attaches oneself to others for selfish ends

SELECTED
BIBLIOGRAPHY

BOOKS

Behari, Bepin. *A Study In Astrological Occultism.* Bangalore, India: IBH Prakashan, 1983.

Behari, Bepin. *Myths and Symbols of Vedic Astrology.* Salt Lake City, UT: Passage Press, 1990

Behari, Bepin. *Solve Your Problems Astrologically.* Bangalore, India: IBH Prakashan, 1988.

Behari, Madhuri and Bepin. *An Introduction To Esoteric Astrology.* New Delhi, India: Sagar Publications, 1986.

Blavatsky, H. P.. *Isis Unveiled, Vols. I & II.* Pasadena, CA: Theosophical University Press, 1976.

Blavatsky, H. P.. *The Secret Doctrine, Vols I–VI.* Madras, India: THP, Adyar, 1971.

Blavatsky, H. P.. *Transactions Of The Blavatsky Lodge.* California: The Theosophy Co., 1923.

Disksnita, Vaidyanatha. *Jataka Parijata* (translation by V. Subramanya Sastri). New Delhi, India: Ranjan Publications.

Dowson, John. *A Classical Dictionary Of Hindu Mythology And Religion.* London: Routledge & Kegan Paul.

Frawley, David. *The Astrology Of The Seers.* Salt Lake City, UT, Passage Press, 1990.

Frawley, David. *From The River Of Heaven, Hindu And Vedic Knowledge For The Modern Age.* Salt Lake City UT: Passage Press, 1990.

Giedion, S. *The Eternal Present:the Beginning Of Architect.* New York, NY: Bollingen Foundation.

Hodson, G. H.. *The Hidden Wisdom In The Holy Bible Vol. I..* Madras, India: TPH, Adyar, 1963.

Jennings, Hargrave. *The Indian Religion Or Results Of The Mysterious Buddhi.* London: George Redway.

Kalidasa. *Uttarakalamrita* (translated by V. Subrahmanya Sastri). Bangalore, India: Sri Mallikarjuna Press, 1981.

Santhanam, R.. *Brihat Parasara Hora Sastra.* New Delhi, India: Ranjan Publications, 1984.

Subba Rao, T. *Esoteric Writings.* Madras, India: TPH, Adyar.

Subrahmanya Sastri, V.. *Varaha Mihira's Brihat Jataka.* Mysore, India.

ASTROLOGICAL JOURNALS

Astrological Magazine. Raman Publications, "Sri Rajeswari," 115/1, New Extension, Seshadripuram, Bangalore-560 020 India.

The Times Of Astrology. "Sri Bhavanam," 9/1040, Govindpuri, P.O. Box 4347, Kalkaji (P.O.), New Delhi-110 019 India.

Index